DISCARDED

INTERNATIONAL POLITICAL ECONOMY SERIES

General Editor: Timothy M. Shaw, Professor of Political Science and International Development Studies and Director of the Centre for Foreign Policy Studies, Dalhousie University, Nova Scotia, Canada

Recent titles include:

Manuel R. Agosin and Diana Tussie (*editors*)
TRADE AND GROWTH: NEW DILEMMAS IN TRADE POLICY

Mahvash Alerassool
FREEZING ASSETS: THE USA AND THE MOST EFFECTIVE ECONOMIC SANCTION

Inga Brandell (*editor*)
WORKERS IN THIRD-WORLD INDUSTRIALIZATION

Richard P. C. Brown
PUBLIC DEBT AND PRIVATE WEALTH

Bonnie K. Campbell (*editor*)
POLITICAL DIMENSIONS OF THE INTERNATIONAL DEBT CRISIS

Bonnie K. Campbell and John Loxley (*editors*)
STRUCTURAL ADJUSTMENT IN AFRICA

Jerker Carlsson and Timothy M. Shaw (*editors*)
NEWLY INDUSTRIALIZING COUNTRIES AND THE POLITICAL ECONOMY OF SOUTH–SOUTH RELATIONS

Steen Folke, Niels Fold and Thyge Enevoldsen
SOUTH–SOUTH TRADE AND DEVELOPMENT

David P. Forsythe (*editor*)
HUMAN RIGHTS AND DEVELOPMENT
THE UNITED NATIONS IN THE WORLD POLITICAL ECONOMY

David Glover and Ken Kusterer
SMALL FARMERS, BIG BUSINESS

William D. Graf (*editor*)
THE INTERNATIONALIZATION OF THE GERMAN POLITICAL ECONOMY

Betty J. Harris
THE POLITICAL ECONOMY OF THE SOUTHERN AFRICAN PERIPHERY

Jacques Hersh
THE USA AND THE RISE OF EAST ASIA SINCE 1945

Steven Kendall Holloway
THE ALUMINIUM MULTINATIONALS AND THE BAUXITE CARTEL

Bahgat Korany, Paul Noble and Rex Brynen (*editors*)
THE MANY FACES OF NATIONAL SECURITY IN THE ARAB WORLD

Matthew Martin
THE CRUMBLING FAÇADE OF AFRICAN DEBT NEGOTIATIONS

James H. Mittelman
OUT FROM UNDERDEVELOPMENT

Paul Mosley (*editor*)
DEVELOPMENT FINANCE AND POLICY REFORM

Dennis C. Pirages and Christine Sylvester (*editors*)
TRANSFORMATIONS IN THE GLOBAL POLITICAL ECONOMY

Tony Porter
STATES, MARKETS AND REGIMES IN GLOBAL FINANCE

Stephen P. Riley (*editor*)
THE POLITICS OF GLOBAL DEBT

Jorge Rodríguez Beruff, J. Peter Figueroa and J. Edward Greene (*editors*)
CONFLICT, PEACE AND DEVELOPMENT IN THE CARIBBEAN

Frederick Stapenhurst
POLITICAL RISK ANALYSIS AROUND THE NORTH ATLANTIC

Arno Tausch with Fred Prager
TOWARDS A SOCIO-LIBERAL THEORY OF WORLD DEVELOPMENT

Nancy Thede and Pierre Beaudet (*editors*)
A POST-APARTHEID SOUTHERN AFRICA?

Peter Utting
ECONOMIC REFORM AND THIRD-WORLD SOCIALISM

Fiona Wilson
SWEATERS: GENDER, CLASS AND WORKSHOP-BASED
  INDUSTRY IN MEXICO

David Wurfel and Bruce Burton (*editors*)
THE POLITICAL ECONOMY OF FOREIGN POLICY IN SOUTHEAST ASIA

Indebted Development
Strategic Bargaining and Economic Adjustment in the Third World

Howard P. Lehman
Department of Political Science
University of Utah

St. Martin's Press   New York

© Howard P. Lehman 1993

All rights reserved. For information, write:
Scholarly and Reference Division,
St. Martin's Press, Inc., 175 Fifth Avenue,
New York, N.Y. 10010

First published in the United States of America in 1993

Printed in Great Britain

ISBN 0-312-09635-6

Library of Congress Cataloging-in-Publication Data
Lehman, Howard P.
Indebted development : strategic bargaining and economic
adjustment in the Third World / Howard P. Lehman.
p. cm. — (International political economy series)
Includes index.
ISBN 0-312-09635-6
1. Structural adjustment (Economic policy)—Developing countries.
2. Developing countries—Economic policy.   3. Debt relief-
-Developing countries.   I. Title.   II. Series.
HC59.7.L35165   1993
338.9'009172'4—dc20   92-47353
                                                             CIP

To Jackie, Katherine and Julia

Contents

List of Tables		viii
List of Acronyms		x
Acknowledgements		xii
1	Introduction: Strategic Bargaining and Economic Adjustment in the Third World	1
2	Strategic Priorities of the International Creditor Regime	30
3	The State and Economic Adjustment Strategies	64
4	The State and Debt Management Strategies	119
5	The State's Distributive Policies Under Indebted Development	167
	Conclusions: The Process of Indebted Development	206
Index		217

List of Tables

1.1	Domestic Economic Indicators, 1974–93	18
1.2	Foreign Economic Indicators, 1974–93	19
1.3	External Debt Indicators, 1974–93	20
1.4	External Debt for Brazil, Kenya and Zimbabwe, 1985–92	23
1.5	External Debt for Brazil, Kenya, and Zimbabwe, 1985–92	23
1.6	Debt Service Payments for Brazil, Kenya and Zimbabwe, 1985–92	23
1.7	Source of Foreign Loans by Type of Creditors for Brazil, Kenya, and Zimbabwe, 1985–92	24
2.1	Debt Indicators for the Baker 15, 1985–88	38
2.2	Commercial Bank Provisioning	43
2.3	Net Resource Transfers, 1985–1988	48
3.1	Origins of Gross Domestic Product in Kenya, 1985, 1990	74
3.2	Kenya's Trade Balance, 1985–1992	76
3.3	Trend of Gross Domestic Product of Kenya, 1985–1992	77
3.4	Zimbabwe's Trade Balance, 1985–1992	91
3.5	Trend of Gross Domestic Product of Zimbabwe, 1985–1992	92
3.6	Brazil's Inflation Rate, 1985–1992	102
3.7	Trend of Gross Domestic Product of Brazil, 1985–1992	108
3.8	Brazil's Trade Balance, 1985–1992	108
4.1	Kenya's Total External Debt by Creditor, 1985–1992	122
4.2	Kenya's Debt Ratios, 1985–1992	122
4.3	Kenya's Debt Service Indicators, 1985–1992	123
4.4	Zimbabwe's Total External Debt by Creditor, 1985–1992	131
4.5	Zimbabwe's Debt Ratios, 1985–1992	132

List of Tables

4.6	Zimbabwe's Debt Service Indicators, 1985–1992	133
4.7	Brazil's Total External Debt by Creditor, 1985–1992	140
4.8	Brazil's Debt Ratios, 1985–1992	140
4.9	Brazil's Debt Service Indicators, 1985–1992	142
5.1	Sectoral Distribution of External Loans Guaranteed by Kenya, 1977–1983	175
5.2	Expenditure by Function of Kenya's Central Government, 1970–1989	178
5.3	Subsidies in the Zimbabwe Economy, 1980/81–1984/85, 1989/90–1991/92	182
5.4	Public Sector Investment Program Expenditures, 1980–84, 1990	183
5.5	Expenditure by Function of Zimbabwe's Central Government, 1982–1989	188
5.6	Expenditure by Function of Brazil's Central Government, 1975–1989	200

List of Acronyms

AMA	Agricultural Marketing Authority
ATRR	Allocated Transfer Risk Reserve
CGT	General Workers' Central
CUT	Central Workers' Union
CZI	Confederation of Zimbabwe Industry
DFCK	Development Finance Company of Kenya
ESAF	Enhanced Structural Adjustment Facility
FIC	Foreign Investment Committee
FORD	Forum for the Restoration of Democracy
ICDC	Industrial and Commercial Development Corporation
ICERC	Inter-agency Country Exposure Risk Committee
ICO	International Coffee Organization
IDA	International Development Association
IFI	International Financial Institutions
IMF	International Monetary Fund
IPC	Investment Promotion Center
ISI	Import-Substituting Industrialization
KANU	Kenya African National Union
LIBOR	London Inter-Bank Offered Rate
MIGA	Multilateral Investment Guarantee Agency
MYRA	Multi-year Restructuring Agreement
NIC	Newly Industrializing Country
OGIL	Open General Import Licensing
PFL	Liberal Front Party
PMDB	Brazilian Democratic Movement Party
PSIP	Public Sector Investment Program
PTA	Preferential Trade Area
OAU	Organization of African Unity
OPIC	Overseas Private Investment Corporation
SAF	Structural Adjustment Facility

List of Acronyms

SAL   Structural Adjustment Loan
SAP   Structural Adjustment Program
UDI   Unilateral Declaration of Independence
ZIC   Zimbabwe Investment Centre

Acknowledgements

It is only appropriate to incur my own personal debts while engaged in a research project on indebtedness. I am in debt to many individuals and institutions for advice and assistance over the course of this study.

The book originated several years ago at the University of Minnesota. I am grateful for the valuable comments I received from Bud Duvall, John Freeman, Gary Wynia, Allen Isaacman, and Robert Kudrle. In the intervening period, I received support and encouragement from Valerie Assetto, Thomas Callaghy, Edward Epstein, John Francis, Stephan Haggard, Don Hanson, Jennifer McCoy, and Carol Thompson.

During my research, I encountered a number of helpful people who contributed to this study by providing needed information and entrance to research libraries: Susan Strange and the library of the London School of Economics; Stephany Griffith-Jones and the library of the Institute of Development Studies at the University of Sussex; and Thomas Bryne and the Institute of International Finance. I also profited from the assistance given to me by the library staffs at the Joint World Bank–International Monetary Fund Library, the Library of Congress, the University of Nairobi and its Institute for Development Studies, the University of Zimbabwe, and the research libraries associated with several government ministries and international banks.

The field research in Kenya and Zimbabwe could not have been accomplished without the resolute support of Dr Nicholas Nyangira, Chairman of the Department of Government at the University of Nairobi, and Dr Rukudzo Murapa, Chairman of the Department of Political and Administrative Studies at the University of Zimbabwe. I thank them both for appointing me as Research Associate.

Many of the individuals mentioned above introduced me to an extensive network of people associated with debt management and economic adjustment strategies. Since I promised confidentiality to the more than 200 respondents who took time out of their busy schedules for interviews, I cannot individually thank them. I am, however, extremely appreciative and grateful for not only their time and input, but their encouragement and genuine interest in this study.

Financial support came from several quarters, including the National Science Foundation (SES–8410519), the University of Utah Research Committee, the University of Utah's College of

Social and Behavioral Science, and its Department of Political Science.

In turning this manuscript into a book, I owe much to Timothy Shaw for his time, patience, and constructive criticisms as series editor and to Clare Wace of Macmillan who helped guide the manuscript into a publishable form.

Parts of this book were originally published in a different version in *World Politics* (1992), 44, pp. 600–644, © The John S. Hopkins University Press; in *Studies in Comparative International Development* (1990), 25, pp. 37–72, © Transaction Publishers; and in the *African Studies Review* (1992), 35, pp. 1–34, © African Studies Association.

Finally, I owe the greatest debt to Jackie, Katherine, and Julia to whom this book is dedicated.

1 Introduction: Strategic Bargaining and Economic Adjustment in the Third World

While the 1970s can be considered the decade of rapid debt accumulation and the 1980s that of economic deterioration in the Third World, the 1990s will be the decade of intense *debt management negotiations* between international creditors and debtor states and *economic adjustment negotiations* between the state and its domestic constituents. Arising from these negotiations are both a paradox and a dilemma for Third World states as they seek to work their way through the maze of indebtedness. The *paradox* for debtors concerns the nature and role of state power during this period of economic decline. On the one hand, state capabilities are considered weak and ineffective in combating political instability, social disunity, and scarcity of economic resources. Yet, the state in the Third World has shown remarkable resiliency in extending and developing its bureaucratic and administrative powers. Is the state, in indebted societies, withering away, losing its control over members of its society as well as foreign interests? Or, has the state been able to adapt to changing circumstances which may permit it some degree of freedom in its negotiations with internal and external interests?

Most indebted states also must grapple with a common *dilemma*. On the one hand, these states feel intense pressure to fulfill their financial obligations to international creditors who control access to capital markets. International creditors often call for the adoption of orthodox adjustment policies as a condition for either new money or rescheduling of debt. Any long-term rupture of the credit supply would weaken further the availability of foreign exchange to private and public sectors and squeeze their investment capacity. Indebted states must always keep one eye on the attitudes and policies of international creditors. On the other hand, imposition of orthodox adjustment measures that strengthen the borrower's credit standing may lead (and already have led) to economic hardships, political instability, and threats to the survival of governing elites. Thus, an adjustment dilemma arises: if the state refuses to offer acceptable concessions or imposes severe demands on the creditors in order to placate internal political groups, it risks retaliation from international creditors, such as the attachments of foreign assets, ruptures in trade lines, and cessation of lending; but if the state readily agrees to creditor proposals for economic adjustment and debt servicing to facilitate a debt agreement, it risks polarization and political mobilization against the state by the domestic groups afflicted by the costs of adjustment. The state, caught in the middle as the central decision-maker in the adjustment process, must formulate a credible bargaining strategy to address the contrasting concerns of international creditors and domestic political interests.[1]

These two issues – the *paradox of state power* and the *dilemma of economic adjustment strategies* – form the framework for the analysis of economic adjustment choices in the Third World. This study presents an *institutional policy approach* to explain the selection of adjustment strategies followed by three developing countries: Kenya, Zimbabwe, and Brazil. This work uses a method recently suggested as a means to relink domestic and international levels, and economic and political forces.[2] This study, in examining the national level, considers the relationship between the state and societal interests as revealed by specific adjustment policies and the distributive effect of adjustment. The state must consider the demands and relative power capabilities of domestic interests who pressure the state to adopt favorable policies. At the international level, the state similarly must respond to the demands and power capabilities of international creditors as they press the state to protect their concerns. The state then is the critical intermediary and decision-maker caught in the cross-cutting pressures exerted by domestic and foreign interests. The state, faced with determining the distribution of adjustment costs to society, must engage in simultaneous negotiations with international creditors and domestic political groups.

For this study, *indebted development* implies the process and policy outcomes of economic adjustment and debt management strategies for Third World states who must interact at both levels of analysis; that is, the primary research question is to explain how indebted states, seeking to resolve the adjustment dilemma, choose a strategy while bargaining with both members of domestic society and foreign creditors.

To understand the adjustment process as interpreted in this book, we need to briefly consider what is meant by orthodox economic adjustment. In a strict economic sense, adjustment often refers to the restoration of the balance in the external accounts and the achieving of such goals as the reduction of aggregate demand, economic liberalization, fiscal restraint, and the integration of the national economy into the world economy.[3] For proponents of orthodox structural adjustment, debtor governments are meant to accomplish two major goals: to minimize the role of the state apparatus in economic development and to implement economic reforms that would reorient the economy toward export-led growth and a return to market forces.[4]

Two significant assumptions support this influential adjustment perspective. The first concerns the perception of the state as an obstacle to economic development since it interferes with the strengthening of the private sector and of the market place. Yet, the state in the developing world has taken on a permanent structure from which, as Thomas Callaghy has noted, the state simultaneously becomes the key obstacle to economic reform *and* the primary instrument through which orthodox supporters shape economic policy.[5] The state remains an integral political and economic force with which to be reckoned though often a poorly managed actor in developing countries. The question is not so much as how to reduce the role of the state as what is the appropriate behavior and scope of the state in reforming the economic structure of a society.

A second assumption of orthodox structural adjustment is the acceptance of specific economic reforms that are meant to liberalize the economy through market forces. Without these particular reforms, orthodox supporters claim that appropriate adjustment will not take place.[6] Given this assumption, they further argue that if a country refuses to properly implement and enforce many if not all of these economic measures then that country lacks political will and the bureaucratic capability to carry them out.[7] Leaders who fail to impose these policies demonstrate their political weakness in forcing the costs of adjustment onto society. This argument fails, in my view, by simplistically assuming that only one form of adjustment could achieve the success necessary to break the pattern of economic deterioration and that state authorities have not the political capacity to make difficult decisions.[8]

Much of the current literature conceptualizes bargaining strategies as revolving around this orthodox interpretation of adjustment. Since international creditors generally favor this form they will use their power of collective action against recalcitrant states. Since states and their domestic constituents, it is assumed, disagree with this conception of adjustment, they will seek to form their own collective action in the form of a debtors' cartel.[9] Two relevant implications for this study arise from this perspective. First, adjustment should be considered not simply as a set of economic policies either to be implemented or opposed. Adjustment is considered here as a process that emerges from the bargaining and negotiating strategies of the state, domestic groups, and international actors. Second, as a process that evolves from bargaining, adjustment should be conceptualized as a changing set of policies that, at times, may reflect an orthodox approach, but, at other times, they may represent a more heterodox perspective. States and international financial institutions should not be considered as being either in conflict against each other nor, if they are not in conflict, in collusion with each other.

The state, in general terms, has *four adjustment strategies* in responding to demands from the two levels: 1) it can accept and implement the orthodox measures imposed on it by external financial actors; 2) it can carry out only partial reforms recommended by those external actors; 3) it can impose a set of adjustment policies (sometimes heterodox policies) as determined by the state itself; or 4) it may refuse to implement any kind of economic adjustment program. Most cases appear to fall in between total acceptance and total rejection of orthodox policies. Many states select an adjustment strategy that includes a mixture of orthodox reforms recommended by external actors and heterodox measures determined by state and societal interests. My perspective of these adjustment strategies is broadly comparable to that of studies edited by Joan Nelson and Paul Mosley, et al. The later study, in particular, refers to slippage – the gap between the terms of an adjustment program and the actual implementation of the program – as a key variable in explaining the adoption of World Bank policies.[10] Adjustment, ultimately, is an issue of relative power among the actors in and out of society.

This study argues that the state remains a relevant actor in the adjustment process by defining its policy agenda, distinguishing available policy options, and determining the implementation of adjustment. The state leads the adjustment process due to its central and authoritative role in society and its decision-making capacity in selecting adjustment policies. The state relies on the articulation of its objectives, its own power capabilities, and determination of its policy tactics as it implements adjustment.

THE PARADOX OF STATE POWER

A central debate in the literature on the state has focused on the *state's relative strength and weakness in relation to society*.[11] It is here where a paradox has emerged that has generated further questions about state power and state-society relations. The Third World is plagued with political instability, coups d'etat, deteriorating economic conditions, and ineffective policy implementation. The current difficulties in meeting scheduled debt repayment deadlines and the pressure to make significant economic adjustments further illustrate the precarious financial status of many states. Yet, Third World societies are well known for their heavily centralized bureaucratic apparatus that consumes a substantial portion of expenditures and capital investments. One indicator of state influence is the steady growth of parastatals in these countries. As they have expanded in number and in function, state power over these firms also has grown. And, in response to rapidly deteriorating economic conditions, many states have enacted wide-scale debt management controls on foreign investment, public borrowing, and public sector investment.

In a recent article, Gabriel Almond criticized recent research efforts that attempt to 'bring the state back in' by arguing that the state had never left the political arena.[12] In a similar fashion, the state in the developing world has been a consistent social force at least since the colonial period. For example, in African societies, the colonial experience contributed toward the formation of a centralized state bureaucracy that continues to intervene in nearly all facets of economic, social, and political life.[13] Many current state institutions and state controls are derived from the colonial governing system. As the colonial powers sought to mould the state to mirror and protect their interests with a set of mercantilist policies so do African states today who continue the tradition of state presence.

The state can be interpreted as being 'strong' in the sense that it has become partially autonomous from societal interests. The relative weakness of domestic economic groups allows more extensive state activity. In the absence of a vigorous private sector, the public sector has had to participate more forcefully in the production, distribution, and consumption of capital and goods. The state seeks to consolidate its power and authority out of an environment of dispersed power. As Donald Rothchild writes in the case of Africa, by the way the state has created marketing boards, immigration controls, the Africanization of the public and private sectors, and parastatal monopolies, the state displays 'a limited but real capacity to affect the activities of domestic and international actors and to enlarge its own sphere of enterprise.'[14] It thus develops an institutional capacity as means to manage and protect its own interests. Rothchild further suggests that 'the state's ability to distance itself from these domestic (or international) class and ethnic interests gives public officials room to overpower or ignore some of the less pressing interest group demands and to expand their administrative functions and powers.'[15] Notwithstanding the recent discussion on the spread of privatization in developing states, Rothchild's comment reflects the rapid extension of parastatal firms throughout Africa.[16] In the absence of a cohesive private sector, the state uses various investment and exchange controls to direct scarce resources to their constituents, sometimes to private groups though often to state-owned enterprises. As semi-autonomous entities with an ability and willingness to negotiate strategically with such influential international financial institutions (IFIs) as the International Monetary Fund (IMF) and the World Bank, some states have maintained their distance from these agencies.

While growth in state institutional capacity reflects a more active state, the absence of effective power and legitimacy reveals a weakening and, perhaps, decaying state. Callaghy's term for this paradox, 'lame Leviathan,' juxtaposes the centralized bureaucratic component of the state to the weak efforts of the state to dominate society.[17] In place of widely perceived legitimacy, the state attempts to use the blunt force of its coercive power to impose its narrow interests on society. Yet, the failure of central state authorities to carve out and protect their own autonomous interests facilitates the take-over, as it were, by any hegemonic interests, domestic or foreign, that exist in society. State capacity, according to this perspective, thus does not reflect its own autonomous set of interests nor the entire interests of society, but only mirrors the class interests that have 'captured' the state.[18]

The weakness of the state often is considered in terms of its negotiation, acceptance, and implementation of an IMF adjustment strategy. Most developing states are unable to respond to their financial crisis without negotiating with the international financial community. This places the state in a position of obligation to international financial institutions, especially to the IMF. Not only must these countries accept IMF conditionality, the implementation of adjustment policies generally imposes hardships on various social and economic groups in society. The end result for many countries is a pattern of ineffective policy implementation. The state, it has been suggested, is unable or unwilling to mobilize those societal interests whose support is required for the implementation of an adjustment agreement. It thus lacks the political will and strength to force the necessary support for policy implementation.

The 'political will' argument does not accurately reflect the capabilities of the state to thwart effectively domestic and international pressures. The paradox of state power or, as Joel Migdal conceptualizes the issue, the 'duality of states,' more appropriately emphasizes the countervailing pressures that exist at two-level negotiating 'games.'[19] In the context of severe indebtedness, the 'political will' argument fails to explain the rise of significant state policies that affect the interrelated components of economic adjustment and debt management, including foreign investment, capital borrowing, public sector investment, and the distribution of costs. Contrary to the argument that developing states only weakly implement policy reforms, this book argues that developing states have shown considerable will in exerting control over their deteriorating economic conditions.[20] While success from adjustment varies widely in indebted states, most attempt to make effective use of their available capabilities. Callaghy has written that 'at the international level, this entails bargaining with external actors for policy flexibility and resources sufficient to allow the development of some form of embedded liberalism. At the domestic level, the major dilemma has been one of insulating the technocratic staff and policies required for adjustment while buffering the socio-political impact of implementing such policies.'[21]

Rather than focus on the state's inability to adjust to the debt crisis, this study focuses on its ability to insert itself in the economic crisis in order to manage indebtedness. In a critical way, the debt crisis has become an important variable in the 'hardening' of the state. The state has responded to indebtedness by providing incentives for export growth, regulating the allocation of foreign exchange, controlling additional foreign borrowing, and overseeing parastatal activities. Thomas Biersteker concluded in a recent study on state power and adjustment that IMF and World Bank adjustment programs facilitate the 'continuation of some forms of intervention (influence and mediation), redirect others (regulation, mediation, and distribution), and reduce those associated with state production and planning.'[22] Similarly, Callaghy writes that 'the main task, in short, is not 'getting the state out' – as much of the IMF, World Bank, and Western rhetoric implies – but finding the state's appropriate role for fostering economic growth and development via both state and private sectors.'[23]

The ambiguity of the strong-weak dichotomy for states weakens the value of relying on this concept. Stephen Krasner presented an early formulation of state power in terms of the state's power to resist private pressure, change private behavior, and change the social structure.[24] The state is considered strong when its governing apparatus generates a set of interests, objectives, and capabilities that is separate or autonomous from societal interests. A weak state, then, is considered as consumed by societal interests, domestic or foreign, which further weakens the effectiveness of state policy. But, since developing states often appear to be strong and weak at the same time, Krasner's conception of state power needs to be altered to explain state-society relations. Eric Nordlinger's critique of Krasner is relevant here. He writes that 'to find that public officials are making public policies that derive from their own preferences is patently significant. And their doing so with societal support behind them is not necessarily less significant than their doing so in the face of societal opposition.' 'The state,' he further argues, 'then has its own 'strengths' to rely upon in addition to those stemming from the support given by societal actors.'[25]

The argument presented here is that a continuum of strong-weak states is not analytically well-suited for the special characteristics found in many developing countries today. Neither state nor societal interests dominate one another in most countries. The two sets of interests have shown the ability, at times, to merge their objectives into the governing apparatus and, at other times, to conflict against each other as two autonomous agents, and still at other times, to cooperate together in order to advance their distinct interests. All of these possibilities occur in the current environment of profound economic stress and political instability. The evidence presented in this book suggests that the analysis of the developing state should focus less on the strong/weak dichotomy and more on the contextual and relational linkages to domestic and foreign societal interests. Understanding these relationships between state and society and the level of autonomy accorded to the state may be advanced by a more specific examination of adjustment policy choices.

My perspective of the *state* derives from its complex relationship with societal interests. The state is an actor that, on the one hand, is to be taken seriously because it has its own strengths and preferences. Yet, on the other hand, it also is contextually bound by specific issue-areas that prevail at any one time in its relation to societal actors. Thus, I take the position that the state is only partially autonomous from societal interests, and its ability to make adjustment decisions is determined by its efforts to compete, thwart, and negotiate with those forces. I agree with Nordlinger's remark that 'taking the state seriously thus entails the bringing together of state- and society-centered analyses in a meaningful manner, in ways that parallel the coexistence and interrelationships between state and society.'[26]

In this framework, the state lies at the centre of the formulation and implementation of the adjustment strategy. It must negotiate and bargain at both levels of politics; ie, with its domestic constituents and with international financial actors. In the Third World (including Africa, where the state is considered weak or soft in comparison to the Latin American state), the state still matters both in terms of its capacity to penetrate society and its capacity to organize the defining principles of society.[27] First, the developing state competes against societal groups for scarce power resources in a society deeply divided across ethnic, racial, and economic lines. The relative weakness of those groups implies that few restrictions can be imposed on the state's capacity to implement its policies.

Lewis Snider's conceptualization of state power is useful to consider at this point. He distinguishes the strategic power of a state from its infrastructural power. The former centres on the scope and size of the country's resource base, which includes military strength, economic wealth, and technological innovation. Infrastructural power focuses on the capacity of the state to penetrate society, extract resources, appropriate resources, and to implement political decisions.[28] For most African countries, infrastructural power is most appropriate as a characteristic of state power. Lacking strategic resources, these states utilize their infrastructure to implement policies in order to exert influence and control over domestic actors. In contrast, Latin American states generally incorporate both strategic and infrastructural power. State capacity, for this study, is the ability of the state to implement changes in domestic society in response to international demands and economic shocks.

Second, the state in the developing world also has the means to shape the organizing principles by setting and changing the parameters of behavior with domestic and foreign actors. In the case of selecting and implementing an adjustment strategy, the state has the capacity as the legal representative during debt negotiations to shape the rules of adjustment and to determine the internal distribution of the costs stemming from adjustment. I view the state as an active agent that is representative of the governance of society through the administration and implementation of decisions. As Rothchild has written in terms of African states, by placing limits on societal demands and implementing public policy across a wide range of issues, the state 'has displayed a limited but real capacity to affect the activities of domestic and international actors and to enlarge its own sphere of enterprise.'[29]

A broad definition of the state can successfully incorporate these state-society linkages. At that level, Bob Jessop's conceptualization is useful. He writes that 'the core of the state apparatus comprises a distinct ensemble of institutions and organizations whose socially accepted function is to define and enforce collectively binding decisions on the member of a society in the name of their common interest or general will.'[30] But, as a means to analyze the set of questions in this book, the state needs to be broken down further into discrete, observable components. Since the state itself does not act, a more accurate and operational definition would focus on individual decision-makers. Thus, the state, for this study, 'refers to all those individuals who occupy offices that authorize them, and them alone, to make and apply decisions that are binding upon any and all parts of a territorially circumscribed population.'[31] The limitations of this narrow definition can be partially offset by recognition of Jessop's broader conceptualization.

THE DILEMMA OF ECONOMIC ADJUSTMENT STRATEGIES

Economic adjustment strategies open a Pandora's Box from which conflicting state, societal, and foreign interests carve out their bargaining positions. They react to the substantial costs of liberalization (such as de-industrialization, unemployment, trade deficits, political instability, and foreign exchange gaps) which threaten state autonomy and state legitimacy with these groups. Adjustment, though demanded by most international creditors and some domestic groups, imposes sufficient costs as to require the state to control the direction and timing of economic policy. Thus, economic adjustment has the unintended effect of empowering the state in relation to societal actors in areas of common concern such as foreign investment, public borrowing, and public sector investment. Simultaneously, as the costs of liberalization increase, the state additionally is empowered over the marginalized groups in society who are adversely affected by state economic policies.

Since adjustment was considered unavoidable by most national and international actors, the *adjustment process has evolved into a complex bargaining strategy between the state and its international creditors on one level, and the state and domestic political groups, on another level.* As Stephan Haggard notes, while international actors pressure the state for the adoption of an adjustment strategy, national interests influence the timing of the policy measures and their scope.[32] My study puts forth an analytical framework which considers the economic objectives of adjustment determined by Kenya, Zimbabwe, and Brazil, the policies chosen by the state to achieve adjustment, and the parts of society which bear the costs of adjustment within the context of pressure exerted by domestic and foreign interests. Adjustment is considered as a series of policies enacted by the state that are molded by the interaction of domestic political groups and international creditors as they seek to control the costs of adjustment in a highly politicized environment.

By conceptualizing the state as the central decision-maker in the adjustment process, this study focuses on the *strategic relationship between the state and relevant domestic and foreign actors.* Using Robert Putnam's two-level game framework as a conceptual starting point helps to specify the interaction among the actors. The central dilemma of the two-level game is that the negotiator must satisfy two imperatives simultaneously: in the case of international debt negotiations, the debtor state must find a bargaining strategy to address the concerns of both international creditors and domestic interest groups. On the face of it, this presents a strategic dilemma for the negotiator, since, as Putnam notes, rational moves at one board may be impolitic at the other.[33] Even though the state essentially maintains two on-going sets of negotiations, we first must delink its specific strategies during bargaining before we attempt to link them together.

For debtor governments, the primary objective is to reduce the debt burden so as to enhance domestic economic growth and gain the support of domestic constituents. The set of choices that will be approved by each constituency must overlap sufficiently to produce an agreement acceptable to both sides. The core issue of my argument is how to reach a debt agreement and economic adjustment package that will be ratifiable by international creditors *and* domestic constituents alike. While negotiating debt restructuring with international creditors, the debtor government must simultaneously contend with an internal game (at Level II). The game, according to interest group politics or class conflict, involves three players – labour, capital, and government – whereby the latter seeks to retain power, and labour and capital seek to maximize their gain, wages and profit, respectively. In electoral politics, the government's goal of retaining power may be met by satisfying the demands of a majority of the voting populace through the distribution of benefits in a growth economy. In the context of the international debt crisis, a debtor government may choose between shifting the burden of the debt to the external environment (such as debt repudiation), thus enhancing the prospects for short-term growth, but risking retaliation by international creditors; and meeting the external debt obligation through imposing austerity measures, thus enhancing the prospects of new infusions of capital and eventual growth.[34] If austerity is followed, as has been the case for much of the last decade, the familiar problem of the distribution of the costs of austerity then comprises the domestic game. This choice produces a dilemma for the state: economic growth can help to ensure the government's survival, but if austerity is required to achieve that growth, the government risks a defection of labor and capital, and an eventual loss of power. On the other hand, if the state chooses to shift the burden of austerity to the external sector, it risks retaliation which also will threaten domestic economic growth.

Although comprising a fundamentally different game at Level II than a sovereign government, international creditors must also contend with an internal game in seeking ratification by constituents. During recent periods of debt rescheduling, a primary objective of international creditors has been the maintenance of the quality of their assets. Although this objective is accepted widely among international financial institutions, different organizations have contrasting policies in seeking to achieve this goal. For international banks, bank negotiators must grapple with diverging interests between banks with extensive foreign loans and other banks with smaller amounts. The former banks have a greater incentive to remain committed to accommodation with debtor governments while the latter banks often seek to defect from any debt agreement.[35] The internal game for international creditors becomes more complex as they also must deal with crucial third parties, including the IMF and bank regulatory agencies. Many international banks have lent new money as a component of IMF programs and they have come to rely on IMF agreements to ensure interest repayment. Yet, as debtor governments became increasingly unable to comply with IMF targets, the link between the standby programs and the rescheduling demands of commercial banks became threatened.

Still another third party is the regulatory agencies of advanced industrialized countries. Through a form of collective action, these agencies recently have implemented new rules about the quality of assets in loan portfolios which are felt by creditors to weaken their financial position.[36] Many writers have emphasized the collective power of the international creditor regime, especially the apparent close relationship between the IMF and international private banks.[37] I assert, however, that international creditors are constrained by the power capabilities of the debtors, the international economic environment, and the competitive characteristics of the creditor regime. During periods of prolonged financial mismanagement, uncertainty, and economic decline, international creditors turn inward to reassess their own strategies, tactics, and objectives. Given any lengthy refusal by a debtor state to submit to an IMF-imposed adjustment program, creditors have broken away from the IMF-led international regime to form a more limited, though powerful international creditor regime.

STRATEGIC BARGAINING AND ECONOMIC ADJUSTMENT

Economic adjustment constitutes a series of state and creditor policy moves that are derived from lengthy negotiations and bargaining talks. The two groups often engage in discussion out of fear for a worse-case scenario in which either the state or the creditors face a worsening economic situation. Callaghy writes perceptively that 'palpable fear' is a driving force for international creditors that 'many of the economic reform programs currently underway in the Third World will fail completely unless fundamental changes are made.' 'On the other side,' he continues, 'a number of Third World leaders are beginning to realize that some movement toward neo-orthodox adjustment is imperative to avoid becoming increasingly marginalized.'[38]

We can better understand the learning that has taken place at both levels of politics by reviewing the strategic bargaining positions of states and creditors. I focus on five *components of strategic bargaining* as applied to the adjustment process: 1) the *objectives* that the state, domestic groups, and international creditors set for themselves in the negotiations; 2) the *strategic choices* available to the players which provide a broad though useful simplification of the 'fundamental nature of an issue area'[39]; 3) the *power capabilities* the actors command that could be used to put pressure on the parties in order to reach a favorable outcome, or to resist the other parties' pressure; 4) the *tactics* used by the actors as they seek to deploy their capabilities; and 5) the *constraints* that limit the range of choices for each actor.[40] Strategic bargaining refers to a process in which the choices of one actor are determined by the choice selection of the other actor and the outcome is achieved through negotiations between or among the players.[41]

Although some scholars have criticized the use of game theory as a metaphor because of its looseness in application[42], I contend that the complexities of bargaining at two levels of political interaction involving contrasting objectives and numerous players limit the utility of a rigorous game theory model. A modified game theoretic model provides a valuable framework to understand this interactive relationship. Several scholars already have considered its application to rescheduling negotiations (what might be considered as Level I negotiations between the state and international creditors).[43] And some have looked at the problem of collective action among each group of players: creditors and debtors.[44] I will expand their application to include the overlapping games at both levels: Level I (creditor-state bargaining) and Level II (state-domestic groups bargaining).

The formulation of economic adjustment strategies meets many of the conditions of the model of strategic bargaining. First is a clear sense of the players involved in the negotiations and their bargaining strategies. Actors have identifiable interests that are self-defined; that is, actors have the ability to demarcate and express their own interests and objectives. Second, the major players have revealed their willingness to negotiate. They have agreed that debt management (of which economic adjustment is a component) can meet some of their common objectives, yet they also have agreed to disagree over other defined areas. These negotiations can be considered as an example of a 'mixed-motive' game since, as each side seeks benefits from the manipulation of and constraints on the behavior of the other, neither side for very long will follow a strict conflictual strategy.[45] Indeed, over a period of time the players recognize the constraints imposed on their choice selection and they attempt to adjust to these changing conditions. Debt management negotiations provide an opportunity for the participants to experience iterative and learning behavior and to react in such a way as to strengthen their own position.

The book makes a contribution in this area by relaxing several important assumptions of game theory which strengthens the utility of strategic bargaining in understanding economic adjustment. First, game theoretic models often assume that the actors have a known range of options from which to choose a policy and that they have an equal opportunity to make that decision. Game theory tends to ignore the nature of power relations between actors.[46] But, the ability to create new options, to make choices, and to constrain the choice selection of other actors relies on the relative power of these actors. A second modification to a game theoretic model is the relaxation of the rationality assumption. In many theories of bargaining, emphasis is centered on the assumption of individual rationality as each negotiator tries to maximize his own utility. Each actor is assumed to have perfect information and is able to assign individual values to set preferences based on that information. This assumption needs to be relaxed since individual decision-making is viewed as the outcome of interdependent interaction between two or more actors. By depending on the expected choice of an opponent, the other actor will obtain less than perfect information about the opponent and thus will be constrained from selecting the optimal solution that will maximize his/her utility because the actor depends on expected rather than known choices of the opponent. Conditions of mutual dependence distort the range of alternative options available to the other actor, the other's preference ordering, and the probability distributions affecting the other's choice.

Third, by relying on bargaining in which individual choices are made in an interdependent relationship, decision-making should be construed as an iterative process. Players present proposals and 'bargaining moves' in their attempt to take advantage of the opponent's own moves.[47] Unlike other game theory assumptions which emphasize fixed utilities and pay-off matrices, the strategic bargaining model used in this book reflects moves and counter-moves altering the players' utilities and preferences. Learning derives from repeated exposure to the tactical policy moves of the opponent and, more specifically, how those moves affect the actor's own moves and use of power capabilities. Since bargaining, by definition, requires a mutual willingness to negotiate, bargaining provides a continuous opportunity for players to learn about each other and to reach an agreement as to strengthen their own position. Thus, each side is pursuing its interests yet constrained by the power capabilities and tactics pursued by the other.

Introduction

OVERVIEW OF THE INTERNATIONAL DEBT CRISIS

This section provides a brief analysis of several economic indicators which highlight some characteristics and trends of the international debt crisis. Tables 1.1–1.3 illustrate some economic similarities and differences between Africa and Latin America as well as a comparison between those continents and all developing countries. A general feature for most indebted states is their overall poor economic performance. The per capita growth rate in Table 1.1 points to the deterioration in both African and Latin American economies. For Africa, the per capita rate has been negative in all but two years between 1984 and 1993. Latin America has fared only slightly better though its rate still remains far below that of all developing countries. The table on central government fiscal balances provides a general indication of the states' ability to manage their precarious economies. Clearly, all developing countries are faced with fiscal deficits although the deficits (in percent of GDP) have been decreasing. However, African states still have had more substantial deficits than other countries while Latin America has had much better success in lowering their deficits.

In turning attention to foreign economic indicators (Table 1.2), the terms of trade figures for Africa during the 1980s provides a basis for understanding its debt crisis. Since Africa depends heavily on relatively few agricultural commodities to generate foreign exchange, any sizeable decline in the terms of trade is widely affected throughout the economy. Both Latin America's and Africa's terms of trade fell by about 28 percent between 1985 and 1993. The terms of trade for all developing countries decreased by 15 percent.

While Africa's trade balance has been in deficit for many years (in contrast to Latin America's trade position), their current account deficits bring down their current account balance into a substantial deficit. There continues to be a steady outflow of capital, especially from the Latin American countries as they resume interest payments. As a percentage of exports, the current account balance for Latin America and Africa remains a difficult and consistent problem and one that is severer for them than for all developing countries.

Several relevant points can be drawn from Table 1.3 on external debt indicators. First, the total external debt for all developing countries has risen by 65 percent from 1984 until 1993. African debt has had a more spectacular growth, rising by more than a two-fold rate. Latin America experienced a much slower growth through the 1980s since by the early 1980s it already had heavily borrowed from foreign creditors. Second, the source of credit has shifted in both sets of countries over the 1980s. For both Latin America and Africa, the proportion of international private loans has shrunk in relation to official sources. Still, by the early 1990s, there was an inverse relationship in the sources of international credit for Africa and Latin America. Third, by examining several ratios of indebtedness we can detect the relative burden of debt on Africa and Latin America. The main conclusion from analyzing the debt to export, debt to GDP, and debt service payments to export ratios is the rough equivalency of burden shared by Africa and Latin America. Africa, in particular, has experienced spectacular growth in its debt to export ratio as its exports grew slowly while the total debt level rose quickly. The debt to GDP ratio is indicative of the debt burden on the economy as a whole. The Latin American figures reveal a much stronger economy than Africa and a better ability to weather the debt crisis. Finally, the debt service ratio represents actual payments to creditors in relation to exports. In many ways, this is the most relevant indicator of the cost of indebtedness. According to common practice, any time the ratio rises above 20 percent the country's debt burden is considered unmanageable thus undermining the creditworthiness of the economy. While Africa has remained fairly consistent within the range of low- to mid-20s, Latin America has made significant improvements since the late-1980s although the ratio is still more than twice as large as the ratio for all developing countries.

CASE STUDIES

In seeking to explain the selection, evaluation, and sequencing of adjustment strategies, I chose to focus on Kenya, Zimbabwe, and Brazil between about 1985 and the present. A brief comment should be made here concerning the comparison of a major Latin American debtor country with two much smaller African countries. While the previous section noted the substantial difference in absolute indebtedness, the data also pointed out the significant relative debt burden carried by Africa as well as Latin America. Africa's burden of indebtedness has unfairly received much less attention than Latin America's case even though Africa's economy is much more vulnerable and precarious. Another distinguishing feature of their indebtedness is the source of their loans. While Africa owes about 26 percent of its loans to private creditors, Latin America owes around 58 percent. For Africa, indebtedness to private sources should neither be ignored nor merged into the larger portion from official sources. This study considers the countries' indebtedness, their response to that indebtedness, and their economic adjustment strategies in light of all their creditors.[48]

There are several benefits from this comparison of different cases. One is the opportunity to test the utility of strategic bargaining under different adjustment conditions. Strategic bargaining will be shown to take place in all three countries as they respond, in their own way, to the adjustment dilemma. A second advantage from this range of adjustment strategies is made by the claim that these countries represent other countries at their level of development and indebtedness. If this framework of analysis can be applied effectively to Brazil (where 70 percent of its debt is from private sources), it should be equally applicable to other large debtor countries in Latin America. Similarly, if two-level bargaining takes place in Kenya and Zimbabwe (in which over 70 percent of their debt is from official sources), it is likely to occur in other African countries.

Despite significant differences, these countries share important attributes of indebted development. First, each has acquired a significant debt relative to its GDP and debt service payments. All three countries must respond to indebtedness and the need to manage their debt by constructing an economic adjustment strategy. Second, all three have had to undergo two sets of negotiations with international creditors over debt repayments and with domestic groups over the distribution of adjustment costs. Each has established an identifiable adjustment agenda that details their bargaining positions. All three governments publish adjustment and development statements, financing requirements, and policy position papers. Third, officials from the governments and IFIs permitted many in-depth interviews and provided access to official and confidential documents.

An additional benefit from comparing these countries is the range of adjustment strategies selected by the governments. In what may be called a neo-orthodox approach, the *Kenyan* state actively uses its regulatory power and legal controls to promote a growth-oriented economy based on the export sector. Export incentives, trade liberalization policies, and foreign investment incentives have been adopted in accordance with economic orthodox principles. The distributive effects of Kenya's adjustment strategy also are congruent with economic orthodoxy. An examination of the government budget indicates how the costs of adjustment are imposed onto the basic goods sector and state firms that do not generate foreign exchange. However, the state has been slow to reform state-owned firms considered integral to national security, infrastructural development, and the export sector. Kenya follows a generally more consistent orthodox strategy toward international creditors. Those creditors are willing to overlook, for the time being, the rigid one-party political system that monopolizes power in the country because of Kenya's ideological unity and commitment to relatively orthodox and market-oriented economic policies.

Table 1.1 Domestic Economic Indicators, 1974–93

	\multicolumn{10}{c}{Real GDP (Annual Changes, in percent)}									
	1974–83	1984	1985	1986	1987	1988	1989	1990	1991	1992	1993
Developing Countries	4.0	4.5	4.4	3.8	4.5	3.9	3.7	3.5	3.3	6.7	5.4
Africa	2.4	1.4	4.1	1.7	0.8	3.6	2.7	0.9	1.4	2.7	3.0
Latin America	3.1	3.6	3.4	4.3	2.2	0.7	1.0	−0.1	2.8	2.7	4.2

	\multicolumn{10}{c}{Real Per Capita GDP (Annual Changes, in percent)}									
	1974–83	1984	1985	1986	1987	1988	1989	1990	1991	1992	1993
Developing Countries	1.3	2.0	2.0	1.1	2.3	1.5	1.4	1.2	1.3	4.1	3.2
Sub-Saharan Africa	−0.6	−0.7	0.6	0.4	−1.0	−0.2	−1.3	−1.9	−1.8	−1.1	−1.0
Latin America	0.5	1.5	1.3	1.0	1.2	−1.4	−1.3	−2.1	0.8	0.6	2.1

	\multicolumn{10}{c}{Central Government Fiscal Balances (in percent of GDP)}									
	1974–83	1984	1985	1986	1987	1988	1989	1990	1991	1992	1993
Developing Countries	—	−5.2	−4.9	−6.7	−6.9	−6.7	−5.2	−3.3	−4.2	−3.0	−2.7
Sub-Saharan Africa	—	−5.2	−5.4	−7.0	−8.1	−7.8	−7.1	−7.0	−7.8	−5.9	−5.0
Latin America	—	−4.1	−3.8	−5.2	−7.1	−5.7	−6.3	−0.2	−1.1	−0.7	0.2

Source International Monetary Fund, *World Economic Outlook* (Washington, D.C.: IMF, May 1992).

Table 1.2 Foreign Economic Indicators, 1974–93

	Terms of Trade (Annual Changes, in percent)									
	1974–83	1984	1985	1986	1987	1988	1989	1990	1991	1992	1993
Developing Countries	6.0	1.4	-2.4	-18.1	2.5	3.8	1.8	2.1	-2.8	-1.9	0.1
Sub-Saharan Africa	-1.3	9.7	-0.6	-10.2	-6.9	1.1	-3.3	-3.2	-3.4	-2.0	1.0
Latin America	1.4	4.4	-5.6	-10.2	-5.4	-0.7	-0.4	-1.2	-5.2	-0.6	1.1

	Current Account Transactions, 1984–93 (in billions of U.S. dollars)									
	1984	1985	1986	1987	1988	1989	1990	1991	1992	1993
Sub-Saharan Africa										
— Exports (f.o.b.)	21.6	20.8	21.2	22.6	23.4	24.4	26.0	26.6	27.8	29.6
— Imports (f.o.b.)	20.7	20.4	22.7	24.8	27.2	27.8	29.4	30.0	31.1	32.6
— Trade Balance	0.9	0.5	-1.5	-2.2	-3.8	-3.5	-3.5	-3.4	-3.3	-3.0
Current Acc't. Bal.	-3.2	-3.4	-5.6	-6.4	-7.5	-6.3	-7.7	-7.7	-7.1	-6.8
Latin America										
— Exports (f.o.b.)	101.5	96.4	81.1	91.5	105.5	116.5	128.2	126.5	134.6	148.1
— Imports (f.o.b.)	63.6	63.3	64.5	72.4	82.4	87.2	98.4	114.7	129.2	140.5
— Trade Balance	37.9	33.1	16.6	19.1	23.0	29.3	29.8	11.8	5.3	7.6
Current Acc't. Bal.	-0.9	-1.9	-16.4	-9.1	-9.2	-6.1	-4.2	-19.4	-22.4	-23.0

	Current Account Balances, 1974–1993 (Percentage of Exports of Goods and Services)										
	1974–83	1984	1985	1986	1987	1988	1989	1990	1991	1992	1993
Developing Countries	0.3	-4.9	-4.1	-8.0	-0.6	-2.8	-2.0	-0.8	-7.9	-6.1	-5.6
Sub-Saharan Africa	-24.0	-12.0	-13.3	-21.0	-22.1	-24.7	-20.1	-22.8	-22.2	-19.7	-17.7
Latin America	-21.8	-0.7	-1.5	-14.9	-7.4	-6.7	-4.0	-2.5	-11.8	-12.7	-12.0

Source International Monetary Fund, *World Economic Outlook* (Washington, D.C.: IMF, May 1992).

Table 1.3 External Debt Indicators, 1984–93

	1984	1985	1986	1987	1988	1989	1990	1991	1992	1993
Total External Debt (in billions of U.S. dollars)										
Developing Countries	879.1	949.1	1050.2	1173.3	1194.4	1221.8	1280.6	1347.7	1387.9	1450.8
Sub-Saharan Africa	56.2	64.7	86.5	105.2	110.3	113.8	126.1	131.4	133.0	137.4
Latin America	360.3	368.2	381.9	419.1	409.4	410.4	422.4	433.4	435.0	3442.7
Source of Foreign Loans by Type of Creditors, 1984–93 (In percent of total external debt)										
Developing Countries										
— Official	32	34	36	39	40	41	43	43	42	42
— Private	68	63	64	61	60	59	57	57	58	58
Sub-Saharan Africa										
— Official	66	68	69	70	71	69	71	73	74	75
— Private	34	32	31	30	29	31	29	27	26	25
Latin America										
— Official	16	19	22	24	26	28	23	33	33	35
— Private	84	81	78	76	74	72	77	67	67	65
External Debt (in percent of exports of goods and services)										
Developing Countries	137.0	154.5	180.4	167.0	148.2	135.3	126.0	125.7	119.5	112.5
Sub-Saharan Africa	214.1	253.2	323.3	365.3	365.1	362.5	375.1	378.7	367.9	356.1
Latin America	274.9	293.8	247.9	341.5	295.0	267.5	250.7	263.4	247.3	230.1

(table 1.3 continued)

	\multicolumn{10}{c}{External Debt (in percent of GDP)}									
	1984	1985	1986	1987	1988	1989	1990	1991	1992	1993
Developing Countries	34.0	36.4	39.0	38.5	36.4	33.3	31.5	32.1	28.6	26.8
Sub-Saharan Africa	56.6	66.6	80.1	92.6	89.7	89.6	83.6	78.0	75.4	73.5
Latin America	53.1	53.7	51.6	55.6	50.4	43.5	40.0	42.9	35.9	35.8

	Debt Service Payments (in percent of exports of goods and services)									
	1984	1985	1986	1987	1988	1989	1990	1991	1992	1993
Developing Countries	19.3	20.9	22.5	20.1	18.8	16.3	14.3	14.2	14.5	13.2
Sub-Saharan Africa	23.5	22.4	24.7	21.6	22.9	21.6	21.4	22.0	22.7	21.8
Latin America	40.5	42.2	46.1	39.5	43.9	31.4	27.3	31.5	35.3	29.4

Source International Monetary Fund, *World Economic Outlook* (Washington, D.C.: IMF, May 1992).

Zimbabwe provides an interesting contrast to Kenya as a country following a decidedly mixed pattern of economic adjustment. Zimbabwe is one of Africa's most recently independent countries, and the governing elites of the nation have yet to consolidate and solidify their power bases into a united ideological force. Deep ethnic, economic, and political divisions remain as powerful obstacles to a consistent adjustment strategy. In the absence of such ideological unity (as present in Kenya), the government has lacked a consistent bargaining strategy toward either domestic interests or international creditors. In terms of adjustment, the government incorporates two contrasting tendencies. It displays a neo-orthodox approach toward punctual external debt repayment and avoidance of capital account deficits, winning praise from the World Bank for its prudent and stable management of the macro economy. Yet, in efforts to redress inherited economic inequities, it has followed a more heterodox economic approach by actively intervening in the economy with foreign exchange, import, and price controls, and supporting parastatal subsidies and wage increases. While seeking to avoid the internal political ramifications of accepting IMF conditions, the government has failed to attract sufficient foreign capital to serve the interests of the important private sector and, by depleting foreign reserves to finance a growing deficit, the government will soon confront serious economic dilemmas.

Like several other Southern Cone countries, *Brazil* recently has been affected by economic restructuring and political liberalization. The democratization process has unleashed tremendous pressures from domestic political interest groups, weakening the president and influencing the state's adjustment and bargaining strategies. In response to these new domestic forces, Brazil's adjustment strategy has swung from orthodoxy to heterodoxy and back to orthodoxy. The introduction and subsequent failure of several Cruzado Plans, the implementation of an interest payment moratorium, and the rejection followed by acceptance of IMF conditions demonstrate the range of government reaction to these forces. Yet, in many ways, the state effectively has used its vast power capabilities to constrain both domestic groups and international creditors. The 1988 rescheduling agreement indicates Brazil's leverage based on the size of foreign debt, the capacity to implement a moratorium, and its important economic relationship with the United States.

ORGANIZATION OF THE STUDY

The book contains six chapters. Chapter 2 focuses on the dynamics

Table 1.4 *External Debt for Brazil, Kenya and Zimbabwe, 1985–92 (in percent of exports of goods and services)*

	1985	1986	1987	1988	1989	1990[a]	1991[b]	1992[b]
Brazil	361.9	449.9	430.5	313.4	296.4	324.0	326.3	312.3
Kenya	257.6	264.2	347.0	323.1	331.7	307.3	310.3	272.0
Zimbabwe	166.4	165.5	177.9	136.9	143.0	148.6	146.6	142.0

[a] Estimate   [b] Forecast
Source   Institute of International Finance, *Country Reports* for Kenya, Zimbabwe, and Brazil (Washington, D.C.: IIF 1991).

Table 1.5 *External Debt for Brazil, Kenya, and Zimbabwe, 1985–92 (in percent of GDP)*

	1985	1986	1987	1988	1989	1990[a]	1991[b]	1992[b]
Brazil	47.6	42.2	42.0	35.1	25.7	24.9	28.6	33.7
Kenya	67.5	69.4	76.1	72.1	77.3	79.0	83.2	71.7
Zimbabwe	49.3	53.4	54.7	43.5	46.3	47.4	57.2	66.6

[a] Estimate   [b] Forecast
Source   Institute of International Finance, *Country Reports* for Kenya, Zimbabwe, and Brazil (Washington, D.C.: IIF 1991).

Table 1.6 *Debt Service Payments for Brazil, Kenya and Zimbabwe, 1985–92 (in percent of exports of goods and services)*

	1985	1986	1987	1988	1989	1990a	1991b	1992b
Brazil	44.5	56.5	48.1	43.9	40.9	38.9	33.6	31.1
Kenya	33.6	28.4	36.2	32.3	30.8	31.9	30.2	27.9
Zimbabwe	29.8	27.0	32.4	28.0	23.4	22.8	19.7	19.7

[a] Estimate   [b] Forecast
Source   Institute of International Finance, *Country Reports* for Kenya, Zimbabwe, and Brazil (Washington, D.C.: IIF 1991).

of two-level strategic bargaining. After this introductory chapter, the next chapter lays out the strategic objectives of international creditors that shape the response by indebted states over the last several years of the debt crisis. The chapter analyzes the specific rules and policy moves of international creditors as they form and maintain an international creditor regime.

The following three chapters deal more specifically with the empirical cases of the state in Kenya, Zimbabwe, and Brazil. Chapter 3 examines the historical economic performance of the states, their adjustment objectives, and their financing requirements in order to implement adjustment strategies. Since the state interacts with international creditors, the

Table 1.7 Source of Foreign Loans by Type of Creditors for Brazil, Kenya, and Zimbabwe, 1985–92 (in US millions and in percent)

	1985	1986	1987	1988	1989	1990[a]	1991[b]	1992[b]
Brazil								
Total Debt	106080	113703	123678	115402	115061	117729	118005	120911
— Official Creditors	25110	30769	35032	33767	32566	33575	33702	34946
(in %)	(24)	(24)	(28)	(29)	(28)	(28)	(29)	(29)
— Private Creditors	80970	82934	88646	81635	82495	84154	84303	85965
(in %)	(76)	(73)	(72)	(71)	(72)	(72)	(71)	(71)
Kenya								
Total Debt	4139	5024	6036	6074	6416	6863	6685	6348
— Official Creditors	3600	4126	4967	4871	5266	5450	5532	5431
(in %)	(87)	(82)	(82)	(80)	(82)	(79)	(83)	(86)
— Private Creditors	538	898	1069	1160	1151	1413	1153	917
(in %)	(13)	(18)	(18)	(20)	(18)	(21)	(17)	(14)
Zimbabwe								
Total Debt	2148	2533	2939	2585	2777	3029	3271	3538
— Official Creditors	1368	1632	1952	1755	1983	2280	2226	2721
(in %)	(64)	(64)	(66)	(68)	(71)	(75)	(68)	(77)
— Private Creditors	780	901	987	830	794	749	1045	817
(in %)	(36)	(36)	(34)	(32)	(29)	(25)	(32)	(23)

[a] Estimate [b] Forecast

Source Institute of International Finance, *Country Reports* for Kenya, Zimbabwe, and Brazil (Washington, D.C.: IIF 1992).

emphasis in Chapter 4 is on the state's bargaining relationship with international official and private creditors. Chapter 5 examines the distributive effects of the adjustment strategies in the three countries. In particular, the chapter analyzes government budgets in order to identify the sectoral distribution arising from the costs of adjustment.

The concluding chapter seeks to place this book as part of a third wave of studies in analyzing and explaining the international debt crisis. Unlike the previous two waves of research, the current one utilizes a framework of strategic interaction and bargaining between the indebted state, its domestic constituents, and international creditors. The third wave offers a more comprehensive, dynamic, and accurate account of economic adjustment and debt management than did the other waves of the literature. Also, the last chapter offers several research suggestions. Further research along the general lines of the current study could contribute by extending the conceptual framework of strategic bargaining to either more cases or to a more intensive focus on state-society-creditor relations.

NOTES

1. These 'horns of a dilemma' stand in stark contrast to each other in order to present clearly the parameters of the conceptual framework. In reality, as demonstrated later by the case studies, states often move from one option to the other utilizing what others have called 'slippage' in the actual implementation of adjustment policies. See Ch. 5 in Paul Mosley, Jane Harrigan, and John Toye, *Aid and Power: The World Bank and Policy-Based Lending*, Vol. 1 (London: Routledge, 1991).
2. Robert Putnam, 'Diplomacy and Domestic Politics: The Logic of Two-Level Games,' *International Organization* 42 (Summer 1988); Howard P. Lehman and Jennifer L. McCoy, 'The Dynamics of the Two-Level Bargaining Game: The 1988 Brazilian Debt Negotiations,' World Politics 44:4 (July 1992).
3. Wilfred L. David, *The IMF Policy Paradigm: The Macroeconomics of Stabilization, Structural Adjustment, and Economic Development* (New York: Praeger, 1985); C. David Finch, 'The IMF: The Record and the Prospect,' *Essays in International Finance*, No. 175, Princeton University (1989); Richard E. Feinberg and Edmar L. Bacha, 'When Supply and Demand Don't Intersect: Latin America and the Bretton Woods Institutions in the 1980s,' *Development and Change* 19:3 (July 1988):371–400.
4. David, *The IMF Policy Paradigm*.
5. Thomas M. Callaghy, 'Toward State Capability and Embedded Liberalism in the Third World: Lessons for Economic Adjustment,' in Joan M. Nelson, ed., *Fragile Coalitions: The Politics of Economic*

       Adjustment (Washington, D.C.: Overseas Development Council, 1989), p. 116.
6. World Bank, *Africa's Adjustment and Growth in the 1980s* (Washington, D.C.: World Bank, 1989).
7. Stephan Haggard, 'The Politics of Adjustment: Lessons from the IMF's Extended Fund Facility,' in Miles Kahler, ed., *The Politics of International Debt* (Ithaca: Cornell University Press, 1986); Joan M. Nelson, 'The Politics of Stabilization,' in Richard E. Feinberg and Valeriana Kallab, eds., *Adjustment Crisis in the Third World* (Washington, D.C.: Overseas Development Council, 1984).
8. Proponents of an orthodox adjustment strategy argue that the choice for a government is 'between promptly initiating a gradual and orderly adjustment process, on the one hand, or being faced with abrupt and disorderly adjustment, on the other.' J. B. Zulu and S. M. Nsouli, 'Adjustment Programmes in Africa. *Occasional Paper* 34 (Washington, D.C.: International Monetary Fund, 1985), p. 3.
9. Reginald Herbold Green, 'Third World Sovereign Debt Renegotiation 1980–1986 and After: Procedures, Paradigms, and Portents,' *Discussion Paper* 223 (Sussex: IDS Institute, 1986); Guillermo O'Donnell, 'Brazil's Failure: What Future for Debtors' Cartels?' *Third World Quarterly* 9:4 (October 1987).
10. Joan M. Nelson, ed., *Economic Crisis and Policy Choice: The Politics of Adjustment in the Third World* (Princeton: Princeton University Press, 1990) and Mosely, Harrigan, and Toye, *Aid and Power*.
11. Nora Hamilton, *The Limits of State Autonomy: Post-Revolutionary Mexico* (Princeton: Princeton University Press, 1982); Eric Nordlinger, *On the Autonomy of the Democratic State* (Cambridge: Harvard University Press, 1981); Eric Nordlinger, 'Taking the State Seriously,' in Myron Weiner and Samuel P. Huntington, eds., *Understanding Political Development* (Boston: Little, Brown, 1987); Theda Skocpol, *States and Social Revolutions: A Comparative Analysis of France, Russia, and China* (Cambridge: Cambridge University Press, 1979); Peter Evans, et. al., eds., *Bringing the State Back In* (Cambridge: Cambridge University Press, 1985).
12. Almond was making a pointed remark in response to the well-received edited book by Evans, et. al., *Bringing the State Back In*. See Gabriel H. Almond, 'The Return to the State,' *American Political Science Review* 82:3 (September 1988).
13. Ralph Austen, *Africa in Economic History* (London: James Currey, 1987); D. K. Fieldhouse, *Black Africa, 1945–1980: Economic Decolonization and Arrested Development* (London: Allen and Unwin, 1986).
14. Donald Rothchild, 'Hegemony and State Softness: Some Variations in Elite Responses,' in Zaki Ergas, ed., *The African State in Transition* (New York: St. Martin's Press, 1987), p. 120.
15. Ibid., p. 121.
16. Thomas Callaghy and Ernest James Wilson III, 'Africa: Policy, Reality,

or Ritual?', in Raymond Vernon, ed., *The Promise of Privatization* (New York: Council on Foreign Relations, 1988).
17. Thomas Callaghy, 'The State as Lame Leviathan: The Patrimonial Administrative State in Africa,' in Ergas, ed., *The African State in Transition*.
18. Bob Jessop, *State Theory: Putting the Capitalist State in its Place* (Cambridge: Polity Press, 1990), Ch. 9.
19. Migdal focuses on the states' 'unmistakable strengths in penetrating societies and their surprising weaknesses in effecting goal-oriented social changes' in Joel S. Migdal, *Strong Societies and Weak States: State-Society Relations and State Capabilities in the Third World* (Princeton: Princeton University Press, 1988), p. 9.
20. Joshua B. Forrest, 'The Quest for State 'Hardness' In Africa,' *Comparative Politics* 20:4 (July 1988).
21. Thomas M. Callaghy, 'Toward State Capability and Embedded Liberalism in the Third World,' p. 121.
22. Thomas J. Bierstecker, 'Reducing the Role of the State in the Economy: A Conceptual Exploration of IMF and World Bank Prescriptions,' *International Studies Quarterly* 34:4 (December 1990), p. 477.
23. Callaghy, 'Toward State Capability and Embedded Liberalism in the Third World,' p. 118.
24. Stephen Krasner, *Defending the National Interest: Raw Materials Investments and U.S. Foreign Policy* (Princeton: Princeton University Press, 1978), p. 57; Stephen Krasner, 'Approaches to the State: Alternative Conceptions and Historical Dynamics,' *Comparative Politics* 16:2 (January 1984).
25. Nordlinger, 'Taking the State Seriously,' p. 365.
26. Ibid., p. 361.
27. Donald Rothchild and Michael Foley, 'The Implications of Scarcity for Governance in Africa,' *International Political Science Review* 4:3 (1983).
28. Lewis W. Snider, 'Identifying the Elements of State Power: Where Do We Begin?,' *Comparative Political Studies* 20 (October 1987), p. 321. See Migdal, *Strong Societies and Weak States* and Forrest, 'The Quest for State 'Hardness' in Africa' for a similar conceptualization of state power.
29. Rothchild, 'Hegemony and State Softness,' p. 120.
30. Jessop, *State Theory*, p. 341.
31. Nordlinger, 'Taking the State Seriously,' p. 362.
32. Stephan Haggard, 'IMF Conditionality as a Two Level Game: The Case of the Philippines under Marcos,' unpublished manuscript, 1988, p. 36.
33. Putnam, 'Diplomacy and Domestic Politics,' p. 434.
34. In actual practice, there only have been isolated cases in which a borrower government refuses to cooperate with creditors. Both

Mexico and Brazil imposed moratoriums on interest payments, yet within a short period they were back in the fold of the international financial community. At various times, Nigeria, Peru, and Bolivia have challenged creditors by placing restrictions on interest payments. However, in the majority of cases, as the costs of not reaching a debt agreement increase, negotiators on both sides are forced to seek a compromise. See Lehman and McCoy, 'The Dynamics of the Two-Level Bargaining Game,' for discussion on the costs of a no-agreement.

35. For a discussion of the cracks in the creditor cartel resulting from conflicts between small and large lenders, between U.S. and European banks, between banks and the U.S. government, and between banks and the IMF, see Robert Devlin, *Debt and Crisis in Latin America: The Supply Side of the Story* (Princeton: Princeton University Press, 1989), pp. 227–29. The latter occurred as the banks began to view the IMF as a free-rider, while the IMF became a partial hostage to the short-term profit motive of the private banks,

36. In recognition of these constraints on bank strategies, Level I bank negotiators successfully have established the so-called 'menu of options.' The menu approach, expanded in the Brady Plan, was created to increase the likelihood of bank ratification of debt accords. The menu provides a new incentive structure for banks to address the diverging concerns of Level II constituents and to shift away from a defensive posture to one based on renewed participation in lending while protecting the quality of bank assets.

37. Charles Lipson, 'Bankers' Dilemmas: Private Cooperation in Rescheduling Sovereign Debts,' in Kenneth A. Oye, ed., *Cooperation Under Anarchy* (Princeton: Princeton University Press, 1986); Vinod K. Aggarwal, *International Debt Threat: Bargaining Among Creditors and Debtors in the 1980s* (Berkeley: Institute of International Studies, 1987); Devlin, *Debt and Crisis in Latin America*.

38. Callaghy, 'Toward State Capability and Embedded Liberalism in the Third World,' pp. 134–5.

39. Duncan Snidal, 'The Game Theory of International Politics,' in Oye, ed., *Cooperation Under Anarchy*, p. 37.

40. Oran R. Young, 'Strategic Interaction and Bargaining,' in Oran Young, ed., *Bargaining: Formal Theories of Negotiation* (Urbana: University of Illinois Press, 1975); Carlos Fortin, 'Power, Bargaining, and the Latin American Debt Negotiations: Some Political Perspectives,' in Stephany Griffith-Jones, ed., *Managing World Debt* (New York: St. Martin's Press, 1988).

41. Thomas Schelling, *The Strategy of Conflict* (Cambridge: Harvard University Press, 1960); Robert Axelrod, *The Evolution of Cooperation* (New York: Basic Books, 1984); Robert Axelrod and Robert Keohane, 'Achieving Cooperation Under Anarchy,' in Oye, ed., *Cooperation Under Anarchy*; Snidal, 'The Game Theory of International Politics.'

42. Snidal, 'The Game Theory of International Politics,' pp. 29–30.
43. Aggarwal, *International Debt Threat*; Fortin, 'Power, Bargaining, and Latin American Debt Negotiations;' Benjamin J. Cohen, 'Developing-Country Debt: A Middle Way,' No. 173, *Essays in International Finance* (Princeton University, 1989).
44. Lipson, 'Bankers' Dilemmas;' O'Donnell, 'Brazil's Future.'
45. The term, mixed-motive, implies 'the ambivalence of (actor's) relation to the other player – the mixture of mutual dependence and conflict, of partnership and competition.' See Schelling, *The Strategy of Conflict*, p. 89.
46. Fortin, 'Power, Bargaining, and the Latin American Debt Negotiations.'
47. Schelling, *The Strategy of Conflict*, p. 101.
48. Similar efforts toward this end have been made by the authors whose findings were presented in the edited collections by Mosley and Nelson.

2 Strategic Priorities of the International Creditor Regime

Creditors and debtor states interact with each other according to both the specific behavior of individual actors as well as to the general operating rules and norms of behavior found within the context of international finance. While the next three chapters focus on the specific policies stemming from the creditor-debtor relationship, this chapter lays out the strategic priorities of the *international creditor regime*.

This chapter seeks to explain the evolution of the international creditor regime during the 1980s and early 1990s as the Baker and Brady Plans were being introduced and implemented. Explanation of the shifting priorities and strategies pursued in particular by international commercial banks focuses on two related features of the international creditor regime. At a more *specific* level of analysis, individual creditors competed against each other as they sought to protect themselves against the increasing risk during this phase of the international debt crisis. As conflict intensified within the regime, individual creditors often used specific policy moves in pursuit of their own priorities which threatened the apparent unity of the regime. At a more *general* level of analysis, the widespread acceptance of underlying principles, norms, and rules constituting the regime, countered the potential collapse of the regime. By the early 1990s, the reevaluation of expectations by international commercial banks and their recent flexibility in shifting policy positions toward other creditors and debtor states suggest the emergence of a reformulated and, in some ways, strengthened international creditor regime. In an attempt to understand this outcome of creditor behavior, this chapter analyzes the policies undertaken by international banks and other creditors during the 1980s and early 1990s as these actors pursue their strategic priorities. Analysis of creditor policies during this period of rising risk is used here to account for both the inter-creditor conflict and the continued durability and relative leverage of international creditors in debt negotiations.[1]

International creditors generally pursue three competing, though not mutually exclusive, priorities that are conditioned by the perception of risk over time. Creditors then have created bargaining strategies that fit the stated priorities. The most pressing and immediate priority for many creditors (especially commercial institutions) is the maintenance of scheduled payment of fees, commissions, and/or interest from borrowers. During the early 1980s, creditors sought to achieve this priority by raising the amount of financing tied to International Monetary Fund conditions through concerted lending. This was the bargaining strategy labeled *financing and adjustment*.

As risk rose for international banks because of the failure of this strategy to generate repayment, they endorsed a second strategic priority. The medium-term priority under the *adjustment with growth* bargaining strategy of the mid-1980s was the protection of the value of the remaining loans so as neither to impair the debtor's ability to repay nor to damage the creditor's portfolio. Since many creditors, especially US banks, are regulated by national authorities, any consistent weakening of their assets is expected to draw fire from these powerful supervisory agencies which then could further harm the reputation of the creditors in the eyes of investors and stockholders. Creditors introduced creative financing and 'exiting' measures as part of the menu of options. Yet, their strategy remained one of defensive lending.

In order to reinvigorate the international lending environment, many creditors now follow a strategy called *adjustment with debt reduction*. This bargaining strategy intends to restore the basis of lending and borrowing; that is, in the long-term, creditors anticipate that the borrowing states' restored credit standing, initiated by debt reduction, will foster a profitable and stable lending environment. Many creditors now consider long-term economic improvement in the debtor countries as a necessary condition for the resumption of lending, the restoration of debt servicing capacity, and the legitimization of the 'rules of the game' governing international lending.

Each of these bargaining strategies have been utilized by creditors towards Kenya, Zimbabwe, and Brazil. As this book focuses on debtor-creditor relations since the mid-1980s, the two most recent creditor strategies will be analyzed in Chapter Four. Until late 1991, Kenya was extremely successful in facilitating extensive slippage in its adjustment programs by manipulating inter-creditor competition. To a lesser extent, Zimbabwe and Brazil sought to play individual creditors off each other in order to obtain more satisfactory terms of lending agreements. In the cases of Kenya and Brazil, they currently are trying to negotiate within the framework of the 'adjustment with debt reduction strategy'. Zimbabwe always has operated somewhat independently of these creditor strategies. However, as it works toward opening up its economy to the international economic system, the government will be more susceptible to this most recent creditor bargaining strategy.

When we examine the policies and priorities of individual creditors, we can detect, at a general level, a degree of institutionalization of principles, norms, rules, and decision-making procedures that establish a regime.[2] This chapter broadly considers the *international creditor regime* as being constituted of organizations which provide liquid capital to sovereign borrowers. Industrialized governments, multilateral financial institutions (International Monetary Fund, World Bank, Paris Club forum), and international commercial banks are the key official and private creditors in the creditor regime. The regime has operated on the basis of a broad convergence of actors' expectations over the free exchange of capital, the requirements of repayment from sovereign lenders, the protection of private property, and the preservation of stable financial relations.[3] Actors thus enter into a regime with the expectations that common adherence to dominant rules will lead to relative stability which, in turn, is believed to be a basis for profitable transactions. Thus, identifying and agreeing to the collective rules of behavior are considered to be prerequisites to achieving objectives of individual creditors.

Yet, even with a general convergence of basic and fundamental principles of the international creditor regime, individual creditors may readjust their specific policies and bargaining strategies as rising risks are perceived. The possible divergence of the creditors' interests among themselves may weaken the regime especially during periods of economic stress. As the costs of remaining attached to a regime rise for individual creditors, these actors will seek to alter their policies which may lead to a reformulated regime.

Three competing explanations have been suggested to explain the regime's response during this stage of the debt crisis. One argument suggests that the intensive competitive environment of the debt crisis has sufficiently weakened the regime to render it ineffective. This reading of the debt crisis highlights significant rifts among the members which foster individualistic responses to the crisis.[4] Examples include the tension between the IMF and commercial banks where the former has demanded involuntary lending from the latter. Another rift is between commercial banks and creditor governments when national regulatory authorities adversely affect the value of bank assets. A third break in creditor unity has appeared between commercial banks themselves as European banks have developed interests dissimilar to U.S. banks. The major weakness with this approach is the emphasis on conflict over specific creditor policies while ignoring the continued importance of the general convergence of accepted principles of the regime.

A contrasting interpretation of regime behavior asserts that, in spite of internal divisions, the regime as a structure possesses sufficient power resources to continue to manipulate the outcome of debt negotiations with economically impoverished and politically weak debtor governments. Reginald Green labels this negotiating framework as a creditor-centered model which assumes 'a zero, not a positive, sum game and lays down rules of play which create the probability of the actual result being a negative game.'[5] A central weakness with this argument is the assumption of a common creditor negotiating strategy, coordinated policy moves among the creditors, and a dismissive view of debtor power capabilities.

The perspective I use in this chapter suggests a third interpretation of regime behavior. The behavior of the international creditor regime is derived from the interdependent relationship between the regime as a structure at a general level and the regime as composed of individual creditors at a specific level. This argument is based on the view that the international creditor regime itself does not act. Rather, international creditors by specifying their own strategies and priorities act out of self-interest which has led to intra-regime competition and conflict. Two somewhat paradoxical outcomes can be identified from this dynamic relationship. First, during the last few years when the international economy has been under great stress, international creditors, to varying degrees, have attempted to strengthen their position both vis-à-vis debtor governments and other creditors by pursuing competing priorities. In the intensely competitive lending environment, creditors have conflicted over interest payment requirements, asset protection, and debt reduction. For most creditors, the pursuit of these priorities is in response to increasingly higher levels of risk.

A second outcome highlights the paradox. In spite of (or perhaps because of) inter-creditor conflict, the regime, as a structure held together by generally accepted principles, has been reformulated in recent years. Because some creditors have been weakened by the burden of risk and have decided to 'exit' from the regime, the regime as a whole has gained because the remaining members were successful in adjusting to these changes. Those creditors who remain within the regime are the ones better able to absorb or to reduce risk leaving others to exit from the regime. By being able to pursue several priorities, creditors are in a position to take advantage of shifts in their economic and political relationship with debtor governments. The international creditor regime thus has emerged from the most recent bargaining phase as a powerful force in international debt negotiations.

THE FINANCING AND ADJUSTMENT STRATEGY OF THE 1970s

The debt crisis, although crystallized in 1982 when Mexico declared its inability to pay interest owed to international creditors, has its roots extend back into the early 1970s. The initial risk perceived by many international creditors was the growing possibility of non-payment of interest and, later in the 1980s, the deterioration in the debt-servicing capacity for debtor countries. As the creditors' short-term priority of interest payment became jeopardized, the initial creditor response focused on short-term 'damage-containment' policies.[6] One set of policies sought to reduce the risk factor in lending to sovereign governments. Of course, from hindsight, we can agree with Robert Devlin's comment that 'banks' willingness to lend exceeded their actual capacity to evaluate risks.'[7] At the time of the lending boom of the late 1970s and early 1980s, risk assessment had only recently emerged as an important tool within creditor institutions. Most creditors assumed that sovereign governments could not go bankrupt as in cases of personal borrowing. Also, a lending imperative had been quickly established based on the massive amount of capital circulating through the financial system. Moreover, as deregulation of the U.S. banking sector occurred in the 1970s, competition for international loans heated up leading to falling spreads.

Although from our current vantage point we can conclude that creditors made risky decisions, it is also clear that from their perspective the lending environment offered spectacular results. Average commitment fees grew from 0.25 percent to 0.75 percent between 1973 and 1975. Similarly, management fees jumped from nil to 0.5 percent over the same period.[8] Lead banks in lending syndicates also earned profitable returns on their participation in these early loans. During the 1970s, twenty percent of the lead bank's return on loans came from fees that were paid up front.[9] Falling spreads and increases in up front fees and commissions, in part, led to rapid growth in the volume of international loans. Thus, the risk factor was mitigated by the tremendous short-term results of lending to sovereign governments.

The risk factor also was countered by the rapid policy and institutional changes occurring during the 1970s. One was the introduction of floating interest rates in 1969. When short-term interest rates rose faster than long-term rates, floating rates shifted risk to the borrower. Lenders were then able to anticipate the spreads on loans and expected profits. Borrowers were placed in the uneasy position of timing their international loans to changing interest rates. Loans on floating rates for major third world borrowers increased from 18.4 percent of the total external public debt in 1974 to 51.4 percent in 1983.[10]

Syndicated lending was another innovation of this period to minimize risk for creditors. Syndication diversifies individual risk by reducing the exposure of each lender while enlarging the total amount of the loan. This new form of lending encouraged more active participation of smaller banks since syndication tailored the size of the loan to the particular circumstances of each bank. Syndicated Eurocurrency lending to the Third World grew from $3.8 billion in 1972 to $11.7 billion in 1975 to $34 billion in 1978 and finally reaching the peak of $44.9 billion in 1981.[11]

A third risk-reducing innovation was the standard introduction of cross-default clauses into loan contracts. This specifies if the borrower defaults on a loan with a single creditor, the borrower is forced into automatic default on all its loans. Thus, in one policy move, a nations' credit structure and its credit lines face imminent collapse.

A fourth factor which reduced the level of risk carried by international creditors was the emergence of the International Monetary Fund as a primary intermediary between creditors and borrowers. In many cases, IMF approval of economic adjustment programs had to be granted prior to lending contracts with international banks. The major institutional actors had given the IMF a *de facto* enforcement role by insisting that an IMF agreement with associated exchange rate, credit control, and budgetary measures was a precondition for official and commercial borrowings. International creditors perceived the IMF's involvement as partially removing their share of the risk. The IMF thus assumed more of a governmental role by taking considerable responsibility over financing and economic adjustment in the developing world.

Given the assumption of this financing and adjustment strategy that the debt crisis merely reflected a temporary liquidity gap, the provision of additional money to borrowers was considered essential. This policy developed into the 'concerted lending' strategy in which all members of a bank syndicate would agree to provide new money in proportion to their existing exposure. In many ways, the concept of 'new money' was a misnomer since the money was returned immediately to the creditors in the form of interest payments. The arm twisting that occurred behind the scenes by the IMF and industrial governments encountered significant resistance, especially by smaller banks, many of whom wanted to reduce their sovereign debt portfolio. Differences in country exposure influenced the attitudes of individual banks toward the IMF's request. Smaller, regional banks were significantly less exposed than larger, money center banks. In 1982, for the top nine money center banks, their exposure to capital ratio was 2.29 for loans to non-oil developing countries. For regional banks, their ratio was just .69.[12]

In conjunction with additional money, the other major procedural reform during this period concerned the shift from annual rescheduling of external debt to multi-year restructuring agreements (MYRAs). This policy simply recognized the inability of most debtors to remain on a repayment schedule. By rescheduling their debt over several years, creditors and borrowers would, in theory, be more certain of eventual repayment and lessen the risk of non-payment.

The implementation of these policy innovations and procedural reforms accelerated the process of international lending. The Eurocurrency market doubled nearly every four years from $65 billion in 1970 to about $1400 billion in 1984. The Bank for International Settlements reported a tremendous growth in net international lending from $90 billion in 1978 to $165 billion in 1981.[13]

When Mexico declared in 1982 that it would place a moratorium on its interest payments to international creditors, the collective perception of risk from lending dramatically shifted which in turn altered the primary priorities sought by international creditors. The Mexican crisis foreshadowed the emergence of numerous financial crises in other debtor countries. Indeed, the short-term strategic priority failed because, by focusing on the domestic capacity for interest payment, the regime was unable to integrate the hazards of an increasingly difficult international economic environment characterized by high interest rates, low demand for exports, and little new bank lending. In response to these on-going economic crises and rising risk levels, international creditors turned to another strategic priority.

THE ADJUSTMENT WITH GROWTH STRATEGY OF THE MID-1980s

As the international creditor regime implemented these technical policies to facilitate debt repayment, the debt burden for the borrowing countries increased dramatically. As the data indicate in the tables in Chapter 1, the economic crisis in debtor countries continued to worsen by the mid-1980s. Not only were the latter unable to repay the interest, the governments faced political unrest and instability as they attempted economic reforms. Several Latin American debtor countries sought to counter their deteriorating economic conditions by forming a regional program from which to negotiate with international creditors. The Cartagena Conference, first convened in June 1984 and followed by additional meetings in 1985 and 1986, asserted that the debt crisis, as an external force, caused the drastic decline in regional living standards. Thus, the members proposed that renegotiated debt payments be limited to a 'reasonable percentage' of export earnings and that IMF programs be replaced by giving 'priority to needs for growth of production and employment.'[14] The group's proposal, though not successful, had an impact on U.S. policy in the debt crisis. The linkage between economic austerity and political instability in the largest Third World debtors, many of whom had economic and strategic value for the United States, became clearer for the latter.

The *Baker Plan*, initiated in 1985 by the Secretary of Treasury James Baker, was the first formulation of a systematic U.S. debt strategy.[15] The Plan targeted two debtor groups: the fifteen largest debtors consisting mainly of Latin American countries (Baker Plan I) and Sub-Saharan African countries (Baker Plan II).[16] The overall strategy recognized the limited success of market-oriented financing measures while continuing to insist on major internal adjustment policies. Baker Plan I contained three elements. First, it called for the adoption by debtors of comprehensively macroeconomic and structural policies to promote growth, to adjust the balance of payments, and to reduce inflation. Adjustment followed the orthodox model which emphasized reliance on the private sector, the undertaking of supply-side actions to facilitate efficient investment, and liberal international trade policies. The second element was the continued central role for the IMF as the coordinator of policy reforms and sustained capital flows. The World Bank also was asked to increase structural adjustment lending. The Plan proposed a fifty percent increase in the annual disbursements of these institutions, from $6 billion to $9 billion over a three-year period, with the World Bank supplying two-thirds of the increase. Third, the Plan called for commercial banks to extend new lending of about $7 billion annually ($20 billion over three years) to the fifteen major debtors.

Baker Plan II provided even less money than the first one. This plan encouraged the reformulation of the IMF's Structural Adjustment Facility (SAF) for Africa by calling for enhanced collaboration between the IMF and the World Bank. This action brought about the use of cross-conditionality in which IMF's austerity conditions would be applied to the World Bank's negotiated agreements.[17]

The Baker Plan was widely criticized from several different perspectives. Many debtor governments saw the Plan as an attempt by industrialized powers to divide the increasingly strident debtor group by silencing the few big debtors with promises of new money.[18] Moreover, no matter how one sliced the $20 billion over a three year period, the expected debt relief for so many large debtors was not significant. As Cline points out,

Table 2.1 Debt Indicators for the Baker 15[a], 1985–88

	1985	1986	1987	1988
Real GDP (%)	3.7	4.6	2.1	0.7
Per Capita	1.6	1.5	0.8	–1.4
Current Account (% of exports)	0.2	–13.6	–5.8	–6.3
Total External Debt (U.S. billions)	419.3	445.9	489.7	477.2
Net External Borrowing (U.S. billions)	3.4	11.9	10.5	2.6
Net IMF Credit (U.S. billions)	1.6	–0.2	–1.3	–0.8
Net Bank Loans (U.S. billions)	–7.8	–4.7	–1.0	–10.3

Note [a] Argentina, Bolivia, Brazil, Chile, Colombia, Ivory Coast, Ecuador, Mexico, Morocco, Nigeria, Peru, Philippines, Uruguay, Venezuela and Yugoslavia.

Source International Monetary Fund, *World Economic Outlook*, May (Washington, D.C.: IMF, 1991).

$20 billion during that period only represented 2.5 percent of the debtors' existing exposure.[19]

Within a few years, it became clear that the Baker Plan's objectives for the heavily indebted participants in the Plan would not be realized. Table 2.1 illustrates the continued problems that plagued the Baker 15 three years after the Plan's implementation. On the one hand, net external borrowing for these countries increased between 1986 and 1988 following the Plan's call for new money arrangements. On the other hand, official lenders provided the bulk of new lending ($15 billion) in contrast to the small amount by banks.[20]

The Plan also refused to recognize that some countries (especially in Africa) were suffering from such profound economic distress as to prohibit any amount of repayment. Debtors also were dismayed with the new emphasis on *cross-conditionality*. For many debtors who were faced with program implementation and the political consequences of these conditions, relatively small amounts of new money would not mitigate internal discontentment.

Moreover, many of the creditors themselves were not satisfied with either of the Baker Plans. The strategy assumed a degree of cooperation among the commercial banks, multilateral institutions, and creditor governments.

Yet, from the banks' perspective, they were asked to contribute additional money which would go to other creditors as interest payment. At this point in the mid-1980s, commercial lenders were questioning the provision of new money to debtors who were beyond the capacity to pay. Within the next two years, these creditors changed their main priority from obtaining interest payment to protecting their remaining loans by reducing their exposure to troubled borrowers.

The nature of creditor claims changed again as the Baker Plan failed to lessen the economic crisis within debtor nations and also failed to offset the gradual decline in commercial lenders' rate of return on their loans. If in the absence of new lending, the borrower ceases to pay part of the interest due, the creditor faces reduced income. U.S. banks were especially conscious of this condition since their outstanding loans constituted a high percentage of their institutions' total capital. In 1982 U.S. banks had lent about 150 percent of their capital to non-oil exporting Third World countries. The exposure of the top nine U.S. money center banks amounted to 229 percent of their capital.[21] While U.S. banks first would prefer the resumption of interest payments to shore up their deteriorating profit margins, their second best objective was the reduction in the amount of non-performing loans as a means to strengthen their balance sheets.[22]

Banks came under increasing pressure from national bank regulators to reduce their non-performing loans by tightening up accounting and business practices over those loans. The volatility of U.S. bank industry and the heavy exposure of money center banks in the mid-1980s focused regulatory attention on the inadequacy of bank reserves. A primary objective was to force banks to increase their capital base in relation to their exposure of low performing foreign loans. The first step occurred in 1983 when new capital requirements were introduced which raised the primary capital ratio of major U.S. banks from 4.63 percent to 5.35 percent. In June 1985, the minimum level again was raised to equal at least six percent of total assets.[23] The Inter-agency Country Exposure Risk Committee (ICERC), the main U.S. regulatory authority, introduced new guidelines in early 1984 that required banks to establish additional loan-loss reserves called Allocated Transfer Risk Reserves.[24] Under this ruling, banks would have to make provisions against loans to individual countries where a specific risk has been identified. In the first year following such a requirement the ATRR has to cover ten percent of loans rising to fifteen percent in subsequent years. Although 'specific provisions' forced banks to set aside capital, creditors are able to negotiate some tax reductions against these provisions.[25]

In addition to passing judgement on minimum capital requirements, ICERC also has the authority to evaluate and alter the rating of foreign loans held by U.S. banks. Loan reclassification can penalize both creditors and debtors. First, banks immediately would be required to set aside a reserve of ten to fifteen percent against assets whose value had been found to be impaired. Second, such a reclassification, according to an official in the U.S. Treasury, would place that debtor in the same category as Nicaragua, Bolivia, and Zaire, countries which, when provided credit, have to pay higher interest rates and/or fees for those credits.[26] Third, categorizing a borrower's account as value-impaired would make it difficult for the banks to justify to their shareholders rescheduling with a new money component.[27] It would be considered as 'throwing good money after bad' rather than as an attempt to manage the debt crisis.[28]

Bank regulators also have intervened in the accounting practices of U.S. banks for placing loans on a nonaccrual basis.[29] Prior to 1984, banks had to report loan payments that were more than 90 days late at the end of the quarter. Under the new rules, any loan that falls into nonaccrual at any point during the quarter had to be reported as nonaccrual. This policy move pressured banks to encourage full payment of all of the overdue interest before a loan could be returned to accrual basis. Clearly, the implications of this new policy expanded beyond banking accounting practices. Debtors were pressured to meet new deadlines imposed on them by the banks which 'led the negotiations into brinkmanship exercises that clearly distracted attention from the option of changing the rules of the game and ultimately forced most debtors to fall into line with the procedures basically determined by the creditors.'[30]

The policy moves of regulatory authorities in the mid-1980s shaped the responses by individual members of the creditor regime over, at least, the next five years. By intervening directly in the valuation of foreign loans, these authorities placed themselves in a stronger position vis-à-vis private creditors and forced the regulatory agencies in creditor governments to adopt a more uniform standard of capital requirements. This international coordination program (called the Basle Agreement), which began in December 1987, is to be fully implemented by the twelve member countries by 1992.[31] One objective is raising the minimum capital adequacy requirements to eight percent of assets by 1992 and another objective is the creation of a more equitable regulatory framework in order to diminish the competitive inequities that arise from different capital requirements across countries.[32] Since U.S. banks generally had lower capital requirements than continental European banks, the former banks felt a greater burden and hence less inclined to support higher minimum standards. The reason U.S. banks finally supported the Basle Agreement was the plan's 'ironing out' the competitive inequities against non-U.S. banks. Additionally, the increased capitalization of banks would allow them to absorb any losses associated with measures that reduce their exposure to borrowing countries.[33] Higher capital requirements, according to a recent IMF study, increase 'the proportion of a bank's risk borne by shareholders and therefore reduces the potential benefit from high-risk, high-margin investments.'[34]

A turning point in inter-creditor relations was Brazil's decision in February 1987 to impose a moratorium on its interest payments to commercial lenders.[35] The moratorium sent shock waves through the creditor regime by indicating a debtor's unwillingness to accept conditions of austerity and the creditors' inability to stop Brazil. Banks were immediately affected adversely when Moody downgraded the credit rating of most major banks.[36] Additionally, the secondary market in country loans also reflected deterioration in the performance of those loans and the lowered market perception of the debtors' ability to service the debt. In January 1986, the value of debt of the major borrowers stood at around 73 percent of the original value. By October 1987, that figure had sunk to only 46 percent.[37] Individual banks began to exercise their relative power to actively defend their assets and remaining foreign loans.

The primary policy move for many large banks was the provisioning of capital in order to reduce their exposure in relation to their total assets. On May 19, 1987, Citicorp was the first major bank to allocate a substantial provision against possible losses on its outstanding loans. By setting aside $5 billion (a 150 percent increase in its loan-loss reserves), Citicorp sought to protect itself directly against possible borrowers' defaults. By the end of 1987, U.S. banks had added $19 billion to their loan-loss reserves.[38] It is important to note the distinction between writing down a loan and establishing a provision for a loan. The former refers to a reduction in the book value of the asset in the creditor's balance sheet, to a level which reflects the asset's real net present value. Creditors make 'provision against loans by putting aside reserves in low earning, but risk-free assets in order to cover the possibility that repayments of principal or payments of interest might not be made.'[39] If a default occurs, the bad debt would be charged against the previously established reserves rather than reducing the banks' income or capital base. So long as the banks adequately estimated these losses through the reserve account, current earnings are unaffected. However, banks incur indirect costs in foregone additional loans and potential income. Indirect costs may mount because, according to most national bank regulations, provisions must be maintained for at least five years after the most recent rescheduling agreement or episode of payment arrears.

The creation of *large reserves* had a paradoxical effect on the international creditor regime. On the one hand, the new policy move aggravated the tension within the regime in two ways: among the banks themselves and between banks and the official sector. On the other hand, *provisioning* strengthened specific banks by placing them in a stronger position from which to negotiate with debtor governments. First, Citicorp's move forced many U.S. banks to decide whether to exit or to remain by building up reserves. Provisioning is a competitive measure that drove a wedge between relatively small banks and large banks. During periods of economic crisis, small banks would rather withdraw from a hazardous lending environment by using the secondary market (and hence accepting the discounts on their loans) to exit rather than to lay aside relatively scarce capital into reserves. Large banks, on the other hand, since they cannot easily exit due to their substantial exposure, are less likely to accept discounts on the secondary market and, instead, more likely to create reserves to protect their remaining loans. Provisioning also spawned tension between U.S. and non-U.S. banks. Since U.S. banks historically have smaller loan-loss reserves than non-U.S. banks, they, by provisioning, would be forced to contribute more capital to these reserves in order to compete effectively with non-U.S. banks. Banks are subject to such national regulatory, tax, and accounting diversity as to intensify bank competition.[40] In early 1987, European loan-loss provisions averaged between 30 and 70 percent of all debtor loans while the provisions of British, Japanese, and U.S. banks averaged only five percent.[41] A partial equalization of tax and accounting indicators took place by 1989 because of the Basle Agreement. By the end of 1988, average provisioning levels against developing country exposure exceeded 50 percent in all major creditor countries except the United States and Japan. (See Table 2.2). Since U.S. banks historically have smaller loan-loss reserves than non-U.S. banks, they, by provisioning, would be forced to contribute more capital to these reserves in order to compete effectively with non-U.S. banks. Instead, large U.S. banks generally are more willing to lend new money (provided that interest payments would not be postponed) than banks with larger provisions. Such banks, including many European ones, generally are amenable to postponement of some interest payment instead of lending new money. For those creditors, new money loans would require additional capital set aside as loan-loss provisions.[42]

Provisioning also was at the base of a second rift within the regime between private creditors and the official sector. A major concern for official creditors was the reduction in the supply of new bank loans due to the creation of reserves. Banks were unwilling to provide new money to debtor governments since they also would need to set aside additional

Table 2.2 *Commercial Bank Provisioning (end of 1988; unless otherwise specified)*

Country	Range of Provisioning[a]	Tax Deductibility	Gearability[b]
Canada	70–90 75 average	Up to 45 percent	No
France	40–61 51 average	Yes	Yes
Germany	37–77 53 average	No	No
Japan	25[c]	Only 1 percent of rescheduled debt	Partly[d]
United Kingdom	45–85 60 average[e]	Yes	No
United States	36–100 46 average[g]	No[f]	Partly[d]

Notes
[a] In percent of relevant exposure; numbers indicate range for major banks.
[b] Indicates whether provisions are included in the capital base for monitoring asset ratios.
[c] End of March 1990.
[d] Only the non-tax-deductible portion is included.
[e] End of September 1989.
[f] Except those loans against which regulators mandate an Allocated Transfer Risk Reserve.
[g] End of December 1989.

Source   International Monetary Fund, *International Capital Markets*, April (Washington, D.C.: IMF, 1990).

capital against the new loans. The U.S. government earlier had committed itself in the Baker Plan to a new lending program that heavily relied on private creditors. Moreover, the private banks, according to one analyst, wanted to send a message to the IMF and the World Bank that, due to 'excessive pressure' put on them to increase their share of capital, 'the official sector should be doing more to help resolve the debt problem, not only in making financial concessions and in refurbishing conditionality, but also in terms of orchestrating and taking an overall lead in the approach to the Third World debt.'[43]

The rifts that emerged between individual creditors over specific policies never impaired the regime, as a structure, in rescheduling negotiations with debtor governments. Indeed, the various policy moves by creditors to protect and enhance their remaining assets only solidified and strengthened the regime. First, provisioning, in particular, assisted in restoring market confidence in the banks. By bringing actual balance sheets more in line with market perception, provisioning was a response to and recognition of reality. By the end of 1988, the exposure of U.S. banks in non-oil Third World countries had been reduced to $72.9 billion, or 54 percent of bank capital. Exposure of the top nine money center banks was cut to 91 percent of capital.[44] Second, provisioning strengthened the bargaining position of creditors vis-à-vis debtors. By setting aside large sums of capital, creditors improved their ability to absorb any losses due to a debtor's default. Furthermore, capital reserves also meant a reduction in new money which weakened the debtors' bargaining position.

By aggressively pursuing their strategic priority of asset protection, private creditors only affected the *nature* of the loans. The previous series of policy moves did not alter the *value* of those claims from the perspective of the debtors. Increasing loan-loss reserves is quite different from actually writing down the debt. Borrowing countries still were faced with an escalating burden of debt. Within this context of a continuing crisis, multilateral and official creditors intervened directly in debt negotiations by altering their bargaining strategies. For these official sources of capital, repayment is neither the beginning nor the end of their involvement in the economy of debtor countries. Their overall objective has been to restore the foundation for economic growth which, in turn, would enhance creditworthiness and facilitate foreign investment. Debate on this objective has centered on the content of the adjustment process, the conditions attached to loans, and the political role of the multilateral institutions.[45]

Up to about 1987, the IMF provided short-term funds during times of severe economic imbalances in both external and internal accounts. As is well known, the IMF created a set of conditions by which additional loans would be made available upon the borrowers' reaching particular economic targets as determined by the IMF. Although the IMF usually claims that each specific case is different, a definite pattern of policies has emerged. Policies typically have included 1) restraints on demand (reduced government expenditure, limits on credit creation, increased taxation, and restraints on wages and on public sector employment); 2) emphasis on tradeable goods (exchange rate devaluation, price reforms); and 3) raising of medium- and long-term efficiency of the economy (financial reform, import liberalization).[46] A 1986 study of 94 Fund-supported adjustment programs implemented between 1980 and 1984 found several common characteristics: 63 percent of these programs contained wage and salary restraints; 61 percent included transfer payment and subsidy restraints; 55 percent had trade liberalization measures; and 46 percent included personal income tax measures.[47]

In addition to its economic function, the IMF has a *political role in adjustment policies of debtor countries*. Its involvement has shifted from setting up adjustment and stabilization programs to a more political issue of determining the distribution of financial burden and economic risk. The IMF initially was given the pivotal position as central coordinator of adjustment programs and the surveillance of those programs.[48] Because of the growth of the debt burden and of rising risk to members of the creditor regime during the mid-1980s, the creditors were faced with a dilemma. The IMF argued that the amount of external financing must be decided prior to its own approval of an adjustment program. The IMF typically started its analysis with an estimate of available external resources and then determined the economic targets for the borrowing government. Through the policy of concerted lending, the IMF pressured private creditors to raise additional capital. Yet, the private banks insisted that debtor countries first conclude a standby arrangement with the IMF as a precondition to rescheduling negotiations. By the late-1980s, private creditors sought additional protection by relying on IMF conditionality. Yet, these creditors became increasingly concerned that IMF-supported adjustment was occurring at the expense of foreign investment, economic growth, and political stability. Many individual creditors in the international financial community concluded that the short-term focus on adjustment had an adverse effect on growth and, according to one observer, the IMF had become a 'political liability' to international creditors.[49]

Beginning in 1986, the IMF attempted to respond to this perceptual weakness by implementing a number of policy moves to make its lending policies more flexible to the needs of borrowers. Overall objectives included the enlargement of the lending base, lengthening of the time of adjustment, and relaxation of monitoring of compliance by reducing the number of variables of conditionality.[50] This process began in March 1986 with the establishment of the Structural Adjustment Facility (SAF). This fund provides concessional financial assistance to low income debtors. The IMF stipulated a ten-year repayment schedule during which a country could borrow no more than 70 percent of its quota. Between 1987 and 1989, 29 SAF arrangements had been approved with a committed amount of SDR 1.94 billion.[51] As of April 1991, nine SAF arrangements were in effect, totalling SDR 539.42 million.[52]

In December 1987, the IMF created the Enhanced Structural Adjustment Facility (ESAF) which became operational in April 1988. The ESAF more than doubled the amount of new resources available to the poorest member countries by adding SDR 6 billion to the lending base. The ESAF was designed to assist the adjustment efforts of low-income countries who suffer from high levels of indebtedness and who rely heavily on the export of commodities with weak prices.[53] Programs under the ESAF are aimed at strengthening their balance of payments positions and at fostering growth over a three-year period. The terms of the ESAF were identical to those under the SAF, but the former greatly increased access. Approved countries could borrow up to 150 percent of their quota. By early 1991, fourteen ESAF arrangements had been approved with a committed amount of SDR 1.812 billion.[54] In 1988, the IMF introduced a Compensatory and Contingency Financing Facility which provided funds that were contingent on external shocks affecting commodity prices, interest rates, and oil prices.

Despite the introduction of these reforms, which increased borrower access to IMF funds, the debt crisis lurched forward.[55] One indicator of the extent of Third World indebtedness was the number of borrowers in arrears to international creditors. At the end of 1988, 49 countries were in arrears to all creditors with the amount rising $11 billion, to $55 billion over the preceding year.[56] The IMF considered overdue financial obligations as a 'serious problem' since, by 1989, 11 members owed SDR 2.8 billion, a more than five-fold rise in the amount of overdue obligations since 1986.[57] The World Bank did not fare any better. In 1989, eight members were in arrears on their loans totalling $3.24 billion.[58]

In the mid- to late-1980s, the international creditor regime experienced several important rifts between its members. Private and official creditors, as individual members, intensified their competition and placed pressure on each other in an attempt to protect themselves and their remaining assets. This was a period of aggressive defensive policy moves to shore up their individual position against each other and against debtor governments. Yet, the regime's strategy of 'adjustment with growth' failed to manage the debt crisis in an effective and efficient manner. Paradoxically, the establishment of large capital reserves, while strengthening the creditors' bargaining position, also gave the impression to debtors and official creditors that private creditors could afford a limited write down of their outstanding loans. A new, long-term strategy that relied on an actual reduction of debt and a restored creditworthiness became widely considered. At a *specific level*, the policy conflict between creditors that emerged during this period provided a transition to the more *general level* in which international banks have reevaluated their policies leading to a restored convergence of expectations.

Strategic Priorities of the International Creditor Regime 47

THE ADJUSTMENT WITH DEBT REDUCTION STRATEGY OF THE LATE 1980s

The failure of the Baker Plan, the cornerstone of the adjustment with growth strategy of the creditor regime, became clear by the end of 1988. The plan's promise of new commercial lending did little to offset the continued downward slide in the lending environment and in the debtors' ability to repay their loans. Economic indicators for the two geographic regions targeted by the Baker Plan (African debtors who borrowed mainly from official creditors and Latin American debtors who borrowed mainly from private creditors) illustrate widespread economic deterioration by the late-1980s (see the tables in Chapter 1). In terms of GDP per capita growth, African economies only slightly improved by 1989, but generally remained negative. Per capita figures for Latin America, positive before 1987, have been negative since 1988. Current account data provide a similar bleak picture of the economies of these regions. The current account balance as a percentage of exports in Africa dramatically deteriorated by 1986. Though the deficit was cut in half in 1987, the deficit fell back to near the 1986 level in 1988. The Latin American figure continued to be much worse than the percentage for all developing countries.

Debt burden indicators for this period further demonstrate the creditor regime's inability to manage the economic crisis of the debtor governments. In terms of the ratio of external debt to GDP, the ratio of external debt to exports, and the debt service ratio, both Africa and Latin America sustained rates far above the average for all developing countries. By 1985, Africa's ratio of external debt to GDP surpassed even that of the heavily indebted countries in Latin America, and the ratio continued to grow into 1990. Although net financing to Africa had slowed to a trickle, higher import prices, falling export earnings, and deteriorating terms of trade squeezed Africa's capacity to service the external debt. Finally, one of the most politically sensitive economic indicators is the pattern of net resource transfers to debtor countries. Most debtors resent the growing outflow of capital during this period of economic deterioration. Beginning in 1985, there have been significant resource transfers from developing countries to creditors as debt-service repayments exceeded new loan disbursements. By 1988, this figure had more than tripled, to $40 billion.[59] Nearly half of the capital outflow came from Latin American debtors. For Africa, the transfer turned negative by slightly more than $1 billion in 1985. Increases in official development assistance stymied the declining net inflow so that the figure became positive after 1986. (See Table 2.3)

Latin American leaders inserted themselves once again in this debate

Table 2.3 Net Resource Transfers, 1985–1988
(U.S. Billions)

Category	1985	1986	1987	1988[a]
Total Net Transfers	−12.7	−19.4	−18.8	−39.9
Major Debtors	−17.9	−18.9	−14.9	−26.0
Latin America	−14.0	−15.6	−12.5	−20.8
Sub-Saharan Africa	−1.4	1.5	2.6	0.5

Note [a] Estimated.
Source John T. Cuddington, 'The Extent and Causes of the Debt Crisis of the 1980s,' in Ishrat Husain and Ishac Diwan, eds, *Dealing with the Debt Crisis* (Washington, D.C.: World Bank, 1989), pp. 18, 19.

in late-1987 and again in 1988. Following the first attempt by Latin American debtors to place pressure on the international creditor regime in 1984, the political leaders of eight Latin American countries held talks in Acapulco in November 1987. While the *Cartagena Conference* stressed specific proposals to alleviate their debt burden, the Acapulco meeting had a more general objective. These leaders sought to directly link the reduction of external debt to the emergence of political liberalization and democracy in Latin America. As the document called the 'Acapulco Commitment to Peace, Development, and Democracy' suggests,

> the economic crisis undermines democracy in the region because it neutralizes the legitimate efforts of our peoples to improve their living standards. In addition, it is contradictory that those who call for democracy also impose, in world economic relations, conditions and adjustments that compromise that very democracy and that they themselves do not apply in correcting their own imbalances.[60]

The Latin American leaders also put forth renewed calls for the reduction of their debt by seeking to limit the net transfer of resources, establishing interest rate limits, severing links between new money from private creditors and adjustment agreements with official creditors, and objecting to cross-conditionality.[61] According to these debtor states, not only should international creditors take greater and more generous steps to alleviate indebtedness because of financial requirements, creditors should undertake such measures in order to strengthen the transition to democratic rule in many of these countries.

The African debtor governments, with much less political and economic clout than Latin American governments, waited until the end of 1987 to pursue a continental strategy toward the debt crisis. At a special meeting of the Organization of African Unity (OAU) in December 1987, the official government response was considered relatively radical. The OAU, rather than calling for a unilateral repudiation of all foreign debt, argued for a ten-year moratorium on debt servicing. The group also recommended the conversion of official loans into grants, the reduction of interest rates, and multi-year reschedulings of up to fifty years with longer grace periods.[62]

These economic figures and the Third World's collective response to affect the creditor bargaining strategy demonstrate that, by 1988, first, the debt crisis had reached a critical moment for debtor governments and, second, individual members of the creditor regime were unable and/or unwilling to enlarge their burden of risk by extending new loans to troubled debtors. Recognition emerged among many creditors that the debt crisis was a long-term constraint on the economic welfare of the borrowing governments and on the profitability and stability of international banks. In contrast to the early phases of the debt crisis when creditors were preoccupied with a short-term time horizon centered on interest repayment, yearly rescheduling negotiations, and 'quick fix' stabilization programs, by the late-1980s creditors seemed concerned with the possible insolvency of many debtors, the long-term prospects of economic growth and development for the debtors, and the impact on the creditors' balance sheets. Rather than simply assuming and pressuring debtor governments to make their own adjustments to their deteriorating position, the most recent phase in creditor-debtor relations raises and legitimizes adjustment among international creditors themselves. Debt reduction and a restoration of creditworthiness thus have developed into the twin pillars of the regime's new long-term strategic priority. The reevaluation of their strategic priorities has led to a reformulation of the international creditor regime. The fundamental question for international creditors in this shifting regime centers on the distribution of new financial burdens for commercial and official creditors and the appropriate role of the market as a mechanism of debt reduction.

One of the first policy statements advocating this reformulated creditor strategy emerged from the June 1988 summit of industrialized nations held at Toronto. The specific focus of the *Toronto Economic Declaration* was on the poorest countries, most of whom were African. The Declaration recognized that improved domestic policies alone would not revitalize the growth prospects of the poorest countries. The summit participants agreed that the immediate objective must be the increased availability of capital inflow on concessional terms and the reduction of debt. While the debt service burden thus would be eased, these countries also must undertake traditional reforms of liberalization to promote the long-term objective of improved creditworthiness. The Declaration emphasized that the rescheduling of official debt should occur 'within a framework that allows official creditors to choose among concessional interest rates, usually on shorter maturities; longer repayment periods at commercial rates; partial write-offs of debt-service obligations during the consolidation period; or a combination of these options.'[63]

Following the Toronto summit meeting, several Latin American heads of state met once again and issued another declaration. The October 1988 conference held in Uruguay highlighted the close relationship between debt, international trade, and political stability. Although the declaration considered the Toronto summit to represent 'clear progress,' the leaders also wanted the creditor regime to incorporate a broader definition of development into its bargaining strategy. The Declaration of Uruguay stated that

> political stability is enhanced by development, and development requires a significant increase in flows of financing to the region, the opening of international markets to its exports, and the establishment of rules of the game that are both stable and equitable and that permit a sustained and transparent expansion of world trade.[64]

The Latin American debtors were only partially successful in placing their concerns on the bargaining table. The *Brady Plan*, announced in March 1989, did incorporate the objective of renewed financial flows and the long-term strategy of debt reduction. Named for the U.S. Secretary of the Treasury, Nicholas Brady, the plan resulted from the culmination of the trial-and-error approach during the preceding decade. The plan sought to reinvigorate creditor negotiations by having the U.S., the IMF, and the World Bank offer official financial support for negotiated debt reduction. Given the recalcitrant behavior of private creditors and the perception that the escalating debt burden posed a threat to the emerging democracies in Latin America, the Brady Plan was to bring creditors and debtors together. It plan combined remnants of orthodox conditionality with the new money and menu of options components from the Baker Plan. In addition, it included increased emphasis on official multilateral support and debt reduction. As an economic strategy, it built on the Baker Plan by linking higher rates of growth to economic policy reforms under IMF-supervision and by reviewing each rescheduling effort on a case-by-case rather than comprehensive basis. It is, thus, less a departure from the Baker Plan than an enhancement with monetary incentives from official financial sources to assist in negotiated debt reduction. The objective is to have banks agree voluntarily to reduce the value of their claims in return for guarantees on the remaining portion of the debt. To encourage this change in bank behavior, the IMF and the World Bank are providing half of the $25 billion to be made available over the following three years to support debt reduction. About $11 billion will be used to support negotiated reductions in interest payments while the rest will target reductions in the debt principal.[65]

It was hoped that, by reestablishing the IMF as the central coordinator of debt management backed by industrialized governments[66] and by making options more attractive to lenders, creditors would not be motivated to act as free riders. Without some degree of official support of debt reduction, private creditors would tend to 'defect' from the regime; that is, they would minimize their involvement in new money packages either by exiting immediately or by letting other creditors take on new risks. As Max Corden has noted, the free rider problem essentially suggests that individual banks do not have an incentive to provide debt relief because 'a large part of benefits from such relief would spill over to other banks.'[67]

The menu approach attempts to reduce the free rider effect by offering banks several options of which one should best reflect the specific interests and requirements of the individual creditor. *Voluntary* bank participation in new financing packages can be obtained in two ways. First, different techniques to make increased bank exposure more attractive have been established. Currency switching, relending, and new money bonds are examples of incentives to stem the rise of the free rider effect. Second, since banks still are motivated by the reduction in their exposure, mechanisms have been created to facilitate a smooth process to exit from new money arrangements. Debt-equity conversions, exchange offers, buybacks, and exit bonds are some examples.[68]

However, the emphasis on *debt reduction* was a clear break from the previous strategic priority of asset protection. It was one thing for international banks to increase loan-loss provisions against the risks of future defaults. This measure reduced their exposure while strengthening their balance sheets. Debt forgiveness, as initially perceived by many private creditors, gives the wrong signals and establishes inappropriate incentives to debtor governments. Private creditors have several problems with debt reduction.[69] First, the planned reduction unfairly targeted themselves for the inappropriate investments of their loans by the borrowers. The burden of repayment, they argue, should be on the shoulders of the debtors who need to adjust their policies to these economic conditions. Second, non-repayment in the guise of debt reduction could slow the debtors' return to creditworthiness since creditors would not lend new money to those countries if the debtors choose neither to repay nor to make necessary economic adjustments. A third problem with substantial debt relief concerns the process by which reduction is distributed among the creditor actors. Since the Brady Plan emphasizes the role of the market and voluntary participation in debt reduction, private creditors, acting on their self-interest, will only participate if the expected outcome is no worse than their original policy. As Jeffrey Sachs points out, if debt reduction actually brings about a strengthened credit standing, then the value of the claims will rise. 'Therefore, if a voluntary scheme appears likely to work, banks will decide to hold out until creditworthiness is restored, and the goal of debt reduction will not be achieved at all.'[70] Commercial creditors, acting as free riders, would rather wait for participation by other international actors to bear their losses from debt reduction. Some European private creditors are more willing to accept limited debt reduction since their large reserves and national regulatory policies would offset the losses from reduction. However, many U.S. banks are faced with very different regulatory and accounting policies that would not protect them from those expected losses. Fourth, another criticism levied against the Brady Plan is the size of estimated reduction. One analyst calculated that, with the stated goal of a 20 percent average debt reduction, the countries' cost of borrowing only would drop two percentage points.[71] Additionally, even with a relatively minor reduction in debt burden, the target debtor governments are a dozen or so middle-income developing countries. These countries generally are not considered to be insolvent (that is, on the verge of bankruptcy and economic collapse). Most states which are regarded as insolvent (in which case, debt reduction is crucial) are low-income states in Africa which are not automatically covered by the Brady Plan.

Despite these arguments against the Brady Plan, many official creditors and some private creditors supported the plan and the policy of debt reduction. First, in light of the failure of the Baker Plan, the issue in 1989 was the restoration of creditworthiness and a significant improvement in the investment climate, not the punishment of debtors who were unable to repay. If the forcing of debtors to repay substantial portions of their outstanding loans occurred at the expense of economic growth and political stability, then immediate repayment should not be the primary objective. The Brady Plan's supporters argued that, by reducing the net outflow of capital in conjunction with a more reasonable adjustment program, debtors would have needed resources at their disposal. These new resources would assist in eliminating the debt overhang (the unserviceable portion of the debt) and would improve investor confidence in the country.[72] As several economists have argued, if borrowers with a substantial debt overhang are forced to repay, the incentive structure for the borrower changes. A heavy debt burden reduces the incentive for the debtor to undertake economic reform since, by repayment, the debtor would receive little economic benefits. Thus, debt reduction, according to this argument, will enhance adjustment policies since the debtor would be allowed more capital for domestic investment purposes.[73] One observer concluded that the return of flight capital to Mexico in 1990 under the Brady Plan demonstrates the improved government credibility and domestic business confidence brought about by debt reduction.[74]

Second, the process of determining the allocation of new burdens would be both equitable and reflective of a market orientation. Private creditors, international financial institutions, and creditor governments all would share the burden of debt reduction. The various measures that facilitate debt reduction are based on the market perception of the value of the claims instead of a government fiat concerning their value. Additionally, the Brady Plan, in contrast to the Baker Plan, provides legitimacy behind the World Bank's and IMF's reinvigorated role in debt management. The Brady Plan can be most effective when these multilateral institutions are given the resources and authority to guarantee part of the costs to private creditors stemming from debt reduction. Third, some private creditors find the menu approach an attractive and self-interested option by which they may diversify the risks of new lending to debtor governments. Various forms of securitization of debt, debt-equity swaps, bonds, and the secondary market provide specific benefits to individual creditors. Certainly not all creditors consider debt reduction a primary priority, but given the range of innovative options from which to select, many individual creditors will favor reduction. Indeed, as Corden has noted, several arguments suggest that from the collective interest of creditors, debt reduction actually would be cost-effective.[75]

The international creditor regime faced a serious challenge to its cohesiveness as many private creditors sought to exit from the regime. In order for the Brady Plan to work effectively, official creditors, such as the IMF, the World Bank, and the Paris Club, had to take on an expanded leadership role. Each of these actors increased their lending base, provided more concessional terms to the borrowers, and coordinated their policies with other financial actors in order to share the new risks. The *IMF* moved quickly by issuing supportive statements of the Brady Plan and by increasing access to its capital for the specific purpose of debt reduction.[76] In early 1990, it set forth its lending guidelines in the context of the Brady Plan.[77]

First, the Fund directly linked efforts to reduce debt and debt service to medium-term adjustment programs. Second, it set aside 25 percent of a member's access to Fund resources to support the reduction of debt principal. Third, it approved additional funding of up to 40 percent of a member's quota for interest reduction. Fourth, the Fund broke from the previous strategy by approving, under specific conditions, an IMF program prior to an agreement between the member country and commercial creditors. As part of a comprehensive package dealing with IMF funding, the Fund received a fifty percent increase to its resource base in May 1990. After intense negotiations between the IMF and the United States, in particular, the Executive Board of the former agreed to raise an additional $60 billion from its members. This quota increase became urgent since during 1989 the IMF committed almost $10 billion to Mexico, the Philippines, and Venezuela as part of the Brady Plan.

As the largest source of official lending to the developing world, the *World Bank* took an initial step in 1988 to increase its loan-loss reserves from $100 million to $500 million. In fashion similar to the IMF, the Bank issued guidelines in May 1989 concerning its role in the Brady Plan. It first declared that eligible countries receiving Bank support must present a 'clear need' for debt or debt-service reduction and adopt a 'sound' medium-term adjustment program. Second, it will provide a large amount of capital to support efforts involving the reduction of principal. Member countries could borrow either up to 25 percent of their adjustment lending program over a three year period or ten percent of their overall lending program.[78] Third, the World Bank established a new Debt Reduction Facility of $100 million. This facility, funded by the Bank's net income, will assist eligible low-income countries to repurchase commercial bank debt.[79]

The *Paris Club* is the third group in the creditor regime that has expanded its role in official lending. The Paris Club is a 'forum for the informal monitoring of talks and negotiations among the creditor countries themselves and between the creditor countries and individual debtor countries.'[80] It provides preferential debt relief to the poorest countries suffering under persistent debt servicing difficulties. The Club's adoption of the menu approach in the Toronto Declaration preceded the Brady Plan by a few months. Government creditors were given three options for the consolidation of official loans and government-backed credits granted to the poorest countries. One was partial cancellation. Up to one-third of debt service obligations could be canceled, and the remaining would be rescheduled at the market rate of interest over fourteen years, including an eight-year grace period. Second, the Paris Club consolidated the debt at market rates and extended the maturities to 25 years, including a 14-year grace period. Third, debt service obligations would be rescheduled at concessional interest rates with a 14-year maturity and 8-year grace period.[81]

Unlike the previous period during which the international creditor regime pursued a priority of adjustment with growth, the most recent phase in creditor behavior is marked by a recognition of the long-term priority of debt reduction. During the earlier phase of the debt crisis, individual creditors used a defensive strategy against each other which led to pronounced conflict within the regime. Currently, the policies of most creditors appear to reflect their long-term interests for a restoration of lending and borrowing. For many creditors, debt reduction should be considered as a policy move that might lead to an improved debtor capacity to service the debt, a more favorable investment climate, and the resumption of new lending.

CONCLUSION

In understanding creditor-debtor relations throughout the debt crisis, it is crucial to consider the priorities, strategies, and policies of each side during the negotiations. This chapter attempts the first cut by tracing shifts in the *strategic priorities of international creditors* between the introduction of the Baker and Brady Plans. Chapters Three and Four will present the second cut by focusing on economic adjustment and debt management policies of the three debtor governments under review. In response to increasing risk and uncertainty, creditors have pursued three priorities: a short-term emphasis on interest payment, a medium-term focus on asset protection, and a long-term emphasis on debt reduction. For each priority, creditors have adopted a bargaining strategy that evolved from the failure of the previous strategy. As a result of rising risk and failed strategies, two related features of the international creditor regime were revealed. At a *specific level of analysis*, creditors compete over the distribution of risks and over the ability to protect themselves from those risks. As conflict intensified between creditors, they often used specific policy moves in pursuit of their own interests leading to cracks in the regime. However, at a *general level of analysis*, there has been continued convergence among these actors concerning the underlying principles, norms, and rules that constitute the regime. Clearly, by the early 1990s, the creditor regime at a general level has survived the policy conflicts and rifts between creditors and, as a reformulated regime, it has emerged as a powerful force in on-going debt negotiations.

What does this reformulated regime mean for debtor states? *On the one hand*, key policy reforms have pushed the creditor regime's bargaining position closer to that of debtor states. While still calling for economic adjustment in debtor countries, the creditors themselves have made adjustments. The primary change under the current phase of negotiations has been the acceptance of debt reduction as an operational principle in debt negotiations. Many creditors are willing, at this point of the debt crisis, to intentionally reduce the borrowers' debt burden in anticipation of renewed economic growth and future capital borrowing. In part, the gradual acceptance of a long-term strategy incorporating real reductions in outstanding debt reflects the failure of earlier strategies to cope with the debt crisis. In response to the debtors' inability to maintain interest payments and to the creditors' inability to protect the value of their assets, the latter have been forced by prevailing circumstances to alter their priorities and strategies.

Moreover, poorer debtor states, as in Africa, have become a relatively new point of contact with official creditors. While the Baker Plan illustrated the substantial attraction with the largest debtors in Latin America, the Brady Plan and important changes in the lending policy of multilateral institutions reveal a crucial shift toward the poorest indebted states in Africa. The easing of conditionality affecting the length of maturities, interest rates charged, the time frame of adjustment policies, and less rigid linkage with private creditors and the Paris Club suggest a possible new approach to the debt crisis.

On the other hand, the apparent rapprochement between debtors and creditors must be considered within the context of a rejuvenated creditor regime. The ability of many creditors to shift from pursuing one priority to another underscores their power to adjust to long-term risk. The expanded flexibility in offering a wide array of policy moves has strengthened the regime. First, international creditors have a greater capacity to act collectively than do debtors. This is reflected in their ability (and success so far) to isolate rebel debtors by insisting on case-by-case negotiations and by compensating cooperative debtors to preempt a collective action by the debtors. Second, because of the nature of the international creditor regime, creditors have the ability to share the risks of lending with multilateral institutions and creditor governments, and to protect themselves from the risks of future defection (default) through such actions as building up their reserves (thus giving them breathing space and leverage in future negotiations) and the innovative menu of options. Finally, the creditors' control of short-term credits, the attachment of debtors' foreign assets, and cross-default clauses provide a clear leverage to use in debt negotiations. Despite the attempts by Peru in 1985 and Brazil in 1987 to unilaterally take the offensive against the policies of international banks, by the early 1990s, debtors remain in a defensive and reactive posture. The international creditor regime generally has been successful in defining the agenda and setting the bargaining rules in debt negotiations.

This chapter, however, only analyzed the priorities and bargaining strategies of international creditors. While creditor strategies primarily are concerned with exposure to sovereign debt, they have not treated the distributional issues of indebtedness and economic adjustment within debtor states. From the debtors' perspective, the distribution of risk and the costs of debt management are far from equitable.[82] They must continue to grapple with the costs of adjustment within their society. Given that adjustment is unavoidable, what are the available strategies of adjustment that facilitate an 'escape' from indebted development? It is to that question that I now turn.

NOTES

1. Although the focus in this article is on inter-creditor relations, complementary studies should analyze debtor priorities, strategies, and policies as they react to the international creditor regime. Neither creditors nor debtors act in total isolation from the anticipated and real moves of the other. However, it is necessary, as a first cut, to specify and consider creditor priorities and policies.
2. Stephen Krasner, 'Structural Causes and Regime Consequences,' *International Organization* 36 (1982).
3. Benjamin J. Cohen, 'Balance-of-Payments Financing: Evolution of a Regime,' *International Organization* 36 (1982); Charles Lipson, 'Bankers' Dilemmas: Private Cooperation in Rescheduling Sovereign Debts,' *World Politics* 38:1 (October 1985).
4. Robert Devlin, *Debt and Crisis in Latin America: The Supply Side of the Story* (Princeton: Princeton University Press, 1989).
5. Reginald Herbold Green, 'Third World Sovereign Debt Renegotiation 1980–86 and After: Procedures, Paradigms, and Portents,' *Discussion Paper*, 223 University of Sussex: IDS Institute (December 1986), p. 9.
6. Stephany Griffith-Jones, 'The International Debt Problem: Prospects and Solutions,' in Hans W. Singer and S. Sharma, eds., *Economic Development and World Debt* (New York: St. Martin's Press, 1989), p. 3.
7. Devlin, *Debt and Crisis in Latin America*, p. 111.
8. Paul M. Sacks and Chris Canavan, 'Safe Passage Through Dire Straits: Managing an Orderly Exit from the Debt Crisis,' in John F. Weeks, ed., *Debt Disaster: Banks, Governments, and Multilaterals Confront the Crisis* (New York: New York University Press, 1989), p. 77.
9. Devlin, *Debt and Crisis in Latin America*, p. 114.

10. Kari Polanyi Levitt, 'Linkage and Vulnerability: The 'Debt Crisis' in Latin America and Africa,' in Bonnie K. Campbell, ed., *Political Dimensions of the International Debt Crisis* (New York: St. Martin's Press, 1989), p. 28.
11. Ibid.
12. Seamus O'Cleireacain, *Third World Debt and International Public Policy* (New York: Praeger, 1990), p. 208.
13. Bank for International Settlements, *Annual Report* (Basle: BIS, 1987), p. 94.
14. 'Cartagena Conference on 11 Latin Nations Rejects Debtors' Cartel, Proposes Reform,' *IMF Survey*, 13 (July 2, 1984), pp. 201–2.
15. For various perspectives on the Baker Plan, see Christine Bogdanowicz-Bindert, 'World Debt: The United States Reconsiders,' *Foreign Affairs* (Winter 1985/86); Patrick Conway, 'The Baker Plan and International Indebtedness,' *The World Economy* (June 1987); Cheryl Payer, 'The World Bank: A New Role in the Debt Crisis?' *Third World Quarterly* (April 1986); and William R. Cline, 'The Baker Plan and Brady Reformulation: An Evaluation,' in Husain and Diwan, *Dealing with the Debt Crisis*.
16. The original highly indebted countries eligible under Baker Plan I were Argentina, Bolivia, Brazil, Chile, Colombia, Ivory Coast, Ecuador, Mexico, Morocco, Nigeria, Peru, Philippines, Uruguay, Venezuela, and Yugoslavia. Costa Rica and Jamaica later were added to the list.
17. Cross-conditionality occurs when 'acceptance by the borrowing government of the conditionality of the financial agency is made a pre-condition for financial support by another or others' in Stephany Griffith-Jones, 'Cross-Conditionality or the Spread of Obligatory Adjustment,' unpublished manuscript, (1988), p. 12. For additional analysis of the term, see Richard E. Feinberg, 'The Changing Relationship Between the World Bank and the International Monetary Fund,' *International Organization*, 42 (1988).
18. Guillermo O'Donnell, in 'Brazil's Failure: What Future for Debtor's Cartels?,' *Third World Quarterly*, 9 (1987), p. 1159, argues that the main obstacles to a debtors' cartel derive from the ability of creditors to take two simultaneous actions in response to a unilateral move by a debtor: 1) threaten and apply sanctions and 2) make side-payments (differential benefits) to other debtors who might be tempted to follow suit. See also Diana Tussie, 'The Coordination of the Latin American Debtors: Is There a Logic Behind the Story?' in Stephany Griffith-Jones, ed. *Managing World Debt* (New York: St. Martin's Press, 1988).
19. William R. Cline, 'The Baker Plan and Brady Reformulation,' in Ishrat Husain and Ishac Diwan, eds., *Dealing with the Debt Crisis* (Washington, D.C.:World Bank, 1989), p. 176.
20. Devlin, *Debt and Crisis in Latin America*, p. 11.

21. O'Cleireacain, *Third World Debt and International Public Policy*, p. 6.
22. Loans are classified as 'non-performing' when interest arrears exceed three months. Interest then can only be accrued as income on a cash basis. Inter-agency Country Exposure Risk Committee, 'Inter-agency Statement on Examination Treatment of International Loans,' (Washington, D.C., 1983).
23. O'Cleireacain, *Third World Debt and International Public Policy*, p. 187. Capital ratio refers to the amount set aside by banks (in the form of capital reserves and provisions) as a proportion of total assets owned by the institution.
24. An Inter-agency Country Exposure Risk Committee (ICERC), composed of the head of the Federal Deposit Insurance Corporation, the comptroller of the Currency, and the Federal Reserve Board chairman, has the authority to examine categories of loans that have been adversely affected by risk.
25. In contrast to specific provisions, ICERC also allows for 'general provisions' which is based on 'normal business practice of allowing for the fact that there is statistical probability that a certain proportion of loans will encounter problems.' Graham Bird, *Commercial Bank Lending and Third World Debt* (New York: St. Martin's Press, 1989), p. 51. Tax deductions are not usually allowed against general provisions.
26. Interview with U.S. Department of Treasury economist, November 1987.
27. An ICERC position paper defined the value-impaired category as applying when a country has protracted arrearages, as indicated by more than one of the following: a) the country has not fully paid its interest for six months; b) the country has not complied with IMF programs and there is no immediate prospect for compliance; c) the country has not met rescheduling terms for one year; or d) the country shows no definite prospects for an orderly restoration of debt service in the near future. See 'Inter-agency Statement on Examination Treatment of International Loans.' For additional discussion, see C. Fred Bergsten, et al., *Bank Lending to Developing Countries: The Policy Alternatives* (Washington, D.C.: Institute for International Economics, 1985), pp. 25–32.
28. Interview with senior vice president of an American international bank, June 1988.
29. Nonaccrual refers to delayed interest payments which cannot be treated as received for income purposes.
30. Stephany Griffith-Jones, 'Debt Crisis Management, an Analytical Framework,' in Stephany Griffith-Jones, ed., *Managing World Debt* (New York: St. Martin's Press, 1988), p. 24. Also, see Ch. 4 in Matthew Martin, *The Crumbling Façade of African Debt Negotiations* (London: Macmillan, 1991).

31. Tony Porter, 'Regimes for Financial Firms.' Paper presented at the International Studies Association Annual Meeting (April 1992); Ethan Barnaby Kapstein, 'Between Power and Purpose: Central Bankers and the Politics of Regulatory Convergence,' *International Organization* 46 (Winter 1992).
32. Harry Huizinga, 'The Commercial Bank Claims on Developing Countries: How Have Banks been Affected?,' in Husain and Diwan, eds., *Dealing with the Debt Crisis*, p. 137; International Monetary Fund, *International Capital Markets: Developments and Prospects* (Washington, D.C.: International Monetary Fund, 1991), p. 16.
33. O'Cleireacain, *Third World Debt and International Public Policy*, p. 188.
34. IMF, *International Capital Markets: Developments and Prospects*, p. 16.
35. See Howard P. Lehman, 'From Confrontation to Cooperation: Strategic Bargaining in Brazil's Debt Negotiations,' *Political Science Quarterly* (Forthcoming, 1993) for an analysis of Brazil's debt moratorium and debt negotiations with its creditors.
36. Huizinga, 'The Commercial Bank Claims on Developing Countries,' p. 134.
37. Jack M. Guttentag and Richard Herring, Accounting for Losses on Sovereign Debt: Implications for New Lending, *Essays in International Finance*, 172 (Princeton: Princeton University, 1989), p. 30. Cataquet defines the secondary debt market as a 'forum where a bank who no longer wants to hold a loan can sell the asset to another bank in exchange for cash, or conversely,' in Harold Cataquet, 'Country Risk Management: How to Juggle with your Arms in a Straitjacket?,' in Singer and Sharma, eds., *Economic Development and World Debt*, p. 339.
38. O'Cleireacain, *Third World Debt and International Public Policy*, p. 189.
39. Bird, *Commercial Bank Lending and Third World Debt*, p. 51. See Ch. 3 in Bird for an extended discussion on the implications of provisioning for banks, debtor governments, regulatory authorities, and official creditors.
40. For differences between American and non-American bank regulations and their impact on bank strategies, see Bird, *Commercial Bank Lending and Third World Debt*; Huizinga, 'The Commercial Bank Claims on Developing Countries.'
41. O'Cleireacain, *Third World Debt and International Public Policy*, p. 207.
42. Stephany Griffith-Jones, 'Conclusions and Policy Recommendations,' in Griffith-Jones, ed., *Managing World Debt*, p. 378.
43. Bird, *Commercial Bank Lending and Third World Debt*, pp. 66, 71.
44. O'Cleireacain, *Third World Debt and International Public Policy*, p. 6.

Exposure refers to the amount of outstanding loans to debtor countries as a percent of bank capital.

45. From among many recent examples of the literature on the domestic politics of stabilization and adjustment, see William L. Canak, ed., *Lost Promises: Debt, Austerity and Development in Latin America* (New York: St. Martin's Press, 1989); Stephan Haggard and Robert Kaufman, 'The Politics of Stabilization and Structural Adjustment,' in Jeffrey Sachs, ed., *Developing Country Debt and the World Economy* (Chicago: University of Chicago Press, 1989); Howard Handelman and Werner Baer, eds., *Paying the Costs of Austerity in Latin America* (Boulder: Westview Press, 1989); Joan M. Nelson, ed., *Fragile Coalitions: The Politics of Economic Adjustment* (New Brunswick: Transaction Press, 1989); Joan M. Nelson, ed., *Economic Crisis and Policy Choice: The Politics of Adjustment in the Third World* (Princeton: Princeton University Press, 1990); David Felix, ed., *Debt and Transfiguration? Prospects for Latin America's Economic Revival* (Armonk, NY: M.E. Sharpe, 1990); Bonnie K. Campbell and John Loxley, eds., *Structural Adjustment in Africa* (New York: St. Martin's Press, 1989); Paul Mosley, Jane Harrigan, and John Toye, *Aid and Power: The World Bank and Policy-based Lending* (London: Routledge, 1991).
46. Wilfred L. David, *The IMF Policy Paradigm* (New York: Praeger, 1985); Justin B. Zulu and Saleh M. Nsouli, 'Adjustment Programs in Africa,' *Occasional Paper* 34, (Washington, D.C.: International Monetary Fund, 1985).
47. International Monetary Fund, 'Fund-Supported Programs, Fiscal Policy, and Income Distribution,' *Occasional Paper* 46 (Washington, D.C.: International Monetary Fund, 1986), pp. 2, 22–23.
48. Richard E. Feinberg and Edmar L. Bacha, 'When Supply and Demand Don't Intersect: Latin America and the Bretton Woods Institutions in the 1980s,' *Development and Change*, 19 (1988).
49. Devlin, *Debt and Crisis in Latin America*, p. 228.
50. Ibid., p. 230; O'Cleireacain, *Third World Debt and International Public Policy*, p. 122.
51. International Monetary Fund, *Annual Report* (Washington, D.C.: International Monetary Fund, 1989), p. 60. In 1989, 1 SDR = $1.29.
52. 'Ten Countries Drew on IMF Resources,' *IMF Survey*, 20:12 (June 10, 1991), p. 188.
53. World Bank, *Annual Report* (Washington, D.C.: World Bank, 1988), p. 39; International Monetary Fund, *Annual Report*, p. 34.
54. 'Ten Countries Drew on IMF Resources,' p. 188.
55. In any event, between 1984 and 1989, the average annual amount of IMF funds committed to borrowers was only $4.88 billion (Ibid., p. 60).
56. 'World Bank Report Reviews Initiatives to Reduce Debt and Debt Service,' *IMF Survey*, 19 (January 8, 1990), p. 13.

57. International Monetary Fund, *Annual Report*, p. 45.
58. O'Cleireacain, *Third World Debt and International Public Policy*, p. 116.
59. John T. Cuddington, 'The Extent and Causes of the Debt Crisis of the 1980s,' in Husain and Diwan, eds., *Dealing with the Debt Crisis*, p. 18.
60. 'Acapulco Commitment to Peace, Development, and Democracy,' 1987, p. 6.
61. Ibid., pp. 19–22.
62. Brooke Hyde, 'Summit on the Debt Moratorium,' *West Africa* 3670 (December 14, 1987), pp. 2429–30.
63. World Bank, *Annual Report*, 1988, p. 28; International Monetary Fund, *World Economic Outlook* (Washington, D.C.: International Monetary Fund, 1988), p. 38.
64. 'Latin American Declaration Deplores Adverse Impact of Debt, Protectionism,' *IMF Survey*, 17:21 (November 14, 1988), p. 354.
65. Edward R. Fried and Philip H. Trezise, eds., *Third World Debt: The Next Phase* (Washington, D.C.: The Brookings Institution, 1989), p. 7.
66. By the end of 1989, there had been a substantial increase in forgiveness of official development assistance by industrialized governments, including the United States ($1 billion), France ($2.3 billion), Germany ($1.5 billion), and Canada ($424 million). See Stanley Fischer and Ishrat Husain, 'Managing the Debt Crisis in the 1990s,' *Finance and Development* 27 (June 1990), p. 26.
67. W. Max Corden, 'The Theory of Debt Relief: Sorting out Some Issues,' *Journal of Development Studies* 27:3 (April 1991), p. 139.
68. Buy-backs permit countries to repurchase their debt at a discount for cash. Debt-equity swaps involve a purchase of a debt instrument in the secondary market in exchange for an equity investment in the borrowing country. Debt exchanges involve the transformation of existing debt instruments for new debt instruments denominated in domestic or foreign currency. Exit bonds are issued by a debtor government to a creditor bank in place of a bank credit. Michel H. Bouchet and Jonathan Hay, 'The Rise of the Market-Based 'Menu' Approach and its Limitations,' in Husain and Diwan, eds., *Dealing with the Debt Crisis*, p. 151; John Williamson, *Voluntary Approaches to Debt Relief* (Washington, D.C.: Institute for International Economics, 1988).
69. For statements representative of the views held by the international banking community, see Institute of International Finance, *The Way Forward for Middle-Income Countries* (Washington, D.C.: Institute of International Finance, 1988); Institute of International Finance, *Improving the Official Debt Strategy: Arrears are not the Way* (Washington, D.C.: Institute of International Finance, 1990).
70. Jeffrey Sachs, 'Making the Brady Plan Work,' *Foreign Affairs*, 68 (Summer 1989), p. 95.

71. S. Islam, 'Going Beyond the Brady Plan,' *Challenge*, 32 (July–August 1989), p. 49.
72. Fischer and Husain, 'Managing the Debt Crisis in the 1990s,' p. 25.
73. Ibid.; Helmut Reisen, 'The Brady Plan and Adjustment Incentives,' *Intereconomics* 26:2 (March/April 1991), pp. 69–73; Jeffrey Sachs, 'The Debt Overhang Problem of Developing Countries,' in Ronald Findlay, ed., *Debt, Growth, and Stabilization* (Oxford: Blackwell, 1988).
74. Reisen, 'The Brady Plan and Adjustment Incentives,' p. 73.
75. Corden provides three arguments favoring debt reduction. 1) Investment capacity argument: the debtor would use the savings from reduction for internal investment which in turn would improve its capacity to pay in the future; 2) Default forestalling argument: debt reduction would prevent the debtor from defaulting; and 3) Incentives argument: this is the debt overhang hypothesis mentioned above (Corden, 'The Theory of Debt Relief: Sorting out Some Issues,' pp. 137–139).
76. International Monetary Fund, *Annual Report*, pp. 23, 25.
77. 'Fund Acts to Strengthen Debt Strategy,' *IMF Survey*, 18 (May 29, 1990), p. 161.
78. Ishrat Husain, 'Recent Experience with the Debt Strategy,' *Finance and Development*, 26 (September 1989), p. 15.
79. Fischer and Husain, 'Managing the Debt Crisis,' p. 26.
80. Jean-Claude Trichet, 'Official Debt Rescheduling: The Paris Club,' in Bogdanowicz-Bindert, ed., *Solving the Global Debt Crisis*, p. 109.
81. Ten African countries had received preferential treatment under this new strategy as of 1989 with each given repayment periods of 15 to 20 years (Ibid., p. 118; 'Paris Club Implements Menu Approach for Low-Income Countries, *IMF Survey*, 18 (April 3, 1989), p. 103).
82. For a critical assessment of the Toronto Declaration, see G.K. Helleiner, 'International Policy Issues Posed by Sub-Saharan African Debt,' *The World Economy* 12:3 (September 1989).

3 The State and Economic Adjustment Strategies

INTRODUCTION

By the early 1990s, the international creditor regime successfully has adapted to the rising risks of non-payment, declines in the value of their assets, and the threat from international financial instability. As debt negotiations continue into the 1990s, the regime's continued success will depend on the creditors' capacity to act collectively while preempting collective action by debtors, the ability to share the risks of lending with international institutions and creditor governments, the ability to protect themselves from default, and the leverage gained through control of future credits.[1]

However, the perception of international creditors as powerful entities with the capacity and willingness to impose their will on debtors is overstated. To be sure, international banks and the Bretton Woods' institutions have enormous resources and influential ties with industrialized governments which they have used (or threaten to use) to punish debtors. Yet, creditors do not act in a vacuum. They respond to the policy moves of the debtors themselves who are engaged in the complex process of economic adjustment. The interaction between debtors and creditors is considered here from a model of *strategic bargaining*. For debtor governments, the primary strategic priority is to reduce the debt burden so as to enhance domestic economic growth and gain the support of domestic constituents without greatly antagonizing members of the international financial community. As stated in the first chapter, states have, in theory, several strategic options from which to select. In practice, however, most adjustment strategies incorporate a mix of orthodox reforms recommended by IFIs and heterodox measures often suggested by domestic groups. The issue here is not whether debtor governments select and pursue economic adjustment strategies. Rarely does one find a government not making some adjustment to its set of economic policies. The issue is the type and selection of adjustment strategies.

In contrast to some observers who suggest indebted states have a choice between orthodox adjustment or chaotic adjustment, I argue that states generally have two broad strategies from which to select: orthodoxy or heterodoxy. States thus not only have the capacity to influence domestic and international actors, they have the capacity to adopt and direct adjustment policies to achieve their specific development objectives. A simple two by two game theoretic model is suggestive of these adjustment options available to states. Indebted states have two available strategies in their bargaining with international creditors: *cooperation* – implementation of incentives that facilitate new investments, new borrowing, or good relations with the International Monetary Fund; or *defection* – the unilateral action by states to block repayments or to disrupt foreign investment in the country. Indebted states also have two general strategies in negotiating with domestic interests. Cooperation with those interests suggests that the government shifts the burden of adjustment to the external sector, thus providing more capital for internal development. Defection implies the government seeks to meet the external debt obligation through the imposition of austerity measures on domestic interests. Such measures generally include wage repression, substantial price increases, and reduction in government subsidies.

Of course, in reality states do not only have two discrete strategic options. As ideal-types, these options merely reflect two contrasting strategies. *Slippage* in policy implementation can be a viable tactic in which states gamble with IFIs as a means to obtain external financing with only partial policy compliance. In these cases, states determine that their power capabilities outweigh the expected punishment meted out by the external creditors.[2] This chapter considers three cases in which the state undertakes adjustment consisting of a fluid mixture of reforms. Adjustment is politically difficult for states since generally reforms will leave domestic actors or foreign creditors unsatisfied. For that reason, a review of these cases will illustrate the often times inconsistent implementation of economic adjustment policies.

ECONOMIC ADJUSTMENT STRATEGIES

The state itself does not make economic policy, but rather policy is shaped by the governing apparatus in conjunction with contending coalitions and societal groups. Coalitions, writes Otwin Marenin, 'combine a variety of groups, each having its own base and means of identification, into a common purpose – that of creating, reproducing and controlling the state.'[3] Contending coalitions seek to institutionalize and restructure their collective interests often incorporating relevant state agencies (such as the

Central Bank, the Ministry of Finance, and the Ministry of Planning and Development) as their vehicle of expression.

Thus, the state is composed of particular organizations, and the state's interests are institutionalized in coalitions. Douglas Bennett and Kenneth Sharpe refer to this relationship as 'embedded orientations' in which interests are derived from an institutional complex found within the state.[4] According to Mancur Olson, the interests of coalitions stem directly from the dilemma between cooperation to obtain collective benefits and individual attempts to extract greater benefits by evading the costs of certain policies.[5] Peter Gourevitch presents an interesting alternative framework which seeks to explain policy choices. He argues that coalition preferences and the coalitions' relative influence on the government explain the range of policy choices.[6] In his study on state responses to international economic crises, he focuses on the 'politics of support' for economic policies among societal actors within the state. In terms of this study, critical factors in understanding the selection and implementation of adjustment strategies are the objectives and power resources of important societal members.

Consistent with this conception of the state, I argue that the state interacts with these members in determining a relatively orthodox or relatively heterodox economic adjustment strategy. In this study, two broad coalitions are considered as a reflection of ideal-type models of economic development. The *established coalition* contains members who share the assumptions of and are influenced by an orthodox economic perspective. This approach is premised on several crucial assumptions concerning economic stability and economic growth. Great emphasis is placed on the market mechanism as an efficient means to translate individual preferences into society's objectives. The orthodox perspective further promotes a liberal trade and foreign currency exchange system which is based on the comparative advantage of internal endowment factors. Finally, the perspective calls for a removal of constraints, including government interference in the market system, which are seen as raising the cost of economic transactions. Government involvement in the economy, it is argued, unfairly competes against the private sector for scarce foreign exchange. An orthodox perspective seeks to stabilize, in the short-run, balance of payments position and to adjust, in the long-run, the management of the economy by improving efficiency.[7]

The comprehensive list of macro-policy measures derived from this developmental perspective includes the free exchange of foreign currency, the promotion of the export sector, import liberalization, reductions in protectionism, and a wide range of incentives to attract foreign investment. Among other distributive policies, this approach includes reductions in state subsidies, the elimination of parastatals, the relaxation of foreign currency allocation regulations, and cuts in government budget deficits. In other words, an orthodox strategy seeks to increase the level of exports and control domestic demand through liberalizing all facets of the national economy and eliminating the government deficit through expenditure control and encouraging foreign investment. Societal groups that would benefit from these policies often include agricultural exporters, international business elites, state monetary authorities, and those concerned with a solid international credit standing. They are in general agreement with a policy emphasis on an unencumbered flow of capital, a vigorous private sector, and a concentrated effort to correct the balance of payments.[8] Government authorities that support these objectives and measures often maintain strong links to the international financial community and share adjustment objectives with the IMF.

The second *alternative coalition* takes a quite different tack. In contrast to an orthodox perspective, the interests of this coalition are shaped by an heterodox economic approach. Wilfred David sets apart the heterodox from the orthodox perspective by suggesting that a widening gap exists between the need for short-term balance of payments stabilization and long-term economic development.[9] The capacity of the state first to stabilize the economy and then make long-term adjustments is constrained by structural rigidities. The structural causes of economic crises are found in the depressed condition of foreign exchange availability, the unequal relationship between the core and the periphery, and the declining terms of trade. More specifically, this argument suggests that, in light of excessive import needs and inadequate export levels in developing countries, state economic policy should increase domestic supply rather than suppress demand. Orthodox stabilization measures are criticized as being narrowly conceived by ignoring their long-term distributive consequences. An essential difference between this model and the orthodox perspective is the former's emphasis on redistribution to the mass society rather than distribution favoring foreign investors and large producers. In presenting criticisms of the orthodox model, Miles Kahler points to a shift in goals to 'other than immediate current account equilibrium, particularly economic growth and distributional or poverty alleviation goals.'[10] John Loxley more specifically suggests that heterodox economic policies take into consideration food production, land reform, price controls, and the relationship between urban and rural sectors.[11]

The heterodox coalition represents usually less competitive, domestically-oriented, and non-tradeable producers often found in state-owned enterprises and protected industrial/manufacturing sectors.[12] These groups often see themselves in direct competition with foreign investors and more competitive private sector interests. The heterodox model contains an implicit pessimism against an export-led model of economic development. Price controls, import controls, and trade protectionism are used as ways to strengthen state power and to provide a basis for internal development. Government intervention takes on a renewed role in this approach as the only viable force to generate foreign exchange, to establish capital-creating industries, and to ease structural bottlenecks. This model of development would advocate an active government in controlling the allocation of scarce foreign currency. The private sector either is too small or it has been tainted by foreign capital involvement. Foreign investment further is regulated often times with restrictive investment codes or dividend and remittance controls. Given the importance of the public sector, state subsidies to parastatals remain substantial.

This chapter will analyze the economic adjustment strategies pursued by Kenya, Zimbabwe, and Brazil. Their adjustment objectives will be examined from the context of state-society relations. Within each country, state and societal interests struggle over the identification, selection, and implementation of orthodox or heterodox adjustment strategies.

THE CASE OF KENYA

If there were an African country that during the first thirty years of its existence displayed many of the characteristics of an orthodox economic strategy sought by international financial institutions and Western governments, most analysts would select Kenya. As an ardent follower of an agricultural export strategy, a vigorous promoter of both direct foreign investment and a domestic private sector, and led by a relatively politically stable regime, the Kenyan government historically has presented itself as an orthodox regime. International bankers, IMF and World Bank officials, and government officials generally agree that its overall economic performance, political stability, and adherence to a market-oriented political and economic ideology have strengthened Kenya's position in the international financial system. One demonstration of Kenya's international reputation is the consistently high ranking it receives on the list of creditworthy African nations in the *Euromoney* Index. However, despite Kenya's policy of international accommodation, the state currently is confronting extensive and prolonged constraints in domestic economic and political spheres: vulnerability to drought conditions, rapid population growth, large marginalized groups, and entrenched economic interests. In this deteriorating economic environment, the state has sought an adjustment strategy that reinforces its perceived position as a responsible debtor nation yet one that is able to respond to growing domestic political pressures.

Kenya's Economic Adjustment Objectives

By the early 1980s, Kenya became one of the first Third World countries to begin to implement a series of measures and programs to adjust to a deteriorating national and international economy. The general thrust of the adjustment program has been to reduce government expenditures, especially parastatal subsidies, liberalize the import system, promote agricultural exports, strengthen the private sector, and attract direct foreign investment.[13] Although all those policies have been discussed in conjunction with World Bank and IMF programs, we should not conclude that the governing coalition in Kenya has displayed political weakness. On the contrary, the state has revealed remarkable strength in putting its interests forward during the adjustment process. In discussions with Kenyan officials, they made clear that they did not dispute the IMF's orthodox interpretation of Kenya's economic decline nor the recommended reforms for economic adjustment.[14] Disagreement has existed, however, over the timing and scope of implementing politically sensitive reforms that may threaten influential domestic interests. Mosley recently presented a convincing argument that Kenya has 'gotten away' with tremendous slippage in its many agreements with the IMF and the World Bank.[15] I now review the state's policy objectives and the impact of these policies on domestic and foreign groups.

Kenya has published a series of government documents outlining the objectives and measures of its adjustment strategy. Two of the latest descriptions of Kenya's strategy – the Fifth and Sixth Development Plans (1984–1988 and 1989–1993) – are examples of a state-led strategy directed towards achieving at least some orthodox objectives. The development plans reveal three major planks in achieving these negotiated objectives. As with the development statements published by Zimbabwe and Brazil, one must treat Kenya's development objectives cautiously. There is a substantial gap between the rhetoric of adjustment and the implementation of adjustment. Nevertheless, Kenya's objectives stand in contrast to those of the other cases in this book.

Private Sector Investment
The first objective is the expected generation of productive resources by shifting from public sector investment to private sector investment. The

plans state that 'without growth in the private sector, there can be no effective or widespread development in Kenya.'[16] As a means to revamp the private sector, the Central Bank in conjunction with the International Finance Corporation prepared a program of financial reforms to develop a private capital market.[17] Another set of reforms to divert capital from the public to private sector would gradually eliminate and/or privatize state-owned enterprises.

As early as 1982, a major government statement on parastatals recommended the gradual shifting of investments from the public to the private sector.[18] The report argued that state firms had become inefficient largely because of the intrusion of domestic political interests in the commercial decision-making process. These vested interests are generally of two kinds: domestic economic groups in the manufacturing sector and Africans benefiting from the anti-Asian stance of the government. Several commercial bankers and IMF officials agreed that one of the most serious problems has been the friction between manufacturers close to the government and international institutions pressing for economic liberalization.[19] The selling of key parastatals would undermine the short-term benefits served by local industrialists and local politicians, many of whom have been close to the administration. A 1986 government document provided an early guideline of the restructuring of state-owned enterprises. The government repeatedly has stated that its intention is to confine parastatal funds to projects that could not be better served by the private sector, that could generate foreign exchange earnings, and that could promise high rates of return.[20]

Another important domestic constraint has been the antagonistic relationship between Africans and Asians. The extension and protection of state firms initially employed many workers, but these firms also represented local African control of key financial and industrial resources. A liberalization of the local market would increase Asian opportunities to advance their economic interests. According to several respondents, the Asian community still maintains controls over commercial and industrial sectors, especially in vital export-oriented firms.[21] More recently, a serious dispute broke out in the mid-1980s between two ethnic groups (Kikuyu and Kalenjin) that erupted into a major financial scandal in 1988. According to a financial advisor involved in Kenya's economic strategy, President Moi (a Kalenjin) precipitated the crisis in 1986 by having the Ministry of Finance and state companies withdraw their funds from three banks owned by Kikuyus. As the managing director of one of the three banks told me, 'why should power be concentrated in the hands of people who do not understand the business of parastatal firms?' He, along with Philip Ndegwa, the former governor of the Central Bank, the author of the report recommending the elimination of parastatals, and a part owner of one of the closed banks, was removed from his position.

Foreign Capital Investment
A second plank of Kenya's adjustment strategy addresses the lack of investment capital in Kenya and calls for a heavy reliance on foreign capital. In addition, the creation and maintenance of a stable and profitable environment for foreign investment would also strengthen Kenya's position with international creditors. Since independence, Kenya increasingly has turned toward international financial institutions for its investment requirements. Indeed, external capital inflows accounting for Kenya's gross investment grew from nearly seventeen percent in 1966 to forty-three percent in 1979.[22] The government has implemented several policies to encourage and protect foreign capital investment. According to the Minister of Industry in 1988, Kenya provides the conditions for protecting foreign investment, generating profits for foreign firms, and repatriating capital gains.[23]

The Foreign Investment Protection Act of 1964 became the foundation for this supportive policy. In August 1983, the Central Bank introduced an incentive policy that allowed the remittance of foreign investors' dividends and profit payments for the previous year. Then, in June 1984, the Central Bank lowered the withholding taxes on royalties and dividend remittances. The 1986 budget included a revision of the Foreign Investment Act to encourage increased inflows of foreign capital directed toward technological investments. The Minister of Finance, in the 1987 Budget Speech, made it clear that 'Kenya has always welcomed foreign investors, whose capital, technology, management, and worldwide marketing skills can add enormously to our own productive capacity and especially our ability to export.'[24]

More recently, the government has favored foreign investors with other concessions. In 1988, the government widened the tax exemptions on private capital investment and promulgated the revised Foreign Investment Protection Act which now makes foreign exchange losses on hard currency investments tax deductible. The government also promised to permit the outflow of unremitted dividends which have accumulated to $5.6 million since 1986.[25] The remittance policy was liberalized again in 1988 by allowing the immediate repatriation of the initial foreign exchange invested while depositing any capital gains from this investment in a government account for five years. In the intervening five years, the foreign investor's gains must be invested in government securities that attract market rates of interest.[26] As another means to attract foreign investment, Kenya recently has signed the Multilateral Investment Guarantee Agency (MIGA) of the

World Bank which guarantees against non-commercial risks to enterprises that invest in signatory countries. In light of the overall deterioration in the investment climate, which had caused the number of American subsidiaries to fall from 140 to 115 since 1982, the government in 1990 began a new campaign to attract foreign capital, especially in the export sector.[27]

However, the government's *public rhetoric* in support of foreign capital investment has been offset by the *actual regulation* of foreign exchange allocation. Kenya still maintains blocked funds from which foreign exchange is made available through petition. Tension is most evident between foreign investors in the export, agricultural sector and those in the domestic, import-substituting industry market. Since the export-oriented agricultural firms hold a competitive edge over state-protected, costly manufacturing interests, their representatives favored increased foreign currency allocation to those firms and down played the use of controls as reasonable and merely regulatory.[28] Yet, the government continues to protect and thus establish investment incentives favoring the domestic market and local firms.

Indigenous industrialists and manufactures tend to support the government's restrictions on foreign exchange to the extent that more capital is then available for local investment. These controls, they argue, are a 'necessary evil' during this 'stage of development.'[29] They provided several reasons for the continual implementation of controls. First, many respondents recognized the current generous remittance policy for foreign dividends and profits. While a central tenet of orthodox economic adjustment holds that the flow of foreign investment should be unhindered, economic and political realities in Kenya dictate that foreign capital should be directed, on a temporary basis, toward the achievement of state investment objectives. Foreign capital interests have gravitated towards the domestic market especially towards local manufacturing industries with the support of the government which encourages commercial banks to lend to import-substituting industries. Any significant liberalization of foreign currency controls would risk the immediate outflow of scarce capital thus leading to a more serious foreign currency crisis.

A second reason concerns the economic competition between the *Asian* and *African* communities. Since Asians dominate the commercial market and control a large share of the industrial sector, most Africans assume that Asians would export their profits out of Kenya. Given the perceived likelihood of massive capital flight among the Kenyan Asian community, the 'risk [from liberalization] is too great and the potential abuse too likely.'[30] Capital flight is indeed a genuine problem. A 1989 report estimated that official plus illegal net transfers amounted to between $500 million and $650 million in 1988; or equivalent to 6.7 percent to 8.7 percent of GDP.³¹ State regulation over this outflow, in addition to the large (nearly $1 billion) foreign bank deposits amassed by Kenyan residents and state enterprises, would strengthen the economy and increase the confidence of foreign companies investing in Kenya.

Export Incentives
Finally, as the third plank of Kenya's adjustment strategy, the country is struggling with a transition to an export-oriented economy as the engine of growth while still clinging to the protective measures of import-substitution. This component is perhaps the most controversial issue of Kenya's adjustment strategy. The state is caught directly in the cross-fire between international financial interests pressing for an open, trade regime and domestic manufacturing interests seeking continued protection of ISI firms. The central government is in the process of reorganizing the economy towards a more substantial export tendency. The Central Bank, in its concern for a resurgence of Kenyan creditworthiness that had fallen following the 1982 coup attempt, called for a renewed export-driven economy. As the managing director of a Kenyan bank commented in an interview, 'the world's competitive market has forced the government to be more competitive in the required struggle to earn foreign exchange. A primary force is the need for foreign exchange and a vibrant export sector demanded by foreign banks.'

As with the shift to an *export-oriented economy* in most developing countries, three reasons shaped Kenya's response. First, the agricultural export sector is the largest economic sector in terms of GDP as well as of export earnings. Given this, it is not surprising that the government has created additional incentives for coffee, tea, and meat production. In terms of comparative advantage issues, the government will continue an interventionist policy towards agricultural exports. The state's increased emphasis on agricultural exports has received strong support from large commercial farming interests who benefit from an outward economic policy as opposed to smaller landowners who target local markets. Another government policy that strengthens exporters is the devaluation of the Kenyan shilling. *Devaluation*, as a typical element of an IMF package of policies, is an important and frequently used state tool. As Mosley argued in a study on the implementation of Kenya's adjustment strategy, price-related policy reforms are easier to implement than institutional changes. Devaluation, as a form of price change, can be implemented without time-consuming institutional reforms that require more difficult negotiations with domestic constituents. Devaluation of the Kenyan shilling not only has garnered support from the IMF, international

Table 3.1 *Origins of Gross Domestic Product in Kenya, 1985, 1990*
(as % of total)

	1985	1990
Agriculture, forestry, and fishing	32.5	28.3
Manufacturing	11.7	11.4
Trade, restaurants, and hotels	11.8	11.0
Transport, storage, and communications	6.7	6.9
Government services	13.9	15.3
Other	23.4	27.1

Source   Economist Intelligence Unit, *Kenya: Country Report*, #2 (London: EIU, 1992).

banks, and industrialized governments, but also received strong backing from agricultural exporters and domestic bankers. Between 1981 and 1985, the currency depreciated by 82 percent in dollar terms. The real exchange rate has continued to depreciate where, by 1991, it was expected to have fallen by more than 50 percent since 1985. Such a massive shift resulted in an income redistribution from non-tradeables to tradeables, especially for agricultural exports. Large agricultural producers benefited from the state's devaluation policy, such as firms exporting tea and coffee. Devaluation is used by the state to spur on export growth although at some cost to domestic industries and importers of capital inputs. During this same period, the real wages in the agricultural sector declined by seventeen percent.[32] The Sixth Development Plan continues this policy by calling for another series of shilling devaluations.

In addition to devaluation as a means to attract foreign investment, the government has introduced a centralized system of export incentives. Since the agricultural sector supplies over three-quarters of Kenya's export earnings, it is not surprising that the government has created additional incentives for coffee, tea, and meat production. The government also established an export compensation plan by which the state pays exporters ten percent of their exports. Another incentive offered is direct export finance and insurance. The government recognizes the attitude of local and foreign bankers who are unlikely to lend money to exporters without government guarantees covering the expected return from the transaction. A third support set up by the state is an institutional system to coordinate export promotion activities, such as the Kenya External Trade Authority and the Investment Promotion Center (IPC). The latter is the key agency in the government's plans to attract foreign business. Created first in 1983, its objective is to formulate investment packages according to the government's development priorities. In its first seven years, the center only processed thirty investment applications worth more than $70 million. Between 1987 and 1991, 229 projects valued at $371 million have been processed by the IPC, of which 85 are operational.[33] The center also is responsible for the Export Processing Zone. Based on similar zones in the newly industrializing countries (NICs) in Asia, Kenya hopes to attract large-scale foreign investments with a ten year tax holiday, 100 percent investment allowance, and duty-free and tax-free incentives.[34] Many other African countries, including Zimbabwe (discussed later in this chapter), have established similar institutional incentives to expand exports. Kenya's prospects are somewhat brighter than its neighbors because of the revival of the East African Community and of its role in the Preferential Trade Area (PTA).

A second explanation for the reliance on an export economy is the widely shared perception that, by the early 1980s, Kenya had reached the upper limits of protected industrial growth. Imports had risen rapidly, in part due to the oil price shocks of the 1970s, but also because of the increased costs of imported capital inputs. With the domestic market satiated with costly and poorly made domestic goods, the export sector became crucial as the engine for the next phase of economic growth. Third, government respondents agreed that only a growing export sector could improve Kenya's debt repayment ability. Since external loans generally are repaid in foreign currency, a critical indicator of repayment capacity is export potential. This is a very great concern for Kenya and its creditors since its debt service in terms of exports steadily increased during the 1980s to where, by 1987, over forty percent of all exports were diverted to finance the external public debt. Even by 1992, the projected debt service figure remains near 30 percent.[35]

As a 'boom or bust' economy, Kenya during the 1980s had periodic bright moments of significant export growth, improved terms of trade, and restricted import growth followed by a disastrous period. As IMF and U.S. Treasury officials claim in interviews, the Kenyan government failed to take advantage of the improved economic climate and, instead, followed a lax policy which diminished its foreign reserves and necessitated a new structural adjustment facility from the IMF. The political imperative at this time was to channel new resources back to the private sector in the form of rising government expenditures. Immediately following strong export performances in 1981 and again in 1986, government expenditures increased 15 percent and 20 percent, respectively, while government revenues failed to keep up with much lower increases.[36] Foreign reserves as a percentage of total imports fell after the bust years, but picked up because of IMF and donor financial support. Moreover, private and government consumption

76   Indebted Development

Table 3.2 Kenya's Trade Balance, 1985–1992 (US$ million)

	1985	1986	1987	1988	1989	1990[a]	1991[a]	1992[b]
Merchandise exports	943	1170	909	1018	926	1011	1020	1100
Merchandise imports	–1270	–1455	–1623	–1802	–1963	–2009	–1890	–1640
Trade balance	–327	–285	–714	–785	–1037	–998	–870	–540

[a] Estimate   [b] Forecast

Source Institute of International Finance, *Kenya* (Washington, D.C.: IIF, 1991).

combined increased, as a percentage of GDP, from 75.2 percent in 1985 to 84.5 percent in 1990, while gross fixed capital formation remained about at the same level.[37]

Despite the government's (and especially the Central Bank's) public support for export-orientation, the government has encountered severe *domestic and foreign constraints* on the implementation of this policy. Under the former is the government's concern about the effect that economic and political liberalization may have upon political stability. In 1987 and 1988, the central government significantly increased its expenditures for public sector wages, expanded the education budget, and continued to promote the costly process of Africanization. These policies, the government intended, were to bring about short-term benefits to important domestic groups especially prior to the 1988 elections. Certainly, the dangerously high population growth rate of four percent and periodic drought conditions in the early 1980s drained away scarce resources and undermined the relative expansion of real GDP of around five percent.[38] In 1985, annual per capita growth only managed an increase of 0.1 percent. Between 1985 and 1990, the average annual per capita rate rose only by 0.62 percent.[39]

Kenya's adjustment strategy also has been affected by foreign constraints, most of which rest outside the control of the central government. In addition to the inability to affect internal climatic variations, the government was vulnerable to coffee price shocks controlled by the International Coffee Organization (ICO). While coffee and tea exports can benefit from higher prices, coffee volumes are constrained by Kenya's quota set by the ICO. This quota only accommodated about 85–90 percent of Kenya's exports with the price of non-quota coffee set at cost.[40] But, with the abandonment of ICO quotas in July 1989, average prices for Kenya coffee fell below average costs. Another external constraint is the inability for Kenya's manufactured exports to break into the markets of

Table 3.3 *Trend of Gross Domestic Product of Kenya, 1985–1992*

	1985	1986	1987	1988	1989	1990^a	1991^a	1992^b
Real GDP (% change)	4.3	7.2	5.9	6.0	4.6	4.5	2.3	−1.5

^{a} Estimate ^{b} Forecast

Source Institute of International Finance, *Kenya* (Washington, D.C.: IIF, 1991).

industrialized countries. Even in the absence of the international recession and rising protectionism, Kenya's exports are relatively expensive and uncompetitive.

Despite the international perception that Kenya was following a correct adjustment program and despite the heavy involvement of the IMF through several Structural Adjustment Programs (SAP), Kenya's adjustment performance has been dismal.[41] At face value, economic growth (measured as real GDP) was strong between 1986 and 1990, with an annual growth rate of 5.6 percent. But one study expects a dramatic decline in GDP annual growth to 2.3 percent in 1991 and followed by a loss of 1.5 percent in 1992. By taking inflation and population growth rates into account, economic growth has been negative for several years. This study concluded that the annual change in gross fixed capital investment rose by nearly nine percent in 1988, but it is expected to plummet by a minus 16.7 percent in 1992. A more direct indicator is that of annual net equity investment which is expected to more than double from the 1984–89 period to the 1990–91 period. However, while Kenya, for an African country, has done extremely well in attracting foreign investment, the annual amount of net equity investment between 1985 and 1989 only stood at about $25 million.

Moreover, trade liberalization, by opening up the economy to competitive foreign capital interests, is jeopardizing Kenya's international trade position. The balance of trade deficit jumped 150 percent between 1986 and 1987 and is expected to expand by another 35 percent by 1991. The growth in the deficit is attributed to a rapid rise in imports by more than 10 percent per year from 1986 to 1990, while exports actually fell by nearly two percent annually in the same period. Moreover, as its need for capital investment expanded, the rate of growth for gross fixed capital was less than five percent per year between 1984 and 1987. Finally, the government is faced with a significant foreign exchange reserve crisis. In its attempt to contain the balance of payments deficit, the government has drawn heavily from the reserves since 1986 which has steadily cut the import cover to less than one half of a month in 1992.

The adjustment measures adopted by the government sought to placate the demands of the international financial community and to protect the established interests of the governing coalition. The government implemented monetary, fiscal, and trade policies that strengthened the position of foreign export interests and domestic agricultural interests who benefited from a strong export policy. This coalition clearly favors expanding the capacity to service the external debt based on agricultural exports and attracting further direct foreign investment. A report on the 1987 government budget noted that the domestic business sector was pleased with the government focus on export and import liberalization rather than on any restriction on foreign currency outflows.[42] Although the interests of both foreign and domestic groups generally overlap, conflicting interests arise in several important areas. The government has allowed considerable slippage in implementing price decontrols in the agricultural sector. Farmers represent an influential voice within the established coalition.

In interviews, several international bankers and IMF officials also were critical of the corruption, bureaucratic incompetence, and political gerrymandering in maintaining inefficient parastatals, industrial protective measures, wage repression, and agricultural marketing boards. In addition, social tension is increasing as demonstrated by repeated calls for civil disobedience against one-party rule and the state's repressive response against demonstrators. While President Moi finally gave in under domestic and foreign pressure by legalizing a multi-party political system, he has delayed in proposing a national convention and in scheduling elections. By early 1992, domestic opposition to the monopolistic control by the Kenya African National Union (KANU) under Moi's control led to the formation of several new political parties. The largest opposition party, the Forum for the Restoration of Democracy (FORD), gathered on January 18, 1992 for its first public meeting and attracted 150,000 people.[43] Another sign of KANU's weakness was the defection of several prominent politicians (including Moi's former vice president, Mwai Kibaki) to FORD.

THE CASE OF ZIMBABWE

In its selection and implementation of a mixed pattern of adjustment, Zimbabwe has had to negotiate simultaneously with international creditors and domestic interests. In contrast to Kenya, the outcome of these negotiations has reflected two developments: first, the government during the 1980s recognized what it saw as a failure of orthodox adjustment strategies in Africa. The poor economic performance under SAPs convinced the Zimbabwe government that it should identify a 'home grown' adjustment path. Second, as one of Africa's most recent independent countries, the governing elites of the nation have yet to consolidate and solidify their power bases into a united ideological force. Ethnic, class, and political divisions remain as powerful obstacles to a coherent adjustment strategy. In the absence of such ideological unity, the government has not been successful in establishing a consistent bargaining strategy toward either societal interests or toward its international creditors. The oft-remarked *incongruity* between early calls for a socialist transformation of the economy and the use and expansion of inherited market capitalism is seen as the basis for the inconsistent approach towards foreign capital.[44]

In terms of adjustment, the government has incorporated two contrasting tendencies. On the one hand, the government displays a *neo-orthodox* tendency toward economic growth, punctual external debt repayment, and avoidance of capital account deficits. It has won praise from a World Bank report for its prudential and stable management of the macro economy.[45] Yet, in efforts to redress inherited economic inequities, the government has followed a more *heterodox* economic approach by raising government expenditures, specifically in the areas of basic goods and subsidy support of parastatals resulting in the expansion of the government budget deficit.[46] From these tendencies have emerged two broad adjustment priorities. The government sought during the 1980s to rely on international finance capital instead of direct foreign investment or the IMF as a primary financial source for its state-driven adjustment strategy. This form of borrowed capital has allowed the government greater internal control over the timing and scope of adjustment. The primary requirement has been the prompt repayment of its external debt. The government's second adjustment priority has been to pay close attention to the rising expectations of the population, especially in terms of the distribution of resources to the marginal groups of society. Because of Zimbabwe's particular historical context, the government has actively sought domestic ratification of the adjustment strategy. This section examines the adjustment objectives in more detail and the internal and external constraints that affect the government's capacity to achieve the objectives.

Zimbabwe's Economic Adjustment Objectives

The government's objectives and adjustment policies have been shaped by the distinctive history of the period of the Unilateral Declaration of Independence (UDI) and the ideological conflict that emerged after independence in 1980. The current regime inherited the traditions of state economic controls, an inward-looking economic strategy, the self-sufficient (mainly white) commercial agricultural sector, and a relatively sophisticated financial structure from the UDI period (1965–79). The Rhodesian government, by necessity of international isolation, developed a relatively sophisticated import-substitution industry with strong financial links to South Africa. The absence of foreign exchange required the regime to impose tight controls over the use of foreign currency and redirected those resources towards internal productive sectors. The UDI government thus was faced with structural rigidities often found in other developing countries: excessive import needs and inadequate export levels. In response to this dilemma, the new government selected a mixed economic strategy incorporating both heterodox and orthodox policies.

Upon independence, these two contrasting ideological perspectives reflecting components of both heterodoxy and orthodoxy dominated economic decision-making. Most of the respondents who have been active in economic decision-making described the conflict as a struggle for power and influence between ideological *radicals* and *pragmatists*.[47] The formers' adjustment strategy is shaped by the policies and objectives of a heterodox model of development as discussed earlier in the chapter. The assumptions and objectives of this model were contained in one of the first official development statements. The 1982 *Transitional National Development Plan* asserted that the government's

> belief is that it is only within the framework of a planned economy that Government is better able to influence and purposefully direct development, create appropriate institutions, and establish the magnitude of investment and its allocation as well as the formation of a pattern of income and wealth distribution in harmony with socialist objectives.[48]

Given the importance of the public sector, state subsidies to parastatals have remained substantial. The private sector has, at times, either been considered too small or been tainted by foreign capital involvement. Foreign investment has been further regulated with often times restrictive investment codes or dividend and remittance controls. The radicals are strongly influenced by the presence of South African ownership in Zimbabwe and the constraints on foreign exchange allocation. This group perceived that the pragmatists, with strong international capital assistance, 'adopted measures that only deepened the neo-colonial structure of the economy and weakened the position of local capitalists vis-à-vis international capital.'[49]

The radical group further argues that a free market system incorporating an open and integrated economy would fail to overcome structural rigidities and bottlenecks. Indeed, a complete liberalization of the economy would increase the economy's vulnerability to external forces and impinge on domestic economic firms and, as one respondent claimed, would entail the surrender of Zimbabwe's sovereignty to market forces.[50] Liberalization, they argued, poses a threat to the state as it could lead to firm closures in the manufacturing sector, rising unemployment, and a major reduction in foreign exchange availability. In addition, the policy was too closely aligned with the austerity measures pushed by the IMF and the World Bank.[51] Instead, the radicals favor the tools of state economic management (such as dividend and remittance controls, import controls, and wage and price controls) in an attempt to balance economic growth with redistribution. Beginning with its first development statement and continuing into 1992, the government also has emphasized land redistribution that would take land away from white commercial farmers and give it to black peasants. The state thus seeks to redistribute income in a way to increase the proportion of domestic content in manufactured goods and to redistribute productive assets (as in land) to protect those people who fail to be absorbed into the employment structure.[52]

While the radical approach was most vocal (especially in the initial years after independence), the pragmatic group was able to off-set complete implementation of radical economic policy. In recognition of the significant degree of foreign ownership in the country (in which about 50 percent of the productive sectors was foreign-owned, and about one-quarter owned by South Africans in 1986)[53] and the severe absence of foreign currency, this group seeks the maintenance of foreign capital ties in order to foster the interrelated policies of foreign borrowing, export growth, and rising investment. An economist for RAL Merchant Bank argued in 1985 that, as a young country, with much illiteracy and many impoverished people, it needed substantial economic growth and maintenance of the capitalist structure in order to address distributive issues. A socialist transformation of society is not likely to occur, according to this respondent, without destroying the productive base of the country, alienating the international financial community, and depriving domestic groups of resources. In interviews, officials from the IMF and World Bank gave strong support to this coalition for their objectives of reducing the government deficit, increasing export performance, shifting incentives away from the protected domestic industries and toward agricultural and mining sectors, and greater cooperation between the state and the private sector. More recently, the Fund and the Bank both assisted in the formulation of and gave their firm backing to the latest five-year economic plan issued in early 1991.[54]

A third important participant in the adjustment process is the president, *Robert Mugabe*. His initial tendency was to support the radical coalition, yet his current attitude toward adjustment remains unclear. While in public he has espoused the arguments and rhetoric of the radical group, in private Mugabe has favored the implementation of more orthodox policies. His role, at the moment, appears to center on the creation of political unity and the promotion of nationalism. Through the inclusion into the cabinet of many members of an early opposition party, the Zimbabwe African People's Union including the party's head and former political rival, Joseph Nkomo, Mugabe has been successful, at least for the time being, in lessening domestic political instability. More recently, Mugabe has acted quickly on persistent claims of government corruption by firing several cabinet members involved in cases of personal corruption.

The interplay of these groups has played a vital role in the formation of the adjustment strategy. Since neither has convinced the other of the appropriateness of its objectives nor its policy measures, Zimbabwe's adjustment has proceeded in fits and starts as suggested in several recent analyses.[55] During the first two years of independence the initial objective was the creation of self-sustaining sources of economic growth that would foster an equitable distribution of economic and political resources. The government initially set an annual economic growth target of eight percent by 1982. Ridiculed by most respondents as unrealistic, one respondent, who was a senior official in the Ministry of Finance involved in these early decisions, argued that the figure was not meant to be a forecast, only a reference point. In any event, the government at that time recognized the importance of rapid economic growth to offset growing internal and external constraints. The goals for the three year plan were 1) narrowing the economic gap between racial groups by redistributing society's assets; 2) providing health facilities, education, and housing; 3) redistributing land to the farmers while developing the agricultural sector; 4) stimulating agricultural and industrial output; and 5) creating a 'socialized means of production and distribution.'[56] The initial financing of this development strategy was established on a mix of internal and external sources of capital. As opposed to Kenya's financing strategy, the Zimbabwe state purposively restricted foreign investments in infrastructural and agricultural sectors, placed limits on capital flight and the allocation of foreign exchange to the private sector, and invested heavily in unprofitable areas of the public sector, including housing, health, social welfare, and education.

Independence in 1980 brought two years of rapid growth due to the effects of ending the war, the lifting of economic sanctions, and the excellent 1980–81 agricultural season. But these positive effects were outweighed in the 1982–84 period by the impact of the world recession on the Zimbabwe economy, three successive drought years, and an economic policy environment that failed to attract business and financial investments. Economic growth data indicate a real growth annual change of 15 percent in 1981, but dropping to −1.3 percent in 1982 and −4.0 percent in 1983. At this time of economic decline, public expectations had risen rapidly in anticipation of the delivery of promises made upon independence. The public pressured the government to build health clinics, schools, refurbish the transportation network, build rural markets, and provide subsidies to keep consumer prices low. The combination of these factors forced the the government to abandon the Transitional Plan which led to the implementation of the First Five-Year National Development Plan. This latter plan backed away from a specific socialist orientation and more broadly called for a 'restructuring and modernisation of the economy, development of human resources and alteration of the structure of ownership.'[57] The most recent indication of government policy is its apparent recognition of a number of pressing problems, including a rising unemployment rate of 25 percent, stagnating exports, upcoming debt repayment deadlines, and a severe reduction of imports; imports now are one-third below the 1982 level.[58]

The current adjustment strategy has been shaped by ideological divisions within society and by the constraints affecting the implementation of adjustment. Although, as I will discuss in the next chapter, the government now is in broad agreement with several IMF adjustment objectives, its specific policies differ sharply from those of the IMF. For this mixed economic strategy to work effectively, the government has enacted adjustment policies overseeing foreign investment, foreign exchange allocation, and international trade.

Direct Foreign Investment
Upon independence, the new government's economic strategy was restricted by the massive presence of foreign capital invested in the productive sectors of the economy and the perceived need to generate domestic support and ratification of the government's adjustment strategy. In the context of socialist rhetoric articulated at the inauguration of the government, multinational corporation investment was seen to strike at the heart of production and thus at the core assumptions of a transitional economy. A former Secretary of Finance said in an interview in 1985 that 'the government was suspicious of foreign investment since it could become a permanent edifice in the economy's foundation.' If direct foreign investment expanded into vital economic sectors, not only would profits

from the investments leave Zimbabwe, but the country would become increasingly dependent and vulnerable on foreign (and South African) sources of investment capital. According to an economist of the Zimbabwe National Chamber of Commerce in 1985, 'why should the government pay repatriation for investments which the government could have done as well?' Government policies on direct foreign investment have intended to establish national control over capital investments in order to allocate resources to social and economic priorities.

In considering government policy toward foreign capital, one first must distinguish existing foreign investment from new investment in Zimbabwe. Despite the anti-foreign capital rhetoric espoused by many government officials (including Mugabe's own statements[59]), the government only implemented partial restrictions on the foreign capital already invested in the country at the time of independence. From the perspective of foreign investors, the greatest barrier was the regulation over dividend and remittance repatriation. At first, the government allowed foreign investors to repatriate fifty percent of their after-tax profits. In March 1984, the government suspended all remittances of dividends, branch, and partnership profits made prior to September 1979. Zimbabwe further suspended income remittances from blocked funds, with a provision for the eventual release of the blocked capital.[60] The Minister of Finance stated in a 1986 Reserve Bank report that the removal of restrictions on the use of blocked funds would burden the already overstretched foreign exchange capacity with additional foreign currency demands for capital and raw materials requirements.[61] In reaction to the continued outflow of capital amounting to Z$150 million in 1986, the government, in May 1987, halved the dividend remittances from fifty to twenty-five percent of after-tax profits. Foreign firms have the option of divesting from Zimbabwe, but the process is complex. Capital can be repatriated either through the purchase of long-term interest-bearing bonds or immediate repatriation but for a heavy discount of 70 percent.

The government had several reasons for its intervention in and control over invested capital. It attempted to subordinate dividend remittances to other claims within the economy's tight supply of foreign exchange. By controlling foreign investments, it could influence the direction of scarce foreign currency to projects identified as high priority. The government further has used the blocked fund accounts as a large reserve held under its control. The Minister of Finance argued in 1990 that this policy resulted, not from any ideological predisposition against foreign capital, but from the severe constraints of the balance of payments.[62] Implicit in this remark was the perception that capital controls would be needed only in the short-term until trade performance improves. Throughout most of the 1980s, domestic industrialists represented by the Confederation of Zimbabwe Industries (CZI) only partially opposed the regulatory structure since, in the final analysis, many domestic firms were being protected from the competitive international market.[63] Another reason for managing investment capital was the apparent success of controls. According to Roger Riddell, 'while institutional controls have become *more* rather than *less* extensive during the 1980s, their effects have tended to make the [manufacturing] sector *more* rather than *less* competitive.'[64] Finally, the radical contingent in government had been demanding strict regulations governing foreign investment. By 'losing' out to the liberal wording of the new Constitution which, in part, protected foreign capital from uncompensated nationalization, the policy on dividend and remittance repatriation was meant to placate this faction.[65]

During the mid-1980s, restrictions also were imposed on foreign investments that occurred after independence. One regulation concerned the definition of 'foreign' investment. By equating 15 percent foreign involvement with foreign ownership, the government sought to minimize foreign domination in the economy as well as to maximize its control over the purposes of investment. A second restriction focused on the bureaucratic process by which foreign investment projects had to be submitted to obtain necessary government approval. A three stage process centered around the Foreign Investment Committee lengthened the approval period up to two or three years. The government also refused to sign bilateral guarantees such as the Overseas Private Investment Corporation (OPIC), claiming such an action represented an infringement on the country's sovereignty. OPIC is designed to improve the investment climate in the developing world by protecting foreign firms against the political risks and possible disruption of flows of remittances and dividends. The government claimed that the country's constitution (and a 1982 investment policy statement) sufficiently protected private investment. Clearly, the government sought to distance itself from a traditional IMF financing package. Unlike Kenya's objective in attracting direct foreign investment to assist in financing adjustment, Zimbabwe attempted, until the mid- to late-1980s, to restrict and control the degree of foreign capital involvement.

However, by the mid-1980s, the government was faced with a number of *regional and national constraints* that impinged upon the level of foreign investment. Debt, drought, and destabilization account for several important causes of Zimbabwe's investment policy change. The drought of the early 1980s had a detrimental effect on food production which was, in part, responsible for the near doubling of the trade balance deficit between 1981 and 1982. Drought conditions also worsened the balance of payments deficit requiring the borrowing of short-term loans to shore up the country's foreign reserves. Foreign reserves had fallen from $170 million in 1981 to just $45 million in 1984. An additional pressure that relied heavily on scarce foreign currency came from the continuing ethnic struggle between the Shonas and the Ndebeles, entrenched in the southern part of the country. The high level of defense spending further reflected the unstable political situation in southern Africa and the priority placed by the government on maintaining the security of the Beira Corridor, the transportation link through Mozambique.

Zimbabwe's regional trade status had become extremely vulnerable due to the South African destabilization strategy in the region. In 1982, more than half of Zimbabwe's imports and exports moved through Mozambique. By 1984, with the Maputo line closed because of instability, Zimbabwe relied solely on South African ports costing Z$10–50 per ton higher than through Mozambique's. Joseph Hanlon estimates that the transport crisis in the early 1980s cost Zimbabwe Z$5 million per week in lost exports.[66] Due to Zimbabwe's increasing trade vulnerability, South Africa with relative ease disrupted Zimbabwe's trade with slow-downs at the border and demanded large hikes in duties and import surcharges.[67] The costliest effect of South Africa's destabilization strategy was Zimbabwe's heavy financial burden to defend itself and trade routes through Mozambique. As late as 1989, approximately 12,000 troops were deployed across the border with Mozambique, keeping open road and rail lines to the port of Beira and protecting the oil pipeline.[68] In response to dozens of attacks by the Mozambique National Resistance or by South African forces, Zimbabwe was spending by the late-1980s about US$3 million a week.[69] In addition, the United Nations High Commission on Refugees reported that, due to regional instability, 175,000 refugees were residing in Zimbabwe.[70] Reginald Green estimates that, due to destabilization, the loss in Zimbabwe's GDP from 1980 to 1988 was nearly US$8 billion. He calculates that without destabilization from South Africa, Zimbabwe would have had both recurrent and capital budget surpluses.[71]

The country also faces national economic constraints. According to Colin Stoneman, Zimbabwe's strong growth rate had been bought at the expense of low investment and very low job creation.[72] As a percentage over the previous year, gross fixed capital fell by seven percent per year between 1984 and 1987.[73] Zimbabwe, from all economic sources, had not been investing enough to maintain its existing capital stock, let alone create new productive capacity. Furthermore, new investment is considered necessary by many in government as the number of school leavers joining the labor market approaches 200,000 each year while only 30,000 new jobs are created annually. Since independence, it sought to remain creditworthy in the eyes of international banks by keeping to its repayment schedule while pumping resources into social service sectors. In order to revamp the deteriorating infrastructure and to finance a partial liberalization policy, the government needed external financing from a variety of sources including foreign investment.[74]

Faced with a declining investment rate, burgeoning population growth, rising domestic discontent in industry and manufacturing over the inadequate access to foreign exchange needed for imports, and with divestment running at an annual rate of US $75 million in 1988, the government belatedly began to incorporate some incentives favorable to foreign investors.[75] Because of the shift in government policy in favor of foreign capital, a major pillar of the 'home grown' adjustment strategy disappeared. In 1989, the government instituted a more liberal foreign investment code and, in 1990, signed an international agreement guaranteeing foreign investments, both of which had been demanded by foreign investors as measures of the government's approval of foreign investment. The new investment code seeks to reassure investors of government protection of their investments and the unlikely event of reducing the degree of remittability of investment income. The investment code also liberalizes the use of blocked funds, amounting to US$460 million, by allowing foreigners to reinvest those funds in approved projects. Foreign investors now can buy local currency with foreign exchange, at a discounted price, and invest them in new projects. The Reserve Bank is to issue non-negotiable certificates of deposit for subscription by nonresident-controlled firms with the Zimbabwe Development Bank and the Small Enterprises Development Corporation acting as intermediaries. The state decision affecting the allocation of these blocked funds depends on whether the new investment will either a) generate net export earnings or net import savings; b) generate net employment; c) result in adaptable technology transfer using local inputs; or d) result in the decentralization of industry from urban to rural areas.[76]

The new investment guidelines also broaden and relax the definition of 'foreign' investment by increasing the percentage from 15 percent to 25 percent of capital owned by nonresidents. Finally, the government eliminated the bureaucratic Foreign Investment Committee (FIC) and created a Zimbabwe Investment Centre (ZIC) to streamline procedures for investment approval.[77] It recently has been provided with a permanent staff and legal status in making decisions. Decisions are meant to be reached within ninety days instead of the two to three years under the FIC. The results from the creation of the ZIC and from streamlining procedures and liberalizing investment rules have been positive. While in 1989, Z$600 million of new projects were approved, in 1990, the figure more than doubled, to Z$1.4 billion. Currently, around 300 investment projects have been approved of which 60 percent are new.[78]

The *Economic Policy Statement* issued in July 1990 clearly reflects government concern over the lack of foreign investment needed for major infrastructural overhaul. The investment guidelines thus were implemented specifically to increase the investment rate from around 14 percent of GDP to at least 20 percent.[79] Multilateral financial organizations, which had been holding back funds for Zimbabwe, suddenly reopened negotiations for large loans and grants. During spring 1990, negotiations were held with the International Finance Corporation and the African Development Bank for medium-term export finance of US$130 million each to be invested exclusively in the private sector. The World Bank also is anticipated to provide US$420 million over the next five years.[80]

Although the state has liberalized its foreign investment policy, it has done so in order to attract investment while remaining firmly in control of those projects. While these reforms affected the perception among foreign investors that Zimbabwe is becoming more open, the state has reserved for itself controls over this investment.[81] The primary objective of these reforms is to plow the profits from these investments back into the economy rather than to remit them abroad. Investors are allowed to swap foreign currency with local currency, but they only are allowed to repatriate capital after ten years from the date of the swap. The government seeks to attract foreign investment and be in a position to direct it towards development projects determined by the state. The new investment guidelines specifically exclude foreign investment from large-scale commercial farming and services while providing incentives for investments in peasant agriculture, manufacturing, and mining sectors.[82] Moreover, the large pool of blocked funds continues to exist from which the government can draw needed funds.

Local reaction to these reforms has been mixed. According to the Confederation of Zimbabwe Industries in July 1988, industry's main concern was that the liberalization process should be 'gradual and controlled by Zimbabwe, to ensure that the country's industrial base is not irreparably damaged or destroyed.'[83] Even the Governor of the Reserve Bank offered his own qualification of the reforms when he said that 'free competition on the Zimbabwean market will be done when and where constraints facing domestic industry have been reduced or eliminated.'[84] Despite the on-going liberalization process, then, the state continues to play a significant role in influencing the pattern of foreign investment. The nature of state controls has shifted from purely *negative* (ie, preventing firms from undertaking certain action) to somewhat *positive* (ie, providing incentives for firms to invest in state-determined economic and development sectors).

Foreign Exchange Allocation
A recognized cost of restricting direct foreign investment is limited access and availability of foreign exchange. Economic orthodoxy argues that foreign exchange limits inherently follow foreign capital restrictions. Furthermore, as foreign currency becomes a scarce commodity, importers have less capital for their inputs which, in turn, places constraints on the export sector leading to restrictions on economic growth. Yet, government policies suggest that foreign exchange allocation controls are a crucial instrument of state control over national investment objectives. Foreign exchange controls are used in order to enhance state power by weakening private economic power and to loosen the state's reliance on private sources of foreign investment capital. The controls, moreover, free up scarce hard currency for use in priority projects determined by the state. Still, the question concerning the actual process to allocate foreign exchange remains a critical source of social and economic conflict within Zimbabwe.

One battle is between the private sector and public sector over the allocation of scarce foreign exchange. According to one study, the private sector received a thirty-six percent increase in foreign exchange allocations in 1979 over the previous year, which jumped by another forty-seven percent in 1980 followed by only a twenty percent rise in the following year.[85] According to an IMF economist, the restrictive policy toward the private sector continued, since between 1982 and 1985, that sector's foreign exchange allocation dropped by 30 percent. Implicit in the government's controls toward the private sector is a government effort to regulate South African firms embedded in it.

The government has established a number of new parastatals in an attempt to assert control over key economic sectors. Among the most important are the Industrial Development Corporation, the Zimbabwe Development Bank, and the Minerals Marketing Corporation. Each one seeks to develop the economic sectors, but also to control the productive forces through the purchasing of equity in foreign and private companies.[86] Most of these parastatals have greater access to foreign currency than many private firms. According to a managing director of a foreign bank in Zimbabwe, the government has pressured his bank to lend to industrial and agricultural parastatals. In interviews, pro-private sector economists from the Confederation of Zimbabwe Industries and the World Bank both were critical of this policy. Each argued that as the government clamps down on foreign currency allocation and redirects it to the public sector, the consequences will be two-fold: the private sector's share of foreign currency will be squeezed and foreign investment will decrease. Another conflict has arisen between sectoral interests. Given the government's ideological predisposition toward the peasant class and the export strength of the white agricultural class, foreign exchange allocations have benefited the agricultural sector to the detriment of industrial and manufacturing interests. Foreign exchange allocation was slashed during the first six months of 1987 to industrial and commercial sectors by forty percent and fifty-five percent, respectively.[87]

Trade Liberalization
As with previous government adjustment policies, Zimbabwe's trade policy has been shaped by the intra-government ideological conflict. On the one hand, the government, according to several respondents, has expressed export pessimism by not actively encouraging foreign investment, by cutting foreign exchange allocations to export sectors, and by compressing essential imports.[88] The radical contingent in government strongly supports this approach due to its suspicion that a liberal trade system with reduced import controls would increase the country's vulnerability, especially to South Africa. As a landlocked country with critical transportation routes through Mozambique and South Africa, Zimbabwe's export potential is limited. In 1990, South Africa was the largest trading partner with Zimbabwe, importing nine percent of Zimbabwe's exports in exchange for 20 percent of its goods.[89] Not only is the radical group apprehensive of the country's increased vulnerability to South Africa as a consequence of trade liberalization, but it is equally concerned with the potentially growing foreign investments in the manufacturing sector and possible increased unemployment and eventual loss in the country's industrial stock to foreign interests.[90] Domestic manufacturing interests have aligned themselves with this perspective. Generally, they are against liberalization and devaluation as corrective measures since they fear increased foreign competition and higher import costs of capital requirements. Between 1983 and 1986, this group prevailed, in part, as import controls resulted in a decline in imports by 35 percent since 1981.

But, import compression during those years also led to export compression with an 18 percent decline in exports. From the standpoint of the export-oriented, 'pragmatic' group, only an active export policy built on appropriate incentives could ensure economic growth. As with the shift in government policy toward foreign investment, a similar change recently occurred in the government policy toward trade liberalization.

Table 3.4 Zimbabwe's Trade Balance, 1985–1992
(US$ million)

	1985	1986	1987	1988	1989	1990[a]	1991[a]	1992[b]
Merchandise exports	1124	1325	1455	1669	1680	1732	1880	2110
Merchandise imports	−922	−1013	−1973	−1157	−1319	−1511	−1820	−1940
Trade Balance	202	312	382	512	361	220	60	170

[a] Estimate   [b] Forecast

Source Institute of International Finance, *Zimbabwe* (Washington, D.C.: IIF, 1991).

Both changes result from the introduction of Zimbabwe's Structural Adjustment Program in introduced in 1990. A government commission recently recommended the phased removal of import controls and the replacement with a system of tariff protection.[91] In October 1990, the government began to switch critical inputs for industry onto the Open General Import Licensing (OGIL) system, sweeping away administrative allocations of foreign exchange for imports. The initial objective was to place 50 percent of the country's imports onto the OGIL by the end of 1991. Moreover, the 20 percent across-the-board import surcharge will be lowered until it is abolished entirely by 1995. The phasing of imports onto the OGIL has exerted pressure on the balance of payments position. The forecasted result for 1991 is a 40 percent rise in imports since 1989, while exports for that period only grew by 12 percent.[92] Given this pressure on the trade balance, the government slowed the shift of imports onto the OGIL so that only 24 percent of imports had shifted as compared with the initial target of 50 percent.[93]

In light of a deteriorating trade balance, in December 1991, the government expanded the export retention scheme first introduced in September 1990 as part of the trade liberalization strategy. The scheme allows companies to retain a portion of their export earnings to finance imports. The revised plan now expands from original levels of between five percent and 7.5 percent to 15 percent immediately, to 25 percent for the first half of 1992, to 30 percent for the second half of 1992, and to 35 percent for 1993.[94]

The government, in maintaining a flexible management of the exchange rate for much of the 1980s, used devaluation as a supplemental policy. The advent of the current SAP has brought about a more vigorous use of devaluation. In 1991, the value of the Zimbabwe dollar devalued by nearly 50 percent.[95] Agricultural and mining interests support such a policy

Table 3.5 *Trend of Gross Domestic Product of Zimbabwe, 1985–1992*

	1985	1986	1987	1988	1989	1990[a]	1991[a]	1992[b]
Real GDP (% change)	6.7	2.7	–1.4	7.0	5.5	2.1	3.5	2.8

[a]Estimate [b]Forecast

Source Institute of International Finance, *Zimbabwe* (Washington, D.C.: IIF, 1991).

since they generate eighty-five percent of Zimbabwe's foreign exchange and would benefit further from more competitive export costs.[96] The government also introduced a supplementary bonus scheme in 1990 to provide exporters with foreign exchange to finance necessary inputs. Moreover, throughout the late 1980s, Zimbabwe obtained foreign loans from the Export Revolving Fund financed by the World Bank and from international commercial banks to provide revolving funds and export incentives for the mining and agricultural sectors.

After years of a so-called 'home-grown' liberalization strategy, the Zimbabwe government has rejected many tenets and assumptions of the radical coalition in society and has accepted more orthodox adjustment measures. While some analysts argue that economic orthodoxy was imposed on Zimbabwe by the IMF and the World Bank at a time when liberalization was not necessary, economic reforms had indeed been implemented prior to the active involvement by the IMF or the World Bank.[97] A Zimbabwe-designed adjustment program was considered advantageous to policy-makers since it seemed to provide an equitable internal redistribution of goods and services and it went a long way toward satisfying international creditors' demands for a strengthened market economy.

THE CASE OF BRAZIL

Brazil, as with the two previous country examples, also must grapple with the problematic process of indebted development. As with Kenya and Zimbabwe, the Brazilian state has been integrally involved in on-going negotiations with both members of society and of the international creditor regime during the recent period of economic adjustment and external indebtedness. However, much can be said of the differences between a major Latin American debtor and relatively minor African countries. While the scope of indebtedness, the size of the domestic economy, and, in Brazil's specific case, the political transition back to a democratic system, can distinguish Brazil from many other countries, these variables are considered in this study as intervening, albeit, important variables in the negotiating process. A critical factor that Brazil shares with the African cases is that the specific adjustment objectives pursued by the state are derived from its strategic interaction with societal members and the international financial community. Moreover, both Brazil and the African countries moved towards acceptance of SAPs and economic liberalization strategies about the same time; ie, the mid- to late-1980s. This section of the chapter first briefly reviews Brazil's earlier strategic economic decisions. I then turn to a discussion and analysis of the state's national development plans and to their nearly annual 'correction' in the form of economic adjustment programs of the late-1980s and early 1990s that are broadly comparable to the economic reorientation undertaken by Kenya and Zimbabwe.

The so-called 'miracle' growth era of the 1960s and early 1970s had its roots in the strategic decisions made earlier in the 1960s. At that time, compatible with prevailing wisdom, the Brazilian state sought to develop a massive import-substituting industrialization (ISI) strategy based on the accumulation and mobilization of internal savings and significant sources of external capital. The Kubitschek administration actively sought foreign capital in the form of direct foreign investment and private loans. Kubitschek, by breaking off negotiations with the IMF, forced Brazil to seek short-term, high-cost loans from private sources abroad. Brazil considered itself able to finance the balance of payments deficits out of its own reserves and to borrow from non-official sources, avoiding the immediate consequences of adjustment. However, his successor, Quadros, inherited a full-scale debt crisis which left the country with debt service payments of 45 percent of the GDP in 1961 and a 100 percent devaluation of the currency two years later. Even though the government arranged new rescheduling talks with the IMF, the two chronic economic problems plaguing Brazil – inflation and balance of payments deficits – persisted. These two problems added to Brazil's external debt and, simultaneously, shaped the context for a further infusion of foreign capital.

The 1964 coup brought about a reorganization of the state's economic plan, but the outcome only differed in degree. The coup leaders instituted a monetarist program to reduce inflation, reimburse part of Brazil's external debt, restore the level of international reserves, and overcome the balance of payments deficit. At the center of this orientation rested two building blocks of the 'miracle' growth: export-promotion and expanded credit service. Complementing the previous stage of ISI, these economic components reinforced the links to the international financial system. The sources of the required capital lay outside the internal cycle of production and consumption. Fernando Cardoso, making a generalization from the Brazilian context, states that 'the accumulation, expansion, and self-realization of local capital requires and depends on a dynamic complement outside itself: it must insert itself into the circuit of international capitalism.'[98] Michael Wallerstein directly comments upon the boom period and its implications for the political process. He argues that 'the most important change in the economy as import-substitution advances, in regard to political rule, is not the development of heavy industry, or competitive manufactured exports, or the predominance of consumer durables, but the internationalization of the local economy.'[99]

Brazil's Economic Adjustment Strategies

During the late 1960s and early 1970s, Brazil's long-term development objectives were expansionary and *growth-oriented* based primarily on the mobilization of international capital to finance exports and imports for both private and public sectors. The development model focused on the accumulation of foreign capital to finance the production of capital goods by state firms. It was thought that state investments for the exports of manufactured goods would reap benefits for the state in terms of high employment, foreign exchange earnings, and improved trade balances. External financing, the development plan claimed, would free Brazil of outside constraints and the state was prepared to incur the additional cost of borrowing from the private market. Sidney Dell and Roger Lawrence assert that 'those countries able to borrow in private capital markets' (including Brazil) 'acquired a certain freedom of action, since, for the time being at least, the conditions for such borrowing did not impinge upon government policies or performance.'[100] This argument, targeted for newly industrializing countries, similarly was used by Zimbabwe in the early 1980s to justify its heavy reliance on financing from international commercial sources.[101] Indebtedness is a form of investment not made by the state, but, in theory, controlled by state policies. According to Jeffry Frieden, the military rulers during the early 1970s successfully adapted Brazil's development plans to attract foreign bank capital. By the early 1970s, half of industrial investment had been financed by bank loans.[102] Indeed, Eliana Cardoso and Albert Fishlow correctly suggests that, at this time, 'foreign financing increasingly became an instrument of choice.'[103]

Brazil's apparent early success in attracting foreign capital was tested severely by the international recession and oil price shocks of the late-1970s. One indicator of the economic downturn was the inflation rate.

During the 'miracle' period, the annual rate averaged 19.5 percent. But, inflation jumped to an annual rate of 50.5 percent between 1974 and 1980, the era of the Second National Development Plan. At the same time, the rate of growth fell by half and the gross fixed investment rate declined from 15.4 percent in the early 1970s to just 3.4 percent during the late 1970s.[104] Brazil's current account deficit, which had fallen during the last half of the 1970s, increased by 45 percent in 1979.

The *Second National Development Plan* (1975–1980) sought to make short-term adjustments in the financing of the balance of payments. The government combined import repression and export expansion with an internal market recession to correct the trade balance. In following a Keynesian 'stop and go' policy, the government walked a fine line between, on the one hand, the control of inflation and the rise of internal consumption and, on the other hand, the promotion of exports relying on a mounting foreign debt. However, in the final analysis, according to one observer, 'the main objective of the recessionary policy was not to reduce inflation, but rather to balance the trade account and appease the international financial system.'[105] A senior economist in a British bank confirmed the pressure on Brazil to follow an outward, expansionary development strategy. He said that 'if Brazil began to emphasize the domestic market and to downplay the export sector, the banks would not tolerate it. They would fear a rise in inflation leading to a reduction of domestic savings, a drop in exports, and the end to a trade surplus.'

The *Third National Development Plan* (1980–1985) unfortunately began as the second oil price shock occurred, bringing on the international recession of the early 1980s and the 1982 Mexican debt moratorium. The plan's initial optimistic forecasts immediately were set back by the twin escalation of inflation and external indebtedness. The first objective, then, was the reduction of the inflation rate. The government sought to implement a new import substitution policy as a means of reducing imports and controlling the inflation rate by expanding the national production of substitutes for imported oil.[106] Foreign indebtedness was to be countered by a continued expansion of manufactured and agricultural exports. Agricultural production became a primary priority both to improve exports, but also to ease the significant unemployment problem. Yet, both objectives were unable to achieve their objectives in light of a drastic fall in the terms of trade and a significant rise in debt service payments.[107]

During the first three years of the plan, the absence of foreign exchange forced the government to clamp down on the rate of domestic consumption growth in order to channel a greater share of the GDP to the foreign sector. According to one source, domestic savings as a proportion of GDP fell from 23.2 percent in 1978 to 18.8 percent in 1982.[108] The stifling of the growth of imports by state-owned enterprises became a critical policy for the reduction of the balance of payments deficit. The number of state firms, for instance, fell from 521 in 1982 to 374 in 1984 although many firms merely were consolidated without diminishing their scope.[109] The 1980 budget for the agency overseeing state enterprises was cut by 15 percent and the agency's authority controlling their debt level was enhanced. Budgetory support of these firms was restricted to projects already under way and to projects that would reduce foreign energy dependence, such as energy, exports, and import substituting projects.[110]

The attention given to an export-oriented economy intensified following the deteriorating economic developments of 1982. The struggle against rising inflation saw a temporary respite as the rate rose by only one percentage point from 1981. But by 1983, the inflation rate reached 165 percent and despite this high figure, the government continued to borrow short-term and to boost exports at the expense of an unmanageable inflation rate. The annual growth rate of inflation averaged 157 percent during the years of the third plan. The growth of the current accounts deficit in 1982 also pressed Brazil to devalue the cruzeiro by 30 percent in February 1983, the second 30 percent devaluation in four years. The maxi-devaluation made a significant impact on the trade balance and the current accounts deficit. Yet, it did nothing to slow domestic recession and inflation. Indeed, a 30 percent wage cut followed in June 1983.

The objectives for the second half of the development plan necessitated a further reduction in public expenditures. An increasing amount of resources had to be shifted to the payment of interest on foreign loans and to the financing of trade contracts with foreign suppliers. The public sector again became the focal point of international pressure to decrease its budget. The policies reflected the export bias of the government in that two major exporting state firms, Petrobras and Companhia Vale do Rio Doce, did not suffer budget cuts. Indeed, as the expenditure reduction of most state firms amounted to 10 percent and their investment budget was cut by 24 percent, the state pumped more capital into the large, export-generating and foreign exchange-earning projects managed by those enterprises.[111] The success of the government's adjustment policies also was demonstrated by the tremendous growth of merchandise exports. On the one hand, merchandise exports grew at 9.4 percent a years from 1965 to 1980. On the other hand, the 1980–84 level of real imports was lower than that of the 1970–74 period.[112]

The *Fourth National Development Plan* (1986–1990) began as the country embarked on a political transition to democratic rule. The effect of the political liberalization process on development objectives was quite immediate. The unleashing of previously repressed social groups – legitimized by a democratic political system – pressured the government to recognize the inequities in the distribution of the national income and to emphasize social welfare projects. Yet, the plan also optimistically forecast annual growth rates of six to seven percent.[113] Moreover, the plan failed to reflect the harsh economic realities of Brazil by the late-1980s: in just one year (1985 to 1986), the trade balance fell by more than one-third; the current account deficit ballooned from −$274 million to −$5.3 billion; foreign reserves dropped by 45 percent; the annual inflation rate continued at over 250 percent; and Brazil's total foreign debt as a percentage of exports rose from 362 percent to 450 percent, while debt service payments in terms of exports also increased from 46.2 percent to 56.5 percent.[114] The plan, its objectives, economic targets, and policies soon were discarded and replaced in the coming years by a number of radical economic adjustments to which I now turn.

Economic Adjustment Strategies
The *heterodox economic plans* of the mid-1980s and early 1990s reflected the government's abrupt awareness that in order to resuscitate the economy, it had to address the concerns of both major domestic constituents and international creditors. Moreover, the state realized that policies and actions taken either by societal members or by creditors influenced its negotiating stance.[115] Possible resolutions to Brazil's internal and external economic crises were much more complex as the objectives and policies of domestic and international actors became strategically interdependent. Brazil's formulation and implementation of these heterodox plans were determined in large part by the domestic politics of the transition from authoritarian rule and the domestic economic situation. In this very fluid political environment, no economic adjustment program could easily obtain solid political support.

President *Jose Sarney* had been elected vice-president indirectly by an electoral college on a coalition ticket in which he represented a defecting wing of the official (military) party. He gained the presidency when the popular Tancredo Neves died suddenly on the eve of his inauguration in March 1985. The uneasy alliance between Neves' party – the opposition PMDB (Brazilian Democratic Movement Party) and Sarney's new party – the PFL (Liberal Front Party) – produced an atmosphere of uncertainty and hesitant national support for the new president.

Political motivations in the context of the transition influenced economic policy-making as the actors followed strategies to further their own interests. Within the legislature, the PMDB dominated the governing alliance and acted to protect its interests in fighting for a goodly share of the patronage benefits of executive office – which it had been denied for twenty years – as well as to assure its victory in the November 1985 municipal elections and the November 1986 constituent assembly elections which would choose the constitution-writing body.[116] President Sarney, past president of the official party, was viewed suspiciously by many in the PMDB and the center-left in Brazil. Constrained by the pacts negotiated by Neves and dependent on PMDB support in the legislature, Sarney would seek to improve his political capital with the dominant party in his first two years in office.

The private sector, particularly industrialists, had become vocal in its opposition to military rule as participation in economic policy-making decreased and recessionary stabilization policies were emphasized. In the 1984 campaign, the president of the national Chamber of Commerce broke the traditional political silence of the Brazilian private sector and announced his support for Neves.[117] In contrast to other Latin American countries, Brazilian business had not resorted to substantial capital flight, financial speculation and banking activities and, therefore, did not automatically support orthodox economic policies. The powerful Sao Paulo business elite, in particular, represented by FIESP – the Sao Paul Federation of Industries – with its fixed investments in industrial plants and equipment favored easy credit policies and resisted negotiations with the IMF.[118]

Unions, newly revitalized after the end of military rule, were divided into two competing organizations: the CUT (Central Workers Union) had its stronghold in Sao Paulo and was more confrontational toward the government and the CGT (General Workers' Central) had its origins in the official labor movement and was more moderate in its demands. For example, the CUT opposed the Democratic Alliance (PMDB-PFL) negotiated transition with indirect elections, while the CGT supported the gradual transition and has generally been more supportive of the new government's policies.[119] In the context of democratic politics, the unions, along with other popular groups who had been disadvantaged under the previous regime and the parties representing them, put great pressure on the new government to pursue distributive and expansionist policies.

Sarney initially acted with great caution, and seemed reluctant to tackle the job of President. During his first months in office, indecision and internal divisions racked Sarney's government and the Congress authorized direct elections for president, threatening Sarney's tenure.[120] He inherited from Neves a deeply divided cabinet (the result of the Democratic Alliance negotiations) and a socio-economic agenda with

The State and Economic Adjustment Strategies 99

job-creation and growth as the main priorities, and debt negotiations as a lower priority.

Economically, Brazil was enjoying recovery with a GDP growth rate of 8.3 percent in 1985 due to renewed exports and a jump in real wages, and a relatively large trade surplus which allowed Brazil to stay current on its interest payments without new money. But, the outgoing military government had failed to meet the performance criteria of the existing IMF agreement in late 1984 and early 1985, and the negotiations to reschedule $45.3 billion in external debt due in 1985–89 lapsed before the transition.[121] In addition, inflation reached ten percent per month in mid-1985, spurring fears of hyperinflation.

Domestic politics continued to dominate Brazil's economic and debt policy in late 1985 and early 1986 as Sarney and Funaro struggled to stabilize the economy and strengthen the President's political position before the November 1986 legislative elections. Public opinion polls in September 1985 showed a 20 percent drop in presidential popularity since April.[122] Further, the government had hoped to negotiate a social pact with business and labor to gain support for its macroeconomic policy, but had made little progress. Thus, the administration began secretly preparing a bold, new economic plan in the fall of 1985 – a plan that could bring stabilization without recession.

By early 1986, the country faced runaway inflation of 500 percent annually. Roughly following the Argentine model of a heterodox shock treatment of the economy, President Sarney and Finance Minister Dilson Funaro unveiled the *Cruzado Plan* in February 1986 to address the inertial component of inflation without pushing the economy into recession.[123] The Plan imposed a price freeze on both private and public sector prices, and imposed a wage freeze after implementing a 33 percent minimum wage rise and an across-the-board wage increase of eight percent. Further, a wage trigger was set so that when accumulated inflation reached 20 percent, wages automatically would be 'triggered' to rise. Finally, the Cruzado Plan introduced a new currency, lowered interest rates, and continued monetary expansion. Baer and Beckerman note that because of the wage increases immediately preceding the freeze, the Cruzado Plan actually acted as an income plan in favor of labor. This income policy initially was feasible since 'even those sectors caught behind at the time of the freeze were willing to remain briefly at a relative disadvantage for the sake of stabilization.'[124] In fact, real wages increased between 15 to 20 percent in 1986, and real demand increased 23 percent.[125]

Extremely popular with consumers, the plan initially was successful in controlling inflation, cutting a monthly rate of nearly 20 percent to zero.

International media and financial circles initially praised the achievements of the plan, including a booming growth rate. Morgan Guaranty Trust Co. concluded rather prematurely in August 1986 that 'the (Cruzado) Plan has worked wonders for the inflation so far . . . These economic achievements, plus the successful transition from military rule to a democracy with stable policy prospects, provide Brazil (with an) opportunity . . . to be the first Latin American country to recover normal access to the international capital markets.'[126] However, inflationary pressures soon began to emerge. The wild spending spree fueled by the price freeze eventually led to domestic shortages as production approached 100 percent capacity and producers slowed investment in the expectation of an eventual currency devaluation.[127] At the same time, the trade surplus shrunk because producers had diverted goods from the export sector to the more attractive internal sector. But as the price freeze wore on, agricultural producers and ranchers actually withheld products from the market in protest, and the government chose to draw down reserves by importing food rather than relax the price freeze.[128]

By the time of the November 1986 legislative elections, an adjustment was overdue, but the government was reluctant to relax a widely popular price freeze in the middle of a political campaign. The politicization of the Plan is clear in Singer's account that, though the price freeze had been intended by the planners to be temporary (only 3 months) and a tactic to win time to bring prices to their 'equilibrium' level, the freeze soon became the most important element to the political leadership, ensuring popular support for the Plan and themselves.[129] Furthermore, neither Sarney nor PMDB leaders were eager to face the hard decisions to reduce the public sector deficit in the wake of the upcoming elections.

Immediately after the elections, the *Cruzado II Plan* was announced with public sector price hikes, a selective increase in private sector prices, closing of 15 state companies, an interest rate hike, and a return to mini-devaluations of the currency although unions successfully resisted the elimination of the wage trigger. The blatant political timing of the new austerity measures, waiting until after the November 1986 elections to raise prices, caused widespread opposition, including a shocking riot in Brasilia and an unprecedented general strike in December coordinated by the rival CUT and CGT labor confederations. Workers called the economic package 'the worst assault on wages in recent years,' and particularly complained about a new cost of living index which they said was designed to disguise true inflation.[130] The government's renewed calls for a social pact were met with stiff demands from labor, with the CGT demanding in preliminary talks a suspension of debt payments, an end to all contacts

Table 3.6 *Brazil's Inflation Rate, 1985–1992 (% change average)*

1985	1986	1987	1988	1989	1990^a	1991^a	1992^b
227.0	145.2	229.7	638.0	1475.3	2863.9	432.9	446.5

^{a} Estimate ^{b} Forecast
Source   Institute of International Finance, *Brazil* (Washington, D.C.: IIF, 1991).

with the IMF, a wage increase, a quadrupling of the minimum wage, and automatic readjustment of wages whenever accumulated inflation reached five percent.[131]

Producers also came into conflict with the government over the timing and extent of relaxing the price freezes. By December, industrialists who had benefitted from the initial increase in demand claimed that the price freeze now was reducing their profit margins, and they began a campaign of 'civil disobedience,' raising prices without authorization. In January, the dispute became public as producers threatened to raise prices unilaterally if the remaining freeze was not lifted, and Finance Minister Funaro threatened in return to suspend loans to those initiating unauthorized price increases. President Sarney even called the protesting businessmen 'anarchists.' The issue was resolved when the government freed many prices in February, after meeting with a group of business leaders headed by the president of the National Confederation of Industry.[132]

To make matters worse, Sarney reportedly consulted only with the president of the Brazilian Democratic Movement Party (PMDB) before announcing the Cruzado II Plan, unleashing a storm of protest within the party until a full meeting was called to get approval for the plan.[133] This was reminiscent not only of Sarney's announcement of the Cruzado Plan when Congress was out of session, without any prior consultation, but also of the military regime's practice of announcing unpopular decree laws when Congress was in recess. Then, in January, a group of powerful PMDB governors called for the maintenance of the 20 percent wage adjustment trigger and for a tougher stance against commercial creditors in the debt negotiations. In addition, the issue of Sarney's tenure in office began to heat up as members of the PMDB joined with the leftist opposition in calling for direct elections in 1988, as opposed to Sarney's desire to stay in office two more years.[134] The term of office was one of the major issues facing the new legislative/constituent assembly as it began the task of writing a new constitution. As noted below, the politics of the constituent assembly continued to affect executive decision-making as the major parties, as well as the military, jockeyed for power within it.

The economic situation continued to deteriorate in late 1986 and early 1987. Double-digit inflation returned with a monthly rate of 16.8 percent in January, interest rates reached 1,100 percent on short-term lending, international reserves fell from $11 billion to $3.8 billion over the life of the Cruzado Plan, and the trade surplus declined to less than $200 million, less than 25 percent of the amount needed to make the interest payments on the foreign debt.[135] Domestic economic pressure had risen to the extent that a moratorium on interest payments became politically feasible.

The moratorium did nothing, however, to address the renewed inflation unleashed by the Cruzado II Plan and the relaxation of the price freeze in February. Uncertainty and confusion over a follow-up economic policy generated apparently conflicting positions among different actors. Disagreement within the economic cabinet over the government's pricing policy led to the resignations of several economic team members including the head of the Central Bank who had been accused of being too soft in preliminary debt negotiations with private creditors. This strengthened Funaro's position in the short-term even amid speculation that he would eventually be made the scapegoat for the rising inflation. The PMDB seemed torn fearing his replacement by a more conservative economist, but unsatisfied with the lack of a clear economic policy. In early April, three powerful PMDB governors called on Sarney to discuss Funaro's position.[136]

Business leaders increasingly were concerned with skyrocketing interest rates and curbs on domestic consumption. Fearing recessionary consequences, they also began to press for Funaro's removal, even though the alternatives of negotiating an IMF agreement to move the external debt negotiations along also would likely bring recessionary austerity policies. The military became increasingly restive over the 'crisis of authority' and took a more visible role in maintaining order as strikes increased, sending troops to occupy state-owned oil refineries and ports.[137]

The lack of coherence in his economic team probably reflected Sarney's own indecision in the face of conflicting pressures from the majority party, the left, industrialists, unions, and the military, and his personal political ambition. The constituent assembly was preparing to discuss the length of the presidential term and the possibility of re-election – issues which had grown dear to Sarney as he moved from an initially reluctant president to one who strove to guarantee the longest tenure possible to him. At this same time in Kenya and Zimbabwe, Presidents Moi and Mugabe were faced with similar domestic pressures resulting in wavering economic adjustment strategies. For both of these leaders, domestic political unrest increased over their unwillingness to have their countries move quickly towards a multi-party system and to implement economic reforms intended to stem economic decline.

The constituent assembly debate – over the form of government (parliamentary or presidential); the length of term of office; the re-election issue; and the distribution of power between the executive and legislative branches if a presidential system were retained – reflected a larger struggle for institutional political control in Brazil's transition to democracy. According to one view, the original pact negotiated by Tancredo Neves and the PMDB-PFL Democratic Alliance in 1984 envisioned that the constituent assembly task of drafting a new constitution would be the final phase of transition, followed by direct presidential elections three to four years after the 1984 indirect election of Neves-Sarney. However, Sarney and his inner circle, backed by the military which represented continuity in the transition, argued for a five to six year term for Sarney, a strong presidential system, and the military's role in keeping law and order. He, in fact, used the economic crisis to rally support for his position, blaming the economic situation on the 'crisis of political uncertainty' and arguing in a televised speech in May 1987, 'give me a five to six year mandate and full presidential powers, and we can surmount the economic crisis.'[138] Sarney's concern about the length of his mandate may have been directly linked to his decision to declare the debt moratorium. According to one report, 'in hindsight, Funaro's two aides concluded that Sarney's political need to restore PMDB support for his five-year mandate outweighed any economic repercussions from overseas creditors in the moratorium decision.'[139]

In the midst of this political pressure and economic crisis, Sarney named economist Luis Carlos Bresser Pereira, a PMDB activist, as the new finance minister in April 1987. Bresser Pereira brought a more conciliatory attitude to debt negotiations, recognizing that adjustment would be necessary to reach a debt accord.[140] At that time, Bresser Pereira reports, he assumed it would be possible to achieve a six percent growth rate for Brazil and negotiate the debt 'in conventional terms, according to the finance and adjustment approach' put forward by the IMF.[141] Thus, in June Sarney approved a new austerity plan to address the 27 percent monthly inflation rate, reduce public expenditures, and stimulate exports. The so-called *Bresser Plan*, welcomed by the creditors, eliminated the wage adjustment trigger, instituted a new 90-day price freeze, and devalued the cruzado. At the same time, the government announced plans to begin talks with the IMF in July, though reiterating that a formal link between an IMF accord and debt restructuring was still out of the question. Talks with the international banks advisory committee were put on hold awaiting a new proposal from Bresser. The government's 'Macroeconomic Control Plan,' issued in July

1987, claimed that

> the central concern of a strategy such as the one defined in this program is to demonstrate that it is possible to simultaneously attain the goals of economic growth, external adjustment, and price stability. That is, to demonstrate that it is possible to grow at the anticipated rates without coming against the balance of payments restriction, without creating inflationary tensions, and, furthermore, permitting the expansion of domestic consumption at reasonable rates.[142]

During the next two months, (July–August of 1987), Bresser tried to convince the PMDB and Sao Paulo industrialists of the need for an IMF agreement, with little success. Political and business leaders feared a recession resulting from an IMF-approved program, and argued that Bresser should first try for a debt accord not linked to an IMF-approved program.[143] Meanwhile, the anti-inflationary package came unravelled as Sarney refused to cut expenditures in the context of constituent assembly deliberations and tax increases, wage-earners complained about loss of purchasing power, and producers resisted price controls.[144] The inflation rate was over 14 percent for the month of December, with the year-end accumulated rate of 366 percent.

Frustrated by the lack of progress on all sides, Sarney apparently decided in favor of a more orthodox approach to Brazil's economic and debt problems. He replaced Bresser with a man of his own choosing, rather than one imposed on him by the PMDB, and instructed him to 'end the public sector deficit, counter inflation and generate new investments and jobs.'[145] The new Finance Minister, Mailson Ferrera da Nobrega, was a career technocrat with no binding party loyalty, but supported by conservative factions of the PMDB and leading Sao Paulo businessmen. Nobrega faced continuing inflation of 20 percent monthly, rumors of a coup threat in response to inflation and recession, and a new wave of strikes, including the national railway. The December 1988 inflation rate reached a new monthly record of 28.8 percent, pushing the accumulated total for 1988 to 933 percent, compared with 366 percent the previous year.[146] In addition, popular support for immediate direct elections continued to build, with polls showing 60 percent of Rio businessmen and 80 percent of the general public favoring only a four-year term for Sarney.[147]

Given the accelerating inflation rate and the presidential elections in November, Sarney and Nobrega introduced another economic package, the fourth in as many years. Called the *Summer Plan*, its objectives consisted of a general price freeze of short-term duration, the introduction of a new currency, the centralization of all foreign exchange operations in the central bank, the suspension for one year of debt-equity conversions, the targeted reform of the public sector through the reduction in the budget deficit, and the abandonment of wage indexation. The Summer Plan differed in several important ways from the preceding adjustment packages. First, it sought to correct the assumed errors of the Cruzado Plan by discontinuing the wage scaling rule leading the way to free wage negotiations. Second, in line with the IMF's own objectives of public sector reform, the plan tried to attack the budget deficit by limiting expenditures, reducing public sector employment, and offering a privatization program for selected state firms.

In addition to the attack on inflation, the government also used the plan to send a message to international creditors. The government centralized the control of foreign exchange operations in an attempt to unify any possible action to delay or suspend interest payments. This policy move along with the suspension of debt-equity conversion auctions were to convey to creditors that Brazil had to regain control over its foreign reserves. While Nobrega called for an 'understanding' attitude on the part of the creditors, Sarney more directly asserted that a suspension of payments could be considered if the country's reserves fell below an unspecified 'point of equilibrium.'[148]

Two months after the plan's implementation, the results were not much different from the previous shock treatments. The rate of inflation, which had dramatically dropped in January, began to rise to over six percent in March. Many interest groups who earlier expressed reserved support for the program drifted away from the government. Both trade union and business leaders objected to the wage and price freezes.[149] As external support (which had been expected) failed to materialize, the exchange rate freeze brought about a speculative rise in the dollar black market rate and provided an incentive for capital flight. High interest rates (set by the government in hopes that they would dampen inflationary expectations) led to rise of the government's internal debt by 25 percent. Because of this substantial growth, the government failed to meet its target, agreed with the IMF, of eliminating the public sector deficit by the end of 1989.[150]

By April 1989, the government had revoked so many key planks of the Summer Plan that the adjustment efforts were declared to have failed. The government lifted the exchange rate freeze, devalued the currency, and introduced wage and price increases. Moreover, the fight against inflationary expectations had squeezed the economy of any real economic growth. With a weakened domestic economy and uncertainty over the November 1989 presidential elections, international creditors hesitated to make any new commitments to Brazil, forcing the government to delay interest payments.

As the 1980s drew to a close, national accounts data for Brazil show that not only had the economic growth rate slowed down and then plummeted by 1988, but that a succession of adjustment shock programs had failed to reverse the inflationary expectations of both domestic and foreign actors. Capital flight was on the rise, foreign direct investment was stalled, and public resources were switched to meet mounting debt service obligations.[151] The new president, *Fernando Collor de Mello*, shared a dilemma with Sarney: domestic constituents calling for economic relief to move the country out of a recession while international creditors were pressing for timely interest payments and the end of interest arrears. As with Sarney, Collor has attempted to manipulate the weakest actors at each level in order to placate powerful domestic interests without alienating Brazil's international creditors. Brazil's bargaining tactics were similar to those of Kenya's. President Moi attempted to forestall growing domestic opposition by dividing and weakening that group while channeling resources to the stronger domestic interests in the commercial agriculture and manufacturing sectors.

Collor unveiled his version of an economic shock program the day after he took office in March 1990.[152] The plan was designed to reduce inflation sharply through a freeze of financial assets and a reduction in the government deficit. Its fiscal measures included an immediate freeze on bank deposits and the creation of new taxes on capital gains, on wealth, and on agricultural incomes. It was thought that through these new taxes and determined cutbacks in government spending, the budget deficit would be reduced zero percent. Critical to the program's success were structural reforms aimed to raise revenue and reduce spending. Several cabinet ministries were to be dismantled along with the dismissals of federal employees. Moreover, the government was to embark on an ambitious privatization program which was intended to make room for private sector investment and growth.

The *Collor Plan* similarly targeted international creditors. The government had hoped that the plan's domestic policies would strengthen its relationship with the international financial community. The finance minister, Zelia Cardoso de Mello said in July 1990, 'because we are obviously putting our house in order, and not without sacrifices, the potential advantages of Brazil as an investment and trade partner come out more naturally.'[153] Yet, international banks failed to be convinced by the government's actions since the Collor administration allowed interest arrears to accumulate. By July 1990, arrears had been built up to $6 billion and, by September, they had increased to nearly $10 billion.

Yet, after a brief decline in the inflation rate, the monthly rate began to increase during the summer months reaching 12 percent by September. Simultaneously, as the government used tight spending policies, recessionary tendencies forced economic growth to plummet where by the end of 1990, Brazil's GDP had fallen by 5 percent. Even as late as July 1990, Collor denied reports that his plan had failed and that a new plan was being considered. 'There will be no 'Plano Collor II',' he said.[154] Yet, since inflation had only accelerated by the end of the year, the Collor administration formulated another attack on Brazil's 'inflationary culture.'[155] Indeed, the inflation rate for January and February 1991 hovered around 20 percent. The government sought to intensify its attack against inflation by a more complete deindexation of the formal economy and to freeze both wages and prices.

International creditor response to the most recent government anti-inflation plan was not supportive. While the government continued to impose financial restraints on the domestic economy, it still refused to allow banks to obtain the accumulated interest arrears. As one banker commented in early 1991, 'we have already seen this before. Until now we had thought Collor was different.'[156] The plan also targeted foreign investors in Brazil. The government particularly was concerned with the turn around in flows of direct investment. While in 1989 *net inflow* to Brazil amounted to $350 million of direct investment, Brazil in the following year experienced a *net outflow* of $115 million.[157] Collor's adjustment strategy not only failed to persuade international creditors to loosen their demands, his plan also dissuaded foreign investors from directing capital into Brazil. Indeed, as inflationary pressures mounted to over 20 percent in October 1991, Brazilians began to rid themselves of cruzeiros in favor of gold and black market dollars which eroded Brazil's foreign reserves. Foreign reserve levels also fell as the government in agreement with international creditors provided $2.5 billion as a partial depletion in debt service arrears. Moreover, the trade balance continued to shrink in 1991 to its lowest point since 1986, adding to the country's foreign reserve crisis. The change in Brazil's real GDP, which had dropped by four percent in 1990, is expected to grow by only one percent in 1991 and experience no growth in 1992.[158]

By early 1992, the Brazilian government's track record in effecting economic adjustment changes was far from positive. After several economic shock programs, the Sarney and Collor administrations had, at best, limited the crippling consequences of hyperinflation, a mounting budget

Table 3.7 Trend of Gross Domestic Product of Brazil, 1985-1992

	1985	1986	1987	1988	1989	1990[a]	1991[a]	1992[b]
Real GDP (% change)	8.3	7.5	3.6	-0.1	3.2	-4.0	1.0	0.0

[a] Estimate [b] Forecast

Source Institute of International Finance, *Brazil* (Washington, D.C.: IIF, 1991).

Table 3.8 Brazil's Trade Balance, 1985-1992 (US$ million)

	1985	1986	1987	1988	1989	1990[a]	1991[a]	1992[b]
Merchandise exports	25634	22348	26210	33773	34381	31414	31800	34250
Merchandise imports	-13168	-14044	-15052	-14605	-18263	-20424	-21300	-22360
Trade balance	12466	8304	11158	19168	16118	10990	10500	11890

[a] Estimate [b] Forecast

Source Institute of International Finance, *Brazil* (Washington, D.C.: IIF, 1991).

deficit, and a still substantial and intractable foreign debt burden. Faced with these domestic economic and political constraints, the government has demonstrated 'political fatigue.' That is, as each adjustment program failed, the degree of credibility shown by the populace declined leading to an apparent crisis of governance. At the start of each program, the government publicly called for a 'social pact' between trade unions, business associations, and the government. More privately, the government also attempted to construct a similar pact with its international creditors. Unlike the two African cases in this study, the legacy of corporatism in Brazil remains a crucial variable in understanding the state's relationship with domestic constituents. The complexity of the social, political, and economic environment in Latin America requires an elaborate and fluid 'playing field' in contrast to Africa's more narrow and more restricted field of play.[159] Yet, while threats of labor unrest and the pessimistic view held by the business community demonstrate the rupture of any perceived domestic social pact, agreements late in the year with the IMF, the World Bank, and international banks suggest a renewed effort on the part of the government to ensure an international accord with creditors. The government appears ready to negotiate with its creditors if it is able to obtain needed financial assistance based on more flexible conditions. Brazil's relationship with these creditors will be reviewed in more detail in the next chapter.

CONCLUSION

Indebted development is the condition under which states must manage their twin economic crises: domestic economic deterioration and foreign indebtedness. The state, as the primary governing apparatus, is the main intermediary between the two affected groups under indebted development; namely, domestic constituents and international creditors. The state thus is at the locus of interaction with the former in formulating an economic adjustment strategy and with the latter in identifying a debt management strategy. With this role of the state in mind, an adjustment strategy becomes a series of policies made by the state as it responds to the cross-cutting pressures and demands from both groups. The adjustment process clearly is a comprehensive political process in that the state simultaneously pursues policies of economic adjustment and of debt management that will benefit some groups and hurt others. The state is not simply an arbitrator, but an active player in the negotiating process. Economic interests, which may have 'captured' the state, tend to promote either economic orthodoxy or heterodoxy that best serves their interests. However, as the three cases have shown in this chapter, the identification of winners and losers becomes obfuscated by wavering implementation of economic strategies. In all three cases, each state had pronounced misgivings in its prevailing strategy and, by the late-1980s, began to undertake a shift towards economic liberalization.

What this conception of adjustment implies is that indebted states have *strategic options*, albeit constrained, in responding to the condition of indebted development. The case studies in this chapter illustrate a range of adjustment options available to each state. All three countries have utilized various incentives (either positive or negative) as a means to promote exports, regulate foreign exchange, or direct resources toward public sector investment. Through a mixture of economic orthodoxy and heterodoxy that most appropriately reflects the interests of the established coalition, the state has used its power in an attempt to shape the adjustment process. The fluid combination of adjustment strategies (resulting in often inconsistent implementation of policies) is, in large measure, due to the specific requirements set by the state in obtaining political support from diverse and often contrasting domestic constituents. Both *Kenya* and *Brazil* have shown considerable success in parting from policy conditions attached to their SAPs. According to some, since Kenya's active policy of slippage has gone unpunished, it has become a special case.[160] However, Brazil also has parted from the IMF over political sensitive issues such as price freezes and specific items spared from budget cutbacks. In both cases, their economic adjustment strategies are driven less by overt IMF conditionalities and more by their acceptance to the general principles and guidelines of IMF ideology. Until very recently, *Zimbabwe* followed a different set of economic principles; guided more by its domestic constituency than its external creditors. In just the last few years, Zimbabwe's economic strategy can be similarly compared to the two other cases.

This chapter has focused in detail on the state's efforts to respond to its domestic economic crisis. Yet, indebted development also refers to the constraints imposed on state action by the management of the external debt crisis. State response to foreign indebtedness thus must consider the available strategies and policies in its relationship with its international creditors. The next chapter will review and analyze the opportunities and constraints under which these three cases sought to manage their debt crisis.

NOTES

1. Charles Lipson, 'Bankers' Dilemmas: Private Cooperation in Rescheduling Sovereign Debts,' *World Politics* 38:1 (October 1985); Guillermo O'Donnell, 'External Debt: Why Don't Our Governments do the Obvious?' *CEPAL Review* 27 (1985); Howard P. Lehman, 'From Confrontation to Cooperation: Strategic Bargaining in Brazil's Debt Negotiations,' *Political Science Quarterly* (Forthcoming, 1993).
2. See Chapter 5 in Paul Mosley, Jane Harrigan, and John Toye, *Aid and Power: The World Bank and Policy-based Lending* (London: Routledge, 1991), Vol. 1 for elaboration on the slippage concept.
3. Otwin Marenin, 'The Managerial State in Africa: A Conflict Coalition Perspective,' in Zaki Ergas, ed., *The African State in Transition* (New York: St. Martin's Press, 1987).
4. Douglas C. Bennett and Kenneth E. Sharpe, *Transnational Corporations Versus the State: The Political Economy of the Mexican Auto Industry* (Princeton: Princeton University Press, 1985), p. 43.
5. Mancur Olson, *The Logic of Collective Action* (Cambridge: Harvard University Press, 1965).
6. Peter Gourevitch, *Politics in Hard Times: Comparative Responses to International Economic Crises* (Ithaca: Cornell University Press, 1986).
7. Wilfred L. David, *The IMF Policy Paradigm* (New York: Praeger, 1985).
8. Jeffry A. Frieden, 'Capital Politics: Creditors and the International Political Economy,' *Journal of Public Policy*, 8:3/4 (July–December 1988), p. 278.
9. David, *The IMF Policy Paradigm*, p. 120.

10. Miles Kahler, 'Orthodoxy and Its Alternatives: Explaining Approaches to Stabilization and Adjustment,' in Joan M. Nelson, ed., *Economic Crisis and Policy Choice: The Politics of Adjustment in the Third World* (Princeton: Princeton University Press, 1990), p. 52.
11. John Loxley, 'Alternative Approaches to Stabilization in Africa,' in G. K. Helleiner, ed., *Africa and the International Monetary* (Washington, D.C.: International Monetary Fund, 1986), p. 35.
12. Frieden, 'Capital Politics,' p. 278.
13. For economic analyses of Kenya's adjustment strategy, see R. Van Der Hoeven and J. Vandemoortele, *Kenya: Stabilization and Adjustment Policies and Programmes* (Helsinski: World Institute for Development Economic Research, 1987); Nur Calika, 'Kenya's Economic Difficulties Are Worsened by Drop in Coffee Prices,' *IMF Survey* 16:10 (May 1987); M. Godfrey, 'Stabilization and Structural Adjustment of the Kenyan Economy, 1975–85: An Assessment of Performance,' *Development and Change* 18:4 (1987); Paul Mosley, 'Kenya,' in Paul Mosley, Jane Harrigan, and John Toye, *Aid and Power: The World Bank and Policy-based Lending* (London: Routledge, 1991), Vol. 2.
14. Interviews were conducted by the author between 1985 and 1988 in New York, Washington, D.C., London, Harare, and Nairobi. Kenyan embassy officials, June 1988; For the IMF's perspective on adjustment, see J. B. Zulu and S. M. Nsouli, 'Adjustment Programs in Africa,' *Occasional Paper* 34 (Washington, D.C.: International Monetary Fund, 1985).
15. Mosley, 'Kenya,' in *Aid and Power*, Vol. 2.
16. Republic of Kenya, *Development Plan, 1984–1988* (Nairobi: Government Printer, 1983), p. 39.
17. Republic of Kenya, *Budget Speech, 1987–8* (Nairobi: Government Printer, 1987), p. 6.
18. Philip Ndegwa, *Report and Recommendations of the Working Party* (Nairobi: Government Printer, 1982.
19. IMF economist, Standard Chartered economist, June 1988; Bankers Trust banker, Barclays Bank economist, July 1988.
20. Republic of Kenya, *Budget Rationalization Programme* (Nairobi: Government Printer, 1986), p. 22.
21. Kenya Association of Manufacturers official; senior officer of Barclays Bank in Kenya, March 1985.
22. Republic of Kenya, *Development Plan, 1984–1988*, p. 43.
23. Chamber of British Industry, *Kenya: The Opportunities for Investment* (London, 1988), pp. 10–13.
24. Republic of Kenya, *Budget Speech, 1987–8*, p. 8.
25. *African Economic Digest*, 'Kenya,' (September 1988), p. 1.
26. Chamber of British Industry, *Kenya*, p. 13.
27. Economist Intelligence Unit, *Kenya: Country Report* #3 (London, 1990), p. 13.
28. Managing Director of an export center and Executive Director of a

regional trade group, 1985.
29. Managing Director of a Kenyan bank; executive officer of the Industrial and Commercial Development Corporation; senior official of Barclays Bank in Kenya; senior official of the Development Finance Corporation of Kenya, 1985.
30. Official with Barclays Bank in Kenya, 1985.
31. *African Business*, 'Kenya Survey,' 132 (August 1989), p. 42.
32. Van der Hoeven and Vandemoortele, *Kenya*, p. 22.
33. *The Courier*, 'Kenya,' #130 (November–December 1991), p. 16.
34. *African Economic Digest*, 'Kenya,' p. 11.
35. Institute of International Finance, *Kenya* (Washington, D.C.: IIF, 1992).
36. Institute of International Finance, *Kenya* (Washington, D.C.: IIF, 1988), p. 5.
37. Economist Intelligence Unit, *Kenya: Country Profile, 1991–92* (London: EIU, 1991), p. 12.
38. According to an IMF advisor to the Central Bank, the 1984–85 drought necessitated increased imports of food stuffs and a substantial rise in the use of trucks as means to distribute maize throughout the afflicted areas thus adding an additional burden on gas and oil imports (February 1985).
39. Institute of International Finance, *Kenya*, 1992.
40. Institute of International Finance, *Kenya*, 1988, p. 6.
41. Data for this paragraph come from a 1992 report on Kenya by the Institute of International Finance.
42. *Africa Research Bulletin*, 'Budget, 1987–88,' 24 (July 31, 1987), p. 8745.
43. Economist Intelligence Unit, *Kenya: Country Report, #2* (London: EIU, 1992), pp. 7–8.
44. Colin Stoneman and Lionel Cliffe, *Zimbabwe: Politics, Economics, and Society* (London: Pinter, 1989); Christine Sylvester, *Zimbabwe: The Terrain of Contradictory Development* (Boulder: Westview Press, 1991).
45. World Bank, *Zimbabwe: A Strategy for Sustained Growth* (Washington, D.C.: World Bank, 1987), p. xiv.
46. A World Bank report noted that government spending as a percentage of GDP had risen from 34 percent in 1979/80 to 43 percent in 1986/7 (ibid., p. xiv). Since then, the figure again has continued to rise to around 49 percent of GDP in 1991 (Institute of International Finance, *Zimbabwe*, (Washington, D.C: IIF, 1991)).
47. Ronald T. Libby, *The Politics of Economic Power in Southern Africa* (Princeton: Princeton University Press, 1987), ch. 2.
48. Republic of Zimbabwe, *Transitional National Development Plan* (Harare: Government Printer, 1982), p. i.
49. T. Mkandawire, 'Home Grown Austerity Measures: The Case of Zimbabwe,' *Africa Development* 10 (January–June 1985), p. 260.

50. Official from the Zimbabwe Mission to the United Nations, 1988.
51. Tony Hawkins, 'Time to Grasp the Nettle of Reform,' *African Economic Digest Special Report* (April 1989), p. 2.
52. Peter Robinson, 'Relaxing the Constraints,' in Colin Stoneman, ed., *Zimbabwe's Prospects* (London: Macmillan, 1988), p. 349.
53. Joseph Hanlon, *Beggar Your Neighbors* (London: James Currey, 1986), p. 305.
54. *Africa Research Bulletin*, 'Five Year Economic Reform Program,' 28 (February 1991), p. 10295.
55. Reginald Herbold Green and X. Kadhani, 'Zimbabwe: Transition to Economic Crises, 1981–1983,' *Report to the Group of 24* (New York: UNDP/UNCTAD, 1985); I. Mandaza, ed., *The Political Economy of Transition, 1980–86* (Dakar: CODESRIA, 1986); O. I. Nyawata, 'Macroeconomic Management, Adjustment, and Stabilisation,' in Colin Stoneman, ed., *Zimbabwe's Prospects*, (London: Macmillan, 1988); Colin Stoneman, 'The Impending Failure of Structural Adjustment: Lessons from Zimbabwe,' paper presented at the Canadian Association of African Studies (May 1990); Colin Stoneman, 'Zimbabwe Opens Up to the Market,' *Africa Recovery* 4 (October–December, 1990); Roger C. Riddell, 'Zimbabwe,' in Roger C. Riddell, ed., *Manufacturing Africa: Performance and Prospects of Seven Countries in Sub-Saharan Africa* (London: James Currey, 1990).
56. Republic of Zimbabwe, *Growth with Equity* (Harare: Government Printer, 1981), p. 2; Republic of Zimbabwe, *Transitional National Development Plan* (Harare: Government Printer, 1982), p. 24.
57. Republic of Zimbabwe, *First Five-Year National Development Plan, 1986–1990* (Harare: Government Printer, 1986), p. 2.
58. *Africa Research Bulletin*, 'Zimbabwe: Economic Policy Dilemmas,' 26 (February 28, 1989), p. 9430.
59. Robert Mugabe said in a July 1987 speech to Parliament that further investment is unnecessary when foreign investors already own many of the country's resources. 'The more we have them,' he said, 'the more the dividends we shall be remitting abroad and the more the indebtedness' (Economist Intelligence Unit, *Zimbabwe: Country Report*, #4 (London: EIU, 1987), pp. 13–14).
60. Blocked funds are monies due and payable to nonresidents which are blocked in local banks by exchange controls.
61. Reserve Bank of Zimbabwe, *Quarterly Economic and Statistical Review* (Harare: Government Printer, 1986), p. 23.
62. Republic of Zimbabwe, *Economic Policy Statement: Macro-Economic Adjustment and Trade Liberalisation* (Harare: Government Printer, 1990), p. 18.
63. Tony Hawkins, 'Time to Grasp the Nettle of Reform,' p. 8; Stoneman, 'Zimbabwe Opens Up to the Market,' p. 23.
64. Riddell, 'Zimbabwe,' p. 358.
65. Jeffrey Herbst, *State Politics in Zimbabwe* (Berkeley: University of

California Press, 1990), p. 127.
66. Hanlon, *Beggar Your Neighbors*, pp. 193, 189.
67. Riddell, 'Zimbabwe,' p. 394.
68. Holman, 'Zimbabwe: Financial Times Survey,' *Financial Times* (August 21, 1989), p. 1.
69. Reginald Herbold Green, et al., 'Children in Southern Africa,' report prepared for UNICEF, 1989, p. 20.
70. Economist Intelligence Unit, *Zimbabwe: Country Report*, #3 (London: EIU, 1990), p. 13.
71. Green, et al, 'Children in Southern Africa,' p. 22.
72. Stoneman, 'Zimbabwe Opens up to the Market,' p. 22.
73. Institute of International Finance, *Zimbabwe* (Washington, D.C.: IIF, 1991).
74. One report concluded that the financial requirements for Zimbabwe's adjustment program amounts to $2.7 billion in foreign exchange to finance imports and improvements to the country's infrastructure (*African Economic Digest*, 'Harare Concessions,' 11:37 (September, 1990), p. 21).
75. One financial analyst estimated that for Zimbabwe's economy to grow at the development plan target rate of five percent per year, the economy needed to invest 25 percent of GDP and, in 1989 figures, a shift of the order of Z$1 billion into investment was necessary (Holman, 'Zimbabwe,' p. II).
76. *African Business*, 'Chidzero Gives Nod to Blocked-funds Trading,' 132 (August 1989), p. 47.
77. Republic of Zimbabwe, *The Promotion of Investment: Policy and Regulations* (Harare: Government Printer, 1989), p. 5.
78. Tony Hawkins, 'Few Signs of Improvement,' *Financial Times*, August 30, 1991, p. 24.
79. Republic of Zimbabwe, *Economic Policy Statement*, p. 17.
80. Jan Raath, 'We'll Do It Our Way,' *The Banker* 140 (May 1990), p. 76.
81. According to a recent World Bank report on investment in Zimbabwe, the main concern for investors should not be the rate of profitability arising from remittance controls. The report argues that Zimbabwe's allowed figure is in line with most other countries' policies. The real and troubling concern is the uncertainty with the government's policy direction toward foreign investment. (Mansoor Dailami and Michael Walton, 'Private Investment, Government Policy, and Foreign Capital in Zimbabwe,' *Working Paper* #248 (August) (Washington, D.C.: World Bank, Policy, Planning, and Research,1989), p. 62).
82. Republic of Zimbabwe, *The Promotion of Investment*, p. 4.
83. Hawkins, 'Time to Grasp the Nettle of Reform,' p. 8.
84. *African Business*, 'Zimbabwe Survey,' 142 (June 1990), p. 26.
85. Whitsun Foundation, *Money and Finance in Zimbabwe* (Harare: Whitsun Foundation, 1983), p. 120.

86. Hanlon, *Beggar Your Neighbors*, Ch. 16.
87. *African Economic Digest*, 'Special Report: Zimbabwe,' (April 1987), p. 1.
88. Zimbabwean economist based in London, 1988; American economist for an international financial resource organization, 1988.
89. Institute of International Finance, *Zimbabwe*, 1991.
90. World Bank, *Zimbabwe: A Strategy for Sustained Growth*, p. 124.
91. *Africa Research Bulletin*, 'Zimbabwe: Economic Policy Dilemmas,' 1989, p. 9431.
92. Institute of International Finance, *Zimbabwe*, 1991.
93. Economist Intelligence Unit, *Zimbabwe: Country Report*, #2 (London: EIU, 1992) p. 25.
94. Ibid., p. 25.
95. Institute of International Finance, *Zimbabwe*, 1991.
96. Tony Hawkins, 'New Strategy Sought as Growth Slows,' *Financial Times* (September 17, 1987), p. II.
97. For the former perspective, see Stoneman, 'The Impending Failure of Structural Adjustment: Lessons from Zimbabwe,' 1990, p. 6.
98. Fernando Henrique Cardoso, 'Associated-Dependent Development,' in Alfred Stepan, ed., *Authoritarian Brazil: Origins, Policies, and Future* (New Haven: Yale University Press, 1973), p. 163.
99. Michael Wallerstein, 'The Collapse of Democracy in Brazil: Its Economic Determinants,' *Latin American Research Review* 15:3 (1980), p. 33.
100. Sidney Dell and Roger Lawrence, *The Balance of Payments Adjustment Process in Developing Countries* (New York: Pergamon Press, 1980), p. 40.
101. See the next chapter in this book for a discussion on Zimbabwe's financing strategy.
102. Jeffry A. Frieden, 'The Brazilian Borrowing Experience: From Miracle to Debacle and Back,' *Latin American Research Review* 22:1 (1987), p. 99.
103. Eliana A. Cardoso and Albert Fishlow, 'The Macroeconomics of the Brazilian External Debt,' in Jeffrey D. Sachs, ed. *Developing Country Debt and Economic Performance*, Vol. 2 (Chicago: University of Chicago Press, 1990), p. 284.
104. Marta Bekerman, 'The Impact of the International Environment on Brazil: From Miracle to Recession,' unpublished manuscript (November 1982), p. 24.
105. Luis Bresser Pereira, *Development and Crisis in Brazil, 1930–1983* (Boulder: Westview Press, 1984), p. 181.
106. Secretariat of Planning, *Third National Development Plan, 1980–1985* (Brasilia, 1979), p. 14; interview with Banco Real director, 1985.
107. The terms of trade dropped by 45 percent between 1977 and 1981 while debt service payments as a proportion of merchandise exports rose from 51 percent in 1977 to 91 percent in 1982. See Jeffry A. Frieden,

Debt, Development, and Democracy: Modern Political Economy and Latin America, 1965–1985 (Princeton: Princeton University Press, 1991), p. 128.
108. Economist Intelligence Unit, *Brazil: Country Profile, 1990–91* (London: EIU, 1991), p. 11.
109. Secretariat of Planning, 'Brazilian Monthly Economic Indicators,' (July 1984).
110. Secretariat of Planning, *Fiscal Policy: Performance in 1980 and Guidelines for 1981* (Brasilia, 1981), pp. 5, 6.
111. Lloyds Bank, *Brazil: Economic Report* (London: Lloyds Bank, 1984), p. 8.
112. Cardoso and Fishlow, 'The Macroeconomics of the Brazilian External Debt,' p. 335.
113. Economist Intelligence Unit, *Brazil: Country Profile, 1990–91* (London: EIU, 1990), p. 11.
114. Institute of International Finance, *Brazil: Special Report* (New York: IIF, 1990).
115. For the theoretical framework concerning two-level games, see Robert Putnam, 'Diplomacy and Domestic Politics: The Logic of Two-Level Games,' *International Organization* 42 (Summer 1988); and for an interpretation and empirical application of this model, see Howard P. Lehman and Jennifer L. McCoy, 'The Dynamics of the Two-Level Bargaining Game: The 1988 Brazilian Debt Negotiations,' *World Politics* 44:4 (July 1992).
116. The continuity of appointments in the federal bureaucracy was striking. One study showed that during Sarney's first year in office, only 15 percent of some 4500 federal appointments were first-time officials without prior ties to the military. See Eul-Soo Pang, 'Debt, Adjustment, and Democratic Cacophony in Brazil,' in Barbara Stallings and Robert Kaufman, eds., *Debt and Democracy in Latin America* (Boulder: Westview Press, 1989), p. 131.
117. Sylvia Maxfield, 'National Business, Debt-led Growth, and Political Transition in Latin America,' in Stallings and Kaufman, *Debt and Democracy in Latin America*, pp. 84–5.
118. Jeffry Frieden, 'Classes, Sectors, and the International Financial Relations of Mexico, Brazil, Argentina, and Chile,' *Comparative Politics* 21:1 (October 1988).
119. Maria Helena Moreira Alves, 'Trade Unions in Brazil: A Search for Autonomy and Organization,' in Edward Epstein, ed., *Labor Autonomy and the State in Latin America* (Boston: Unwin Hyman, 1989).
120. William C. Smith, 'The Travail of Brazilian Democracy in the 'New Republic,'' *Journal of Interamerican Studies and World Affairs* 28:4 (Winter 1986/87), p. 44.
121. World Bank, *Brazil: A Macroeconomic Evaluation of the Cruzado Plan* (Washington, D.C.: World Bank, 1987), p. 26.
122. *Latin American Weekly Report*, October 4, 1985, p. 8.

123. See Luiz Bresser Pereira and Yoskiaki Nakano, *The Theory of Inertial Inflation: The Foundation of Economic Reform in Brazil and Argentina* (Boulder: Westview Press, 1987).
124. Werner Baer, Dan Biller, and Curtis McDonald, 'Austerity Under Different Political Regimes? The Case of Brazil,' in Howard Handelman and Werner Baer, eds., Paying the Costs of Austerity in Latin America (Boulder: Westview Press, 1989), p. 36; Werner Baer and Paul Beckerman, 'The Decline and Fall of Brazil's Cruzado,' *Latin American Research Review* 24:1 (1989).
125. *The Economist*, 25 April 1987, pp. 9–11.
126. *World Financial Markets*, August 1986, cited in *Latin American Times* 7:10 (March 30, 1987), p. 13.
127. Baer and Beckerman, 'The Decline and Fall of Brazil's Cruzado,' p. 53.
128. Pang, 'Debt, Adjustment, and Democratic Cacophony in Brazil,' p. 134; Baer, Biller, and McDonald, 'Austerity Under Different Political Regimes? The Case of Brazil,' p. 36.
129. Paul Singer, 'Democracy and Inflation in the Light of the Brazilian Experience,' in William L. Canak, ed., *Lost Promises: Debt, Austerity, and Development in Latin America* (Boulder: Westview Press, 1989), p. 34.
130. *Latin American Regional Report*, January 8, 1987, p. 2.
131. *Latin American Weekly Report*, 12 February 1987, p. 12; *The Economist*, 25 April 1987, pp. 9–11.
132. *The Economist*, 25 April 1987, pp. 9–11; Smith, 'The Travail of Brazilian Democracy in the 'New Republic,'' p. 56; *Latin American Weekly Report*, 22 January 1987, p. 10; *Latin American Weekly Report*, 19 February 1987, p. 10.
133. *The Economist*, 25 April 1987, p. 10.
134. *Latin American Weekly Report*, 29 January 1987, p. 8; *Latin American Weekly Report*, 19 February 1987, p. 4.
135. *Latin American Weekly Report*, 26 February 1987, p. 11; *Latin American Weekly Report*, 5 March 1987, p. 1.
136. *Latin American Weekly Report*, 5 March 1987, p. 4; *New York Times*, 27 April 1987, p. 23.
137. *Latin American Weekly Report*, 9 April 1987, p. 10; *Latin American Weekly Report*, 23 April 1987, p. 8; *New York Times*, 27 April 1987, p. 23. The 9 July 1987 issue of the *Latin American Weekly Report* reported that when labor groups demonstrated against the government austerity program, the military warned that 'as defenders of the institutions, the armed forces ''will not allow these groups to continue their disturbance and aggression,'' (p. 2). The sensitivity of Sarney to the military's views seems to be reflected in a report on the meetings of the president: the two ministers most consulted by Sarney in his two years in office were the head of the SNI (the powerful military intelligence) and the head of the President's

military household (*Latin American Weekly Report*, 23 April 1987, p. 8).
138. David Fleischer, 'The Constituent Assembly and the Transformation Strategy,' in Lawrence S. Graham and Robert H. Wilson, eds., *The Political Economy of Brazil: Public Policies in an Era of Transition* (Austin: University of Texas Press, 1990), pp. 250–251.
139. Pang, 'Debt, Adjustment, and Democratic Cacophony in Brazil,' p. 137.
140. Alan Riding, 'New Brazil Minister Reviving Austerity,' *New York Times*, 4 May 1987, p. 38.
141. Luis Carlos Bresser Pereira, 'A Brazilian Approach to External Debt Negotiation,' *LASA Forum*, 19:4 (Winter 1989), p. 6.
142. *Macroeconomic Control Plan*, (Brasilia: Ministry of Finance, 1987), July, p. 22.
143. Pang reports that nearly 500 companies in Sao Paulo went bankrupt in April ('Debt, Adjustment, and Democratic Cacophony in Brazil,' p. 137).
144. Ibid., p. 138.
145. *Latin American Regional Report*, 11 February 1988, p. 3.
146. *Latin American Regional Report*, Feb. 9, 1989, p. 2.
147. *Latin American Weekly Report*, 21 January 1988, p. 2; *Latin American Weekly Report*, 18 February 1988, pp. 4–5.
148. *Latin American Regional Report*, Feb. 9, 1989, p. 6.
149. *Latin American Weekly Report*, January 26, 1989, p. 1; *Latin American Regional Report*, February 9, 1989, pp. 2–3.
150. *Latin American Regional Report*, June 1, 1989, p. 6.
151. Economist Intelligence Unit, *Brazil: Country Profile*, 1990–91, p. 14.
152. Institute of International Finance, *Brazil: Special Report*, July 30, 1990; *Latin American Weekly Report*, March 29, 1990, p. 2; Economist Intelligence Unit, *Brazil: Country Profile*, 1990–91.
153. *Latin American Regional Report*, August 16, 1990, p. 3.
154. Ibid.
155. Ibid.
156. *Latin American Regional Report*, March 21, 1991, p. 5.
157. *Latin American Regional Report*, February 14, 1991, p. 3.
158. Institute of International Finance, *Brazil: Country Report* (Washington, D.C.: IIF, 1991).
159. See Julius E. Nyang'oro and Timothy M. Shaw, eds., *Corporatism in Africa: Comparative Analysis and Practice* (Boulder: Westview Press, 1989).
160. Mosley, 'Kenya,' p. 289.

4 The State and Debt Management Strategies

INTRODUCTION

Indebted development is conceptualized in this book as a wide-ranging series of attempts by debtor states to create, implement, and sustain economic adjustment and debt management strategies. The question should not be whether such states have sufficient political will to make hard adjustment decisions; rather, the question is, given that adjustment is unavoidable, how can we explain the selection and implementation of two complementary adjustment strategies: one that targets domestic economic reforms or the other that is oriented toward external debt management? The previous chapter examined the first side of the question; that is, state economic objectives and policies that impinge on domestic interests. This chapter will analyze the second side of the question; that is, the state's debt management policies as they impact upon international creditors. As noted in Chapter One, the state, caught in the center of often countervailing pressures, becomes empowered to respond to these pressures and demands. Through a mixture of economic orthodoxy and heterodoxy, the state uses its power in an attempt to shape the adjustment process. Towards international creditors, states choose between a) *cooperating* with creditors – by meeting debt obligations often through the imposition of austerity measures – and b) *defecting* – by selecting debt repudiation or interest non-repayment in order to pursue domestic economic growth. Of course, as demonstrated in the previous chapter on the state's negotiating strategies toward economic adjustment, these two strategic options reflect ideal-types. State bargaining stances on debt management often involve considerable slippage.

All three countries under review have sought to use state power to advance and protect the interests of the established governing actors. Although each of them has approached international creditors differently, each also has sought to control and regulate the effects of foreign indebtedness. This chapter will analyze the growth and structure of external indebtedness and the states' relationship with international creditors.

DEBT MANAGEMENT STRATEGIES OF KENYA

The national leadership, first under Kenyatta and sustained under Moi, supported an open international strategy as a means to maintain access to foreign capital, technology, and markets. Given the leadership's emphasis on export growth and international trade, the state provided institutional safeguards and incentives for foreign investors. The state also has undertaken steps to liberalize certain components of its economy in order to attract additional foreign capital and to expand its export base while centralizing other components as a means to protect its credit standing among the international financial community. Although it is not entirely willing to implement controls that go against free trade and the uninterrupted flow of foreign capital, the costs of liberalization have forced Kenya to set up temporary controls.

Although Kenya hesitated during the 1970s to embark on on a policy of heavy borrowing from foreign sources, the sudden unravelling of its debt capacity by the early 1980s took state officials by surprise. A shift in the state's role as a central figure in debt management occurred as the debt burden expanded, combined with weakening terms of trade and deterioration of the export market. Kenyan officials realized at this time that an export-oriented strategy (as discussed in Chapter Three) could not be sustained and thus could not be expected to generate funds sufficient to carry a manageable debt load. The state borrowing apparatus moved in quickly to manage the external debt. By 1982, the organizational responsibilities for debt reporting were clarified though not implemented. In the following few years, an External Debt Unit (later called the External Debt Management Committee) was established in the Ministry of Finance which prepared an external borrowing plan.[1] Specific measures then were taken, including a limit on public sector borrowing of six percent of the budget deficit and a requirement that all parastatal borrowing be incorporated in the Forward Budget and approved by the Ministry of Finance. Government ministries must now submit their list of priorities for Treasury approval.[2] Additional policy changes took place in 1988 with the publication of the Sixth Development Plan. The document extends the government's debt management policy to include a 'comprehensive inventory of all public sector external loans,' the 'identification of loans in which debt service is in arrears,' and the evaluation of 'implications of different volumes of existing and new borrowings based on a critical assessment of their impact of such debt on the economy.'[3] In his 1990 Budget Speech, the Minister of Finance further stated that in the future, the debts of parastatal firms, even those guaranteed by the government, would not be honored 'without a thorough investigation of the circumstances behind the payment default.'[4] These controls are not intended to discontinue foreign borrowing or to discourage foreign investment, but they are meant to bring the economy back into balance which would enhance the state's international credit standing.

Kenya has long recognized the valuable role played by foreign finance capital in the form of project finance loans, trade loans, and balance of payments bridge loans. In recent years, as its trade balance and current account balance fell further into deficit, the country has obtained foreign loans and grants as means of financing its economic adjustment strategy. Kenya's total external debt increased by 80 percent between 1984 and 1989.[5] It is projected to rise by only seven percent from 1989 to 1990 where after total debt is meant to drop by almost eight percent by 1992. The proportion of official and private *sources of borrowing* has remained about the same since the mid-1980s. As has been the case for many years, official creditors (IFIs and official bilateral creditors) met almost all of Kenya's external financing requirement at about 80 percent of total borrowing. While Kenya's total debt to the IMF and the World Bank has only somewhat fluctuated over the last five years, its borrowings from other multilateral creditors, especially the International Development Association (IDA), have grown from $520 million in 1984 to a forecast $1956 million in 1992, an annual growth rate of 30 percent. The second largest source of external funds, after multilateral creditors, is bilateral creditors. Kenya has long been a favored recipient of official development assistance. However, recently revised figures suggest a downward slide into the mid-1990s as donors doubt the government's willingness to undertake political and economic reforms. Private creditors make up the third largest source of foreign borrowing. Private creditors are expected to provide an increased amount in new net financing in support of increasing imports for large investment projects through 1990 followed by declines in the next two years. See Table 1.7 for a comparison between Kenya, Zimbabwe, and Brazil over the differences and similarities in their sources of foreign loans.

While the net inflow of new loans has been reduced to a trickle, the repayment of previous loans has become a detriment to Kenya's economic equilibrium. A troubling indicator of Kenya's debt position is the total debt service. Its annual payments for amortization and interest are expected to grow by forty percent between 1984 and 1990, from $518 million to $712 million. In spite of the rapid accumulation of external debt, Kenya's debt servicing requirement is intended to drop slightly in absolute terms through 1992. By obtaining more concessional terms on new loans, Kenya's debt

Table 4.1 Kenya's Total External Debt by Creditor, 1985–1992
($ million)

	1985	1986	1987	1988	1989	1990[a]	1991[b]	1992[b]
Creditors								
Total Multilateral								
Creditors	1857	2075	2371	2374	2543	2949	3051	3019
IMF	521	460	400	455	416	483	541	494
World Bank	751	931	1128	973	889	871	711	569
Others	585	684	843	946	1238	1595	1799	1956
Official Bilateral								
Creditors	1743	2051	2596	2497	2723	2501	2481	2412
Private Creditors	538	898	1069	1160	1151	1413	1153	917
Total External								
Debt	4139	5024	6036	6074	6416	6863	6685	6348

[a] Estimate   [b] Forecast

Source   Institute of International Finance, *Kenya: Country Update* (Washington, D.C.: IIF, 1991).

Table 4.2 Kenya's Debt Ratios, 1985–1992

	1985	1986	1987	1988	1989	1990[a]	1991[b]	1992[b]
Total External Debt								
(in US$ million)	4139	5024	6036	6074	6416	6863	6685	6348
Debt Ratio								
(% GDP)	67.5	69.4	76.1	72.1	77.3	79.0	83.2	71.7
Debt Ratio								
(% Exports)	257.6	264.2	347.0	323.1	331.7	307.3	310.3	272.0

[a] Estimate   [b] Forecast

Source   Institute of International Finance, *Kenya: Country Update* (Washington, D.C.: IIF, 1991).

service as a percentage of exports generally has been decreasing from a high of 36 percent in 1987 to a projected low of about 28 percent by 1992.

At one level, the financing policy of Kenya's adjustment reflects the government's strong support for participation by foreign investors, donor

Table 4.3 Kenya's Debt Service Indicators, 1985-1992

	1985	1986	1987	1988	1989	1990[a]	1991[b]	1992[b]
Total Debt Service ($ million)	540	540	630	607	596	712	651	651
Debt Service Ratio (% exports)	33.6	28.4	36.2	32.3	30.8	31.9	30.2	27.9

[a] Estimate [b] Forecast

Source Institute of International Finance, *Kenya: Country Update* (Washington, D.C.: IIF, 1991).

governments, the IMF and World Bank, and international private creditors. At another level, however, Kenya has used its special relationship to international creditors to its economic advantage by playing creditors off each other while remaining relatively autonomous from the harshest demands for adjustment. For international creditors, Kenya's ideological unity and commitment to relatively orthodox and market-oriented economic policies have outweighed, until 1991, their criticisms of the rigid one-party political system that has monopolized power in the country. However, increasing criticism against the government's policy of repressing political opponents has been escalating which is threatening the party's hold over society by bringing about political instability and undermining Kenya's relationship with foreign capital interests.

Relationship with the Donor Countries

For many of its donors, Kenya has represented the jewel in the crown of international development assistance. As a model of a developing country which has been provided vast sums of capital, technology, and management assistance, donor countries could ill afford to allow disaster to occur in Kenya. A 1987 study on aid coordination in Kenya noted that Kenya's pro-capitalist inclinations 'encouraged donors to support Kenya as an example in Africa of what could be achieved by pursuing liberal economic policies in a democratic framework.'[6] As an annual average between 1982 and 1985, Kenya received over $350 million in gross official development assistance from bilateral creditors. From 1986 to 1989, average annual disbursements from bilateral creditor governments rose to over $500 million.[7] Aid inflows have increased as Kenya's dependence on them also has risen. In 1979, foreign aid only covered 35 percent of the government's development budget. By 1990, the figure was around 90 percent.[8] Between 1984 and 1992, Kenya's external debt to bilateral donors nearly doubled to $2.4 billion.[9]

The donor governments' relations with Kenya have undergone a rapid deterioration since 1991. Even in 1990, an Economist Intelligence Unit report could state that

> donors have accepted that if the government's commitment to some of their desired measures (including not only maize control but also parastatal reform and trade liberalisation) is lukewarm, its commitment to the fundamental principles of market determined exchange rates, interest rates and agricultural prices is total, and there is now a tacit agreement to condone the former in recognition of the latter.[10]

This claim was confirmed by action on the part of official bilateral creditors to make Kenya the prime beneficiary of their debt cancellation programs. In a three-year period (1988-1990), Canada, Britain, the Netherlands, Germany, France, and the United States cancelled over $900 million of official debt.[11] Furthermore, donors felt during the 1980s that Kenya's economic strategy favored their commercial interests as indicated by the common practice of linking aid to expanded trade and investment relations. Between 1982 and 1985, the United States and the United Kingdom provided 14 percent and 11 percent, respectively, of the total disbursements.[12] In addition to its significant commercial role with Britain, Kenya has evolved into a major strategic player with the United States in Eastern Africa. Kenya hosts a large U.S. naval base in Mombassa and a critical electronic listening post. The spread of instability in the Horn of Africa and the Middle East prompted the United States to pressure other donors and the IFIs to continue their assistance of Kenya.

However, Kenya's privileged recipient status is now being threatened, according to several U.S. government aid officials. They claim that the U.S. government has become less tolerant of human rights abuses, government corruption, and inadequate economic reforms.[13] An official with the U.S. Department of Commerce said that the United States is applying pressure on Kenya and telling the Kenyans that 'the United States is the pied piper and we're calling the tune.'[14] By the end of 1991, donor opinion about Kenya experienced a 'sea-change.' In the post-Cold War era, Kenya is less able to use its geostrategic value to Western governments. In losing this primary source of bargaining power, Kenya no longer is able to off-set donor criticism of its human rights policy and of the 'governance' issue. Donor governments have begun to link foreign aid to improvements in governance and economic management.[15] According to one observer, bilateral creditors are losing patience with Kenya's slow pace in undertaking structural economic reforms, especially in the area of the public sector. While the government has made progress, according to this perspective, in decontrolling prices and in trade liberalization, the public sector and parastatals have yet to be reformed.[16] The result was an immediate aid suspension by individual governments in the fall of 1991 and a six-month Paris Club moratorium of aid from November 1991 to May 1992.

Relationship with the IMF and the World Bank

Kenya has had a lengthy and fairly warm relationship with the IMF.[17] Kenya has been a prolonged recipient of IMF funds with a series of standby arrangements running from 1975 to 1986 during which it drew the equivalent of $640 million. It also drew $150 from the compensatory financing facility to cover export shortfalls and cereal imports. There was an interlude in 1986 and 1987 when Kenya, having recovered from the drought and benefited from improved terms of trade, was not under an IMF standby arrangement. However, as a U.S. Treasury official claimed, the Kenyan government did not take advantage of this respite to consolidate its gains, but incurred increased budgetary deficits and expanded domestic credit and money supply, creating the need to return once more to the IMF.[18] This official failed to mention that perhaps the key reason for Kenya's renewed relationship to the IMF was the dramatic fall of Kenya's terms of trade by 23 percent in 1987.

In February 1988, the IMF Board approved a new eighteen month $126 million standby and a Structural Adjustment Facility (SAF) running three years and providing $139 million. At the expiration of the standby in June 1989, outstanding drawings were 215 percent of Kenya's quota, nearing the upper limit of drawings for other African countries. During spring of 1989, another set of negotiations began with the IMF on a three-year Enhanced Structural Adjustment Facility (ESAF) worth $310 million. The conditions attached to the current ESAF were of two kinds: a) ambiguous statements on exchange rate adjustments, market-determined interest rates, and reduction in government expenditures and b) more specific measures dealing with trade of commodities, cuts in government personnel and increased revenue from introducing user charges in education and health care.[19] The Kenya government and the IMF reached agreement following the IMF's evaluation of Kenya's economic performance. Kenya apparently met all IMF targets agreed under the previous SAF program, including the growth rate of the GDP and the lowering of the inflation rate and of the budget deficit.[20] The second tranche under the ESAF became available to Kenya in April 1990 after IMF's satisfaction of met conditions. However, the IMF announced in early 1992 an indefinite delay on the release of $63.2 million as part of its final tranche under the ESAF. From the view of the IMF, the government failed to comply with performance criteria, focusing on the fiscal deficit, the over-expansion in the money supply, and inadequate progress on civil service and parastatal reform.[21]

Despite Kenya's recent setback in its negotiations with the IMF, a still relevant question is knowing that the IMF programs required satisfying conditionalities involving structural adjustments with considerable costs, why did Kenya return to the IMF? One reason is the increased coordination between the IMF and the World Bank as witnessed by *cross-conditionality* indicators. In order to qualify for and obtain funds from one organization, the other also must agree with the economic program. The release of over $400 million in industrial and financial sector lending from the World Bank in 1989 was contingent upon a joint policy framework program with both institutions and Kenya.[22] Another important motivating factor is the common policy and ideological perspective towards adjustment shared by the regime and the IMF. An IMF official said that Kenya and the IMF see 'eye to eye' and have been in total agreement with such measures as price decontrols, import liberalization, and user charge for education and health.[23] Two Kenyan embassy officials confirmed that not only was their country in agreement with the IMF, but it identified its own economic problems before the IMF did and, based on such needs, approached the Fund for a SAF and a standby arrangement.[24]

A related factor is illustrated by the government's willingness to cooperate with the IMF. An academic who worked closely with the government as an economic advisor concluded critically that 'Kenya has abrogated its economic policy decision-making to the IMF.'[25] The government allows significant IMF participation in the policy-making process in the Central Bank and the Ministry of Finance.[26] The IMF officials who monitored Kenya's adjustment performance both concluded in interviews that the country had made sufficient progress toward reaching IMF targets (such as deficit reduction, currency devaluation, and import and export liberalization) to warrant continued cooperation.[27] Although Kenya is experiencing difficulty in implementing some IMF-directed terms, at least one bank economist suggested that it was due more to external economic factors than unwillingness by Kenya's leaders to undertake such policies.[28]

Yet, underneath this veneer of mutual satisfaction lies a crucial tension between the IMF and Kenya. The government has shrewdly and expertly managed its relations with the international financial community. In similar fashion to its deft attention and manipulation of its strategic value to the West, Kenya is able to project its image as a stable country, fully conscious of its economic problems, the necessary economic targets, and the policies needed to achieve them. Through periodic public statements which emphasize its considerable agreement with the broad adjustment objectives of the IMF, the government seeks to aspire to self-selection of IMF objectives while neglecting other IMF economic targets.[29] Kenya thus has been able to draw funds from the IMF and avoid the excessive costs attached to loans from international commercial banks. The IMF also has allowed slippage even on Kenya's own terms. However, recent developments cast doubt on the continued success of Kenya's policy of slippage.

Kenya has had a much rockier relationship with the World Bank than with the IMF. While the latter historically sought to restructure macroeconomic policies, the former defined its role more in terms of institutional reform, sectoral adjustment, and expanding the position of the indigenous private sector. During the early 1980s, the World Bank provided two Structural Adjustment Loans (SAL) with similar objectives: reform of the import licensing process, elimination of the grain marketing board, creation of a comprehensive public investment program, and clearer implementation guidelines. However, Kenyan authorities initially objected to the Bank recommendation that the marketing of maize should be removed from the state monopoly of the National Cereal and Produce Marketing Board and given to the private sector. The government insisted in 1983 that the 'Bank was interfering with the Kenya Government's internal sovereignty by seeking to impose (the policy) on them.'[30] The Bank then suspended the program due to 'substantial delays in implementation' and, according to a World Bank economist, the 'absence of an orderly policy process.'[31] Nevertheless, since 1986, there has been a warming in the relationship. The scope of the current SAL has shifted from comprehensive adjustment objectives to apparently more manageable sectoral targets. The Bank now finds Kenya to be more committed to the program as indicated by the 1989 agreement covering $400 million in industrial and financial sector lending.[32] The release of this money is tied to the liberalization of export and investment incentives as negotiated between the Bank and the government. According to a recent study, the Bank and Kenya have been in agreement about 'what had to be done, but not about when it had to be done.'[33]

In 1991, the Bank showed mixed signals to Kenya concerning its continued financial support. In the fall, the Bank refused to provide $100 million to promote domestic energy production because of claims of corruption issued against the minister of energy.[34] Yet, in September

1991, the Bank's International Development Association (IDA) approved a $100 million credit in support of the education system followed by two new credits issued in November 1991 to the Ministry of Education ($55 million) and to support health sector reforms ($31 million).[35]

Relationship with International Private Creditors

The Kenya government's willingness to work with the IFIs has not gone unnoticed by international creditors and bankers. The signing of IMF programs, Kenya's commitment to its international financial obligations, and the strategic backing of the U.S. and the U.K. have contributed to a positive and beneficial lending environment for international private creditors. Even during the critical period of the mid-1980s, international banks provided trade finance loans and specific state-guaranteed loans.[36] Banks lent short-term, trade finance loans of $70 million in both 1987 and 1988. Kenya still remains a committed borrower from international private creditors. The government borrowed nearly $800 million from that source between 1988 and 1991. All together, Kenya in 1991 owed over $1.6 billion to private creditors. British banks, such as Standard and Chartered and Barclays, have long-standing experiences within the economy as domestic banks and, according to a director of the latter, 'good customer relations pressure loan approval.'[37] A representative of a U.S. bank in Kenya suggested that the most attractive type of loan is trade finance in which the bank acts a financial middleman between foreign traders and Kenyan exporters. Trade finance loans generally are guaranteed either by foreign trade agencies or by the Kenya government thus removing that burden of risk from commercial banks.

While Kenya's relationship with the international financial community generally has been supportive, certain international bankers have expressed concern with the country's intermediate future. They point to increasing internal political pressures arising from growing unemployment, mounting budget deficits, dangerously high population growth rates, and escalating social tension. The scars from the 1982 coup attempt have healed, but another serious uprising will have a long-term detrimental impact on Kenya's ties to the international financial community.[38] Indeed, Kenya's bargaining power with all of its external creditors appears to be weakening. It seems doubtful that the government will be able to contain either the growth of the democracy movement or the repeated calls for genuine economic liberalization. Several observers in interviews were critical of charges of nepotism by government officials, bureaucratic incompetence, and political gerrymandering in maintaining inefficient parastatals, industrial protective measures, wage repression, and agricultural marketing boards.[39] Most bankers would agree with this executive of a Kenyan bank who said that 'although Kenya's credit standing is fairly high, it maintains little control over such reputation. As a purely agricultural-based economy, it has no control over tea and coffee prices. In a very true sense, it is unable to guarantee foreign exchange.'[40]

DEBT MANAGEMENT STRATEGIES OF ZIMBABWE

Since Zimbabwe's independence in 1980, the government's relationship with foreign capital interests often has been labeled as contradictory and conflictual. In part, this contradictory pattern can be explained by the inability of the governing elites to consolidate and solidify their power bases into a united ideological force. The conflict between stated development objectives and actual policy implementation became more dramatic by the late-1980s as the government embarked on a policy of economic liberalization. Yet, the one objective that has remained constant throughout the last ten years has been the effort by the state to exert control over the direction and timing of economic policy. By using regulations over foreign investments, the borrowing process, and public sector investment, and, in the last few years, by permitting a more liberalized policy, the state remains committed to maintain control over its development strategy.

The establishment of a centralized regulatory system in Zimbabwe has roots in the historical evolution of the state reinforced by an ideological leadership that fought against the Rhodesian regime for many years. To speak of the role of the state in the economy, we first must recognize the highly centralized and sophisticated state apparatus already intact at the time of independence.[41] The presence of this kind of state structure had several implications for the post-independence government.[42] First, a foreign exchange allocation system already was in place with years of experience and acceptance when independence occurred in 1980. Second, the powers of the Reserve Bank and the Ministry of Finance increased as government policy controlled the use of foreign exchange and held down import levels. Third, the issue of South African ownership of Rhodesian assets became an influential factor of the current government's aversion towards foreign investment. A crucial objective of the new government was the protection and expansion of nationalist and black capital interests. This policy led to widespread subsidization of industries and manufacturing firms in addition to wage and price controls. Fourth, in reaction to the former regime's emphasis on public investment in productive sectors, the new government shifted its investments toward improving the quality of life for the majority of the population in basic goods and social service sectors. Finally, the government borrowed heavily from commercial sources in the early 1980s, but rigorously kept to the repayment schedule. By maintaining punctual repayment of its loans, Zimbabwe was able to avoid the costs of rescheduling and IMF conditionality (until 1991), while using the capital for development purposes.

Because of Zimbabwe's historical discouragement of foreign investment and limited though vigorous export growth, the government has relied heavily on external financial sources to finance its adjustment strategy. The low level of external indebtedness during the UDI period reflected the effective isolation of Rhodesia's financial requirements from international capital markets. The government placed great pressure on internal financial sources to satisfy the steadily mounting budget deficit. During the 1970s, the government claimed that the foreign component of the public debt remained very small. However, during interviews several respondents from international banks claimed that foreign bank capital reached Rhodesia through private companies and local banks in South Africa.[43] For the most part, however, the government funded its deficits by the sale of government stocks during the early to mid-1970s.

In order to assert its control over the pace and timing of adjustment and to place itself in a position to obtain domestic ratification of the adjustment strategy, the new government at first relied on foreign aid and then turned to international commercial sources for its financing demands. Following independence, Zimbabwe quickly reopened international commercial and financial relations with industrialized states and IFIs. Because of its lengthy period of isolation, the new country was considered by many to be following an underborrowed route of development. The new government used Zimbabwe's widely perceived economic potential within the international financial community as a springboard for new infusions of bank capital. Independence brought not only an expanding public expenditure and budget deficit, but a rapidly rising external debt. At the time of independence, Zimbabwe's external debt was relatively small, but a rapid expansion in external borrowing on commercial as well as concessional terms, together with a large domestic financing requirements and rising interest rates, increased debt servicing costs considerably. The outstanding external public debt jumped four-fold in just one year after independence. The figure grew by nearly fifty percent over the following two years.[44] Since the mid-1980s, the growth rate of Zimbabwe's foreign debt has slowed down considerably. Between 1984 and 1988, the total debt grew by only five percent. But in the next five years (1988 to 1992), its total foreign debt expanded by 37

Table 4.4 Zimbabwe's Total External Debt by Creditor, 1985–1992
(US$ million)

	1985	1986	1987	1988	1989	1990[a]	1991[b]	1992[b]
Creditors								
Total Multilateral								
Creditors	533	619	676	607	596	668	697	1136
IMF	264	234	156	70	29	7	0	130
World Bank	205	280	373	347	353	381	368	498
Others	64	106	147	190	214	280	329	508
Official Bilateral								
Creditors	835	1013	1276	1148	1387	1612	1529	1585
Private Creditors	780	901	987	830	794	749	1045	817
Total External								
Debt	2148	2533	2939	2585	2777	3029	3270	3538

[a] Estimate [b] Forecast

Source Institute of International Finance, *Zimbabwe: Country Report* (Washington, D.C.: IIF, 1991).

percent.[45]

While Kenya, for many years, has sought out multilateral aid, Zimbabwe has relied more on bilateral creditors as well as private creditors. Ever since the 1980 Zimcord agreement by which foreign governments pledged over $1 billion in aid to Zimbabwe, government borrowing policy has been to attract bilateral funds while restricting the credit from the IFIs. The government feared the conditionalities attached to multilateral credits, especially in the form of direct influence by the IMF in reshaping its development strategy. Zimbabwe's use of private commercial credit is quite extensive in contrast to Kenya's policy. Although Zimbabwe's external debt growth has slowed, the government's significant reliance on international commercial capital has put Zimbabwe in an economically difficult position. In recent years, Zimbabwe's ratio of private debt to total external debt has been at least fifty percent more than Kenya's ratio. International bank credit historically is more expensive in terms of higher interest rates and shorter maturity periods than official sources of credit. During the 1980s, interest rates of private credits averaged about ten percent, while official creditors charged only an average of five percent. Maturity data provide similar differences with official credit lines. Zimbabwe faced an average maturity period of ten years on its outstanding debt to private creditors as opposed to the 23 years on debt to official creditors. Moreover, the portion of the

Table 4.5 Zimbabwe's Debt Ratios, 1985–1992

	1985	1986	1987	1988	1989	1990[a]	1991[b]	1992[b]
Total External Debt (in US$ million)	2148	2533	2939	2585	2777	3029	3270	3538
Debt Ratio (% GDP)	49.3	53.4	54.7	43.5	46.3	47.4	57.2	66.6
Debt Ratio (% Exports)	166.4	165.5	177.9	136.9	143.0	148.6	146.6	142.0

[a] Estimate   [b] Forecast

Source   Institute of International Finance, *Zimbabwe: Country Report* (Washington, D.C.: IIF, 1991).

loans consisting of a grant element also distinguished official credit from private credit. Official creditors offered 36 percent in the form of grants, while private creditors only provided two percent.[46]

The combination of expensive capital and restricted repayment periods demands a disciplined method of repayment of loans if the government seeks to avoid rescheduling. As it has continued to borrow from foreign sources over the last few years, the government was faced by the late-1980s with the bunching of loans making repayment difficult. Although, according to one report, Zimbabwe's debt service ratio for 1977–81 was a mere 2.2 percent, the figure steadily climbed until it reached its peak at over 34 percent in 1987.[47] The ratio has since gradually declined to an estimated 19.7 percent by 1992. The rapid growth in servicing the external debt became an increasingly heavy burden on the economy in the 1980s. Even though total debt servicing liabilities peaked by 1987, Zimbabwe is still faced with rising total debt service payments. This implies that if Zimbabwe is to maintain its solid repayment record, an increasing amount of its exports will have to be diverted to repay the loans. While Zimbabwe was spending on average total debt service payments of $400 million between 1983 and 1986, from 1987 to 1992, that figure increased to $485 million. Zimbabwe was very successful in following repayment deadlines, yet at the expense of diminishing foreign currency reserves. In order for the government to sustain substantial repayments, it significantly weakened its foreign reserve position. Since the early 1980s, Zimbabwe's average annual foreign reserves as a percentage of months of imports always has been around one month. Yet, pressures have been increasing as of late within the country to adopt an adjustment strategy that would lower

Table 4.6 Zimbabwe's Debt Service Indicators, 1985–1992

	1985	1986	1987	1988	1989	1990[a]	1991[b]	1992[b]
Total Debt Service (US$ million)	385	413	535	529	454	465	439	491
Debt Service Ratio (% exports)	29.8	27.0	32.4	28.0	23.4	22.8	19.7	19.7

[a] Estimate   [b] Forecast

Source   Institute of International Finance, *Zimbabwe: Country Report* (Washington, D.C.: IIF, 1991).

its vulnerable external financial position without sacrificing the distributive objectives expressed in its development plans.

Zimbabwe's new Structural Adjustment Program (SAP), negotiated in 1991, begins an ambitious five-year plan designed to increase economic growth rates from an average of 3.3 percent in the 1980s to five percent by 1995.[48] In the first stage, the government intends to raise foreign loans to finance imports of capital equipment in order to replace obsolete plants in the manufacturing sector and to boost competitiveness in the export sector. In the second stage, the liberalization program is expected to refinance itself through the increase in export revenue from a re-tooled industry. Given the anticipated mobilization of revenue from exports and net capital inflows (at least $12.5 billion), approximately $3.4 billion will be funded from foreign loans and grants. The total resource requirement during the 1991–95 program amounts to $15.9 billion.[49]

Relationship with the Donor Countries

Soon after independence, donor countries agreed on a massive aid plan called Zimcord that emerged from the Lancaster House conference as detailed in the conference document.[50] They were only too pleased to work with an African country that had a relatively diversified economy, energetic and articulate leaders, and that had the full backing of the UK and other Western powers. Although the impact of the civil war, the costs of demobilization, and the socialist rhetoric of Mugabe instilled doubts in many donor countries, most of these soon vanished as over Z $2 billion in pledges flowed into the country. From the perspective of hindsight, several participants during this period commented in interviews that Zimcord failed to achieve its objectives. At first, the aid program was an admirable 'public relations scheme' which demonstrated the semblance of significant and unrestricted amounts of foreign assistance.[51] Yet, capital from Zimcord did not start to flow until the end of 1982, nearly two years after independence. In the meantime, the government had embarked on development capital borrowing based on the expected and substantial flow of Zimcord aid. Second, much of the aid, which was thought to be cost-free, turned out to be rigidly tied to imports from donor countries. Zimcord failed to free up foreign exchange as it was intended. Rather, the government had to borrow more resulting in 'bloody lending.'[52]

During the mid-1980s, several important donors became increasingly disenchanted with Zimbabwe's political and economic policies. The UK ended its Commodity Import Program and, in 1986, after a diplomatic snub of a U.S. delegation in Zimbabwe, the U.S. terminated AID funds to the country. Eventually, Zimbabwe came to realize that it could not long afford to upset these two countries since its trade with them amounts to about 20 percent of the total.[53] More recently, Zimbabwe has been seeking friendlier economic ties with donor governments. The average annual disbursement figure from bilateral creditors between 1988 and 1991 was nearly $220 million. During this period, repayments actually exceeded disbursements leading to a net outflow of capital from Zimbabwe.

Donor support for Zimbabwe's adjustment program, negotiated in the late-1980s and agreed in 1991, is expected to significantly increase annual aid flows. The government was successful during a May 1991 meeting with creditor governments to obtain a provisional agreement of about $700 million in 1991. At a Paris Club meeting in February 1992, Zimbabwe asked for, and received, an additional $300 million in assistance. The Zimbabwe government justified its request on the grounds of an unexpectedly large inflow of imports on the Open General Import Licensing system and the reoccurrence of extensive drought conditions. Because of the latter, the government estimates that an additional $510 million is needed in 1992 and 1993 for imports, water-related projects, and to off-set shortfalls in agricultural exports.[54] According to a donor report from the February 1992 meeting, the agreement reflects their 'continued confidence in the Zimbabwe structural adjustment programme,' specifically in the implementation of the adjustment plan in its first year.[55]

Relationship with the IMF and the World Bank

Zimbabwe has had several different programs with the IMF, yet, they often collapsed due to fundamental policy disagreements between the two sides. A 1982 Article IV report from the IMF included demands for a substantial reduction of government subsidies, increases in the consumer price of maize meal, promotion of foreign investment, and limits on the growth rate of current expenditures.[56] In March 1983, the IMF provided a stand-by facility to cover the additional costs from unexpected imports of food during a drought. The IMF continued to push for policies that would cut the budget deficit and parastatal subsidies. According to several respondents who were senior officials in the Ministry of Finance during this period, the IMF agreement broke down largely due to the size of the budget deficit. Although these officials claim that the government agreed with most points of the IMF, it disagreed over the speed of reducing the deficit and the 'inevitable clamping down on growth and development.'[57] Given the government's ideological intensity soon after the liberation war and the emergency situation of the drought, the regime felt it could not comply with IMF demands while financing development projects, health clinics, schools, and defense. As one Zimbabwe Treasury official said, 'the IMF has shown itself to be insensitive to social issues.'[58] According to Colin Stoneman, 'where, however, (the government) sees IMF demands for 'liberalisation' in pursuit of short-term balance as threatening its ability to maintain long-run expansion, it is able to prefer direct controls to achieve the balance, even if at a temporarily lower level of activity because of denial of IMF funding.'[59]

During the late-1980s, the government objected to the stringent conditions of a comprehensive package that must be carried out over just eighteen months. Instead of risking the costs which liberalization would incur, such as unemployment and de-industrialization, the government had favored a gradual state-controlled approach to adjustment. Nevertheless, the government complied voluntarily with some IMF restraints on imports, but it was unwilling to limit the expansion of health and education projects. Ironically, it also continues to repay its loans to the IMF. Total repayment to the IMF between 1986 and 1991 amounted to US $300 million which led to a net outflow from Zimbabwe to the IMF.[60] Zimbabwe was able to by-pass direct IMF conditionality, for the most part, because of its particular advantages in terms of a large private sector, diversified economic base, strong domestic support, and additional sources of finance capital.[61] Due to these advantages as well as Zimbabwe's noteworthy repayment efforts, the IMF has given firm backing to the government's adjustment strategy to reform the economy.[62] Crucial to the financing of its five-year SAP was negotiating an agreement with the IMF. In January 1992, the IMF approved an Extended Structural Adjustment Facility (ESAF) amounting to $484 million over three years.

Zimbabwe also has been the recipient of several World Bank loans, totalling hundreds of thousands of dollars and, as of 1992, the government owes $500 million to the Bank. Some of these have supported the reform of agricultural services towards communal areas and others provided funds for manufacturing, transport, and energy sectors. In 1983, the World Bank assisted in the financing of an Export Revolving Fund. This was designed to promote manufactured exports by providing that sector with additional foreign exchange for required imports of raw materials and capital equipment. In the mid-1980s, Zimbabwe negotiated with the World Bank to supply its export industries with new money to purchase vital supplies, but the government felt deterred by the Bank's preconditions. However, in 1989, the Bank took the step of suspending the export fund facility valued at $125 million because of disagreements over the government's trade policies and large budget deficit.[63] Until very recently, World Bank officials held decidedly mixed views toward Zimbabwe's adjustment strategy. According to them, while the government displayed greater awareness for the need of public sector reform, it failed to design a coherent plan that would liberalize the trade regime, prices, and industry.[64]

Zimbabwe's recent policy measures to liberalize the economy through its 'home-grown' adjustment program are actually similar to the World Bank's earlier policy recommendations. Given the government's new, overt liberalization program, the Bank, in early 1990, approved loans that amounted to nearly $150 million for agricultural and urban development projects. Zimbabwe's relationship with it continued to improve following the government's 1990 budget and economic policy statement. These documents reconfirmed the government's commitments to a reduction in the budget deficit, cuts in government subsidies to parastatals, recommendations to promote foreign and private investment, and statements regarding trade liberalization.[65] After Zimbabwe's successful negotiations with the IMF that produced an ESAF in 1992, the Bank agreed to disburse $105 million of its promised $175 million.[66]

Relationship with International Private Creditors

Soon after achieving independence, the new regime negotiated a number of loans from international private sources.[67] The country's external debt quickly ballooned as both international creditors and the government actively pursued each other for transactions. There are a number of reasons for Zimbabwe's initial reliance on this form of foreign capital. According to a senior official in the Ministry of Finance in 1985, 'the market was awash with money . . . and the government used any money, no matter the expected use, for short-term uses.' The government immediately identified several priorities which required borrowed capital. It came under mounting pressure from the high expectations held by the public for the immediate establishment of social welfare, education, health, and job-generating programs. The new government also used this capital to finance capital development projects, such as the Hwange Thermal power plant, dams, electrification, and road construction. During the first two years, foreign bank capital helped to finance the demobilization of the guerrilla armies stemming from the civil war and a resolution to the conflict with the Ndebele in southern Zimbabwe.

The government also turned to international private creditors, in part, as a reaction to the slow and disappointing disbursement of Zimcord funds. At that point, the government could either have encouraged direct foreign investment or contracted with international creditors. It chose the latter because, according to several former senior officials in the Ministry of Finance in 1985, private creditors (especially commercial banks) mainly are concerned with interest repayment which can be controlled and manipulated through government policies. Banks are able to quickly provide liquid capital with very clear terms. In contrast, other international businesses are more rigid as they bring in outside managers, hire employees, construct buildings, and take out profits.

After an initial post-independence honeymoon, in 1983, the government began to realize that its borrowing policies had led to serious debt servicing problems and a depletion of foreign exchange reserves.[68] By 1984, Zimbabwe's foreign debt to private creditors amounted to 40 percent of the country's total foreign debt of which only about 15 percent consisted of short-term loans.[69] Bankers initially were impressed by Zimbabwe's repayment ability and its refusal to reschedule or refinance any part of its public external debt. Yet, as the repayment schedule evolved into a burden for the government by the late-1980s, bankers became worried that the government was starving the private sector of foreign exchange while investment levels remained low.[70] The Finance Minister confirmed their view in 1987 when he said that 'we had no choice but to cut [foreign currency allocations to the industrial and commercial sectors]. We mean to meet our debt obligations.'[71]

The government became especially concerned about the short-term debt to international commercial banks as it jumped from 23 percent in 1984 to 60 percent in 1991. The government gambled through the late-1980s that borrowing from private creditors would pay off in terms of strong economic growth. However, with an annual economic growth rate averaging only three percent between 1986 and 1990, the gamble partially failed. As short-term loans became due, Zimbabwe's balance of payments position became strained which led, in part, to negotiations with the IMF in 1991.[72] The government's current borrowing strategy is to obtain the most acceptable and concessionary loans available by international banks and subject the borrowing process to strict government regulations.[73] Yet, the government is returning to active borrowing from private capital markets to partially meet its financing requirements of its SAP. While the government has annually borrowed nearly $60 million from international commercial banks over the last four years, the government will seek an additional $90 million to cover the adjustment program's financing requirements.[74] Given the private creditors' historically positive relationship with Zimbabwe, the creditors most likely will reach an agreement with the government.

Zimbabwe's debt management strategy underwent a dramatic transformation in 1991 in the sense of a formal agreement to a multi-billion dollar financing plan. Rather than fearing adverse interference by IFIs in the implementation of its adjustment strategy, the government appears satisfied that it can maintain control. Under the consistent and stable leadership of the technocratic minister of finance, Bernard Chidzero, the government remains confident of its bargaining strength. Of course, a continued positive relationship with its international creditors heavily depends on the government's performance in matching the economic targets set by the ESAF.

DEBT MANAGEMENT STRATEGIES OF BRAZIL

Indebted development – the condition under which states must negotiate adjustment and debt management strategies with domestic constituents and foreign creditors – can be clearly identified in the case of Brazil. The previous chapter traced and evaluated the government's domestic economic adjustment strategies. In this section, we focus on its strategies and tactics in managing its large external debt.

The absolute size of Brazil's external debt often is considered as the crucial determining factor in a state's relationship with international creditors. In contrast to many debtor states (including Kenya and Zimbabwe), Brazil is indeed carrying a significant foreign debt. However, the size of debt is only one of several variables affecting a state's condition of indebted development. In this section, we focus on the *complex debt negotiations* that derive from a similarly complex setting involving international trade, geostrategic, and financial factors. Since Brazil negotiated debt rescheduling agreements with international creditors (unlike Kenya and Zimbabwe which simply contracted loans), the agreements are far-reaching and their outcomes are directly intertwined with the negotiating position of the international creditors. Moreover, Brazil's debt negotiations during the mid-1980s took place during its transition from military to civilian rule. The African states' relationships with their creditors are more narrowly defined because those states have far less room within which to maneuver. Thus, in analyzing the complex institutional and policy relationship between the Brazilian state and international creditors, this section will not separately examine donors, official creditors, and private creditors.

Growth and Structure of Brazil's External Debt

In absolute figures and in relation to its burden on the economy, Brazil's external indebtedness experienced substantial growth during the 1970s and early 1980s. The government's strong interventionist policy in implementing its massive economic development projects could only be sustained through substantial borrowings from either internal or external sources. The state selected the former financing policy, rather than raising taxes or relying heavily on private domestic savings. As a means to attract foreign loans, it provided guarantees for public enterprises and private companies seeking them. The government passed two federal regulations in the 1960s that laid the foundation for the escalation of foreign debt growth. First, Law 4131 (passed in 1962) permits domestic firms to borrow directly from foreign banks. Second, Resolution 63 (1967) allows domestic Brazilian banks to borrow abroad at medium- or long-term and then to relend the cruzeiro equivalent of foreign currency to domestic borrowers at relatively short-term.[75] Brazil's total external debt in 1980 amounted to $70.8 billion and reached its peak in 1987 at $124 billion where after it is expected to drop slightly to $121 billion in 1992.[76]

Brazil's government has borrowed most of its external debt from international private creditors. The government turned to international capital markets for both infrastructural and balance of payments loans. While in 1970, private creditor loans amounted to about 45 percent of the external debt in Brazil, this figure jumped to 61 percent in 1974 and to 82.5 percent in 1983. Soon after Mexico's repayment collapse in 1982, Brazil's private creditors hesitated in providing additional loans. By 1992, their allocation to Brazil had dropped to 71 percent of its total foreign debt.

An important element of this debt is the amount of short-term, balance of payments loans. The government made growing use of short-term financing mobilized, in part, by foreign branches of Brazilian commercial banks. Such loans initially were used to finance exports and were self-liquidating. By the early 1980s, these short-term loans instead were being re-lent to Brazilian firms at longer maturities and at higher spreads over London Inter-Bank Offered Rate (LIBOR). According to James Dinsmoor, these short-term liabilities had reached $15.1 billion in 1981.[77] The rapid rise of both

Table 4.7 Brazil's Total External Debt by Creditor, 1985–1992
($ million)

	1985	1986	1987	1988	1989	1990^a	1991^b	1992^b
Creditors								
Total Multilateral								
Creditors	12278	14770	16469	15203	13944	13740	12855	12803
IMF	4619	4501	3963	3327	2423	1825	1176	1742
World Bank	5305	7576	9411	8626	8316	8427	8044	7230
Others	2354	2692	3095	3249	3204	3488	3655	3831
Official Bilateral								
Creditors	12832	15369	18564	18564	18623	19835	20847	22143
Private Creditors	80970	82934	88646	81635	82495	84154	84303	85965
Total External								
Debt	106080	113073	123678	115402	115061	117729	118005	120911

^{a} Estimate ^{b} Forecast

Source   Institute of International Finance, *Brazil: Country Report* (Washington, D.C.: IIF, 1991).

Table 4.8 Brazil's Debt Ratios, 1985–1992

	1985	1986	1987	1988	1989	1990^a	1991^b	1992^b
Total External Debt (in US$ million)	106080	113073	123678	115402	115061	117729	118005	120911
Debt Ratio (% GDP)	47.6	42.2	42.0	35.1	25.7	24.9	28.6	33.7
Debt Ratio (% Exports)	361.9	449.9	430.5	313.4	296.4	324.0	326.3	312.3

^{a} Estimate ^{b} Forecast

Source   Institute of International Finance, *Brazil: Country Report* (Washington, D.C.: IIF, 1991).

private creditor loans and short-term finance loans during the 1970s was suggestive of the difficult repayment period of the 1980s. A series of massive rescheduling negotiations, mounting interest arrears, and the 1987 moratorium can all be linked to the strategic borrowing decisions of the previous decade.

As the inflow of net foreign capital began to dry up in the early 1980s, Brazil was faced with a serious *repayment dilemma*: keep current with its interest payments with the intention of maintaining its credit standing with the international creditor regime *or* accumulate interest arrears and utilize the money for other purposes. During the mid-1980s, Brazil implemented the former policy. According to the Ministry of Finance, net transfers abroad between 1983 and 1986 amounted to $45.2 billion in interest or, in equivalent terms, to 3.5 percent of GDP per year.[78] Brazil thus became a capital exporter, a critical problem for a developing country still requiring a large and growing capital base. The burden of such large transfers fell upon expenditure reduction, import contraction, and export growth. Yet, Brazil's trade surplus in 1986 had fallen by one-third over the previous year. At this point, the government turned to the other debt bargaining strategy, that of withholding interest payments. Accumulated arrears steadily increased during the late-1980s to reach over $12 billion in 1991. The growth and size of these arrears have created obstacles in government debt negotiations with international creditors.

Another indicator of Brazil's indebtedness is its debt service ratio. The combination of heavy international borrowing and persistent reliance on imported goods during the 1970s resulted in a rising debt service ratio (in terms of total exports) from 35 percent in 1970 to 65.6 percent in 1979. By 1982, that figure had risen to 78.2 percent, a climb of over fifteen percentage points from the previous year. The growth in the ratio became increasingly critical as international financial obligations impinged upon the level of foreign currency reserves. Foreign reserve coverage of monthly imports fell from 4.1 months in 1979 to only 1.2 months in 1982 and to 1.8 months in 1983.[79] Yet, by the mid- to late-1980s, the government was able to lower the debt service ratio. Regular debt rescheduling agreements, some new money, limited debt reduction, and overall expansion of the trade balance significantly reduced the ratio to a projected figure of 31.1 percent in 1992.[80]

One early observer of Brazil's debt crisis suggests that the debt crisis may not have been brought about by the magnitude of the outstanding debt, but by the *restricted terms of borrowing*.[81] Indeed, there had been a shortening of average debt maturities and a rise in interest rates during the 1970s. The maturity structure changed radically during this period due, in part, to the substantial growth in the private bank composition of the total debt, coupled with an increase in risk arising from instability in the world capital market. Whereas in 1970, 26.3 percent of the loans took over fifteen years to mature, in 1980 only two percent did so. Short- to medium- terms maturity periods rose substantially during this decade. The bunching of loans is indicated by the 45 percent figure of loans in 1980 which had

Table 4.9 *Brazil's Debt Service Indicators, 1985–1992*

	1985	1986	1987	1988	1989	1990[a]	1991[b]	1992[b]
Total Debt Service ($ million)	13053	14205	13805	16164	15896	14125	12160	12022
Debt Service Ratio (% exports)	44.5	56.5	48.1	43.9	40.9	38.9	33.6	31.1

[a] Estimate [b] Forecast

Source Institute of International Finance, *Brazil: Country Report* (Washington, D.C.: IIF, 1991).

to be repaid within five years. By 1985, the average maturity figure had dropped to 8.9 years in 1985.

Brazil also experienced increases in the interest rates charged to its external bank loans. One indicator is the rise of interest rates from the LIBOR level of 6.5 percent in 1977 to 19 percent in 1981. The *World Financial Markets* calculated that, with a concentration of about 80 percent in dollar-denominated loans, the cumulative cost of the interest rate increase for Brazil was $10 billion.[82] Since the early 1980s, the average interest rate on Brazil's external debt dropped to 9.2 percent in 1988 and is expected to decrease to 8.8 percent in 1991.[83]

Brazil's debt experience of the 1980s has thus been quite varied. Prior to Mexico's moratorium of 1982, Brazil actively pursued foreign bank loans in anticipation of continued export expansion. In the face of a severe credit collapse following 1982, the government reacted mainly to the short-term demands from the debt crisis. Yet, since the mid-1980s, Brazil gradually has sought to manage the crisis from a long-term perspective. There has been some limited indication of success. Brazil's total external debt as a percentage of GDP fell from 48 percent in 1984 to a projected 33.7 percent in 1992. Additionally, the ratio of total debt as a percentage of exports also is forecast to drop slightly from 338.8 percent in 1984 to 312.3 percent in 1992. Although the government still owes over $120 billion in foreign loans, the *relative burden* of the debt has become less severe. In the next section, I will review the main debt bargaining strategies that have led to Brazil's current debt position.

Debt Management Strategies of the 1980s

As can be expected from a country with massive indebtedness, Brazil has had lengthy and intense relationships with many different international creditors. In terms of negotiating debt agreements, the main creditor organization has been the International Monetary Fund. During the early 1980s, an IMF agreement was the most influential factor in obtaining capital from international commercial banks and from the Paris Club group of creditor governments. This linkage between IMF-approved adjustment programs and inflow of credit loosened somewhat after the debt rescheduling accord of 1988. Nevertheless, the government's relationship with other creditors remains heavily reliant upon the nature of its ties to the IMF through formal cross-conditionalities.

Following the second oil price shock of 1979 and the failure of Brazil's domestic economic policies of the early 1980s, the government turned to the IMF for new resources and an economic adjustment agreement. The agreement was modelled after the standard IMF accord: avoidance of balance of payments problems by generating trade surpluses and restricting domestic demand by reducing the level of economic activity through cutting of government budget deficits. The IMF agreement made several specific target objectives: a decrease in the public sector deficit from six percent of GDP in 1982 to 3.5 percent in 1983; the gradual elimination of state subsidies granted to agricultural interests; a rise in the trade surplus to $6 billion in 1983; and a modified exchange rate policy to pace devaluations with the rate of inflation.[84]

In return to agreeing with the terms of this accord, the government was to receive external financing from the IMF, commercial banks, and a rescheduled arrangement with Paris Club creditors. The *financing strategy* approved by the IMF contained four parts: 1) the provision of drawings of up to $5.9 billion from the IMF through 1985; 2) the rescheduling of $3.8 billion in debt amortization and interest payments; 3) a $9 billion extension of inter-bank lines between Brazilian and foreign banks; and 4) $13.2 billion in new credits and refinancing with international private banks. The latter figure included a new money facility of $4.4 billion from banks to cover the immediate payment of interest for previous loans and, since international creditors and Brazilian financial authorities rely on export revenues to generate foreign exchange earnings, the agreement provided another $8.8 billion of short-term trade credits to finance raw material imports and Brazilian exports. The total IMF-sponsored package amounted to nearly $30 billion.

Even with the infusion of new money and rescheduling of previous loans, Brazil was not able to fully comply with the IMF agreement as indicated by the seven letters of intent signed between January 1983 and December 1984. Indeed, three months after formal approval of the stabilization program, the IMF suspended a scheduled disbursement of $2 billion because the government had failed to reduce the public sector deficit.[85] An important lesson from this early debt agreement is that while the current account improved, capital flows did not; that is, the government was in a stronger position to improve its trade account than to manage its domestic economy. Brazil's external debt strategy at this time emphasized punctual repayment, a growing trade surplus, and a net inflow of foreign capital. Yet, by the end of period covered by this agreement, the government was faced with a serious domestic economic disequilibrium marked by an average annual inflation rate of 227 percent in 1985.

By 1986, Brazil's debt management strategy began to fray at the edges. A review of the country's external account data illustrates the limited and temporary success it had achieved in the previous years.[86] Although the trade surplus had only fallen by about five percent from 1984 to 1985, that figure dropped another 34 percent in the following year. The trade balance reflected the deteriorating performance of exports and the greater demand for imports as the domestic economy grew at an annual rate of 8.3 percent in 1985 and 7.5 percent in 1986. During this period, the total foreign debt expanded from $106 billion to $113 billion and, more importantly, about half of Brazil's total debt to international private banks ($35 billion) became due in 1985. By 1986, Brazil experienced a dramatic increase in its current account deficit, from –$273 million in 1985 to –$5.3 billion in 1986 due largely to the fall in the trade surplus. Yet, at the very time of a mounting financial requirement, net equity investment plummeted from $1.3 billion in 1985 to just $177 million in the following year. Moreover, investment as a percentage of GDP also had fallen from 23 percent during the late-1970s to 17.7 percent in the mid-1980s.[87] Finally, Brazil's foreign reserves level also sharply deteriorated by 45 percent between 1985 and 1986 as the government redirected those resources to cover the current account deficit. By the beginning of 1987, the government's debt management strategy clearly had suffered from the failure to use the trade surplus to adequately service the foreign debt during the period of deterioration in the domestic economy. At this time, the government turned to a new debt management strategy.

The Debt Moratorium of 1987
Before debt negotiations reopened, further jockeying for position occurred on 20 February 1987, when Brazil declared a moratorium on the interest payments on its medium- and long-term external debt to commercial banks. The moratorium was accompanied by reassurances that it was only part of a longer-term bargaining strategy, and that Brazil would not seek cancellation of the debt or seek concessionary interest rates below market levels. The

government stressed that the suspension was a temporary move to protect the depletion of the country's hard-currency reserves.[88] On announcing the moratorium, minister of finance Dilson Funaro said that 'we didn't break any contractual clauses. We're suspending remittance during the period of negotiations.' President Jose Sarney further stated that Brazil was buying time 'to avoid political instability, recession, unemployment and social crisis,' and that payments would be resumed once the negotiations with creditor banks were complete.[89]

The government's decision to suspend payments on only medium- and long-term commercial bank debt reflected a decision-making process fully cognizant of the potential ramifications of a comprehensive moratorium against multilateral institutions, foreign governments, and private banks. President Sarney and his advisers feared that a moratorium against the industrial governments would risk a cut-off of export-import bank credits, while a moratorium against the multilateral banks (IMF, World Bank, IDB) would jeopardize future loans Brazil hoped to receive for infrastructural investment.[90]

The banks took action to forestall the spread of the moratorium to other countries and to protect themselves in any event. The banks apparently feared two things: the *spread of the moratorium to other large debtors* and the *pressure bank regulators placed on the banking community* to tighten up accounting and business practices over deteriorating loans.[91]

Based on these fears, the banks implemented several decisions to limit the negative effects of the moratorium. First, they introduced a series of graduated sanctions to pressure Brazil to lift the moratorium, and thereby to prevent the reclassification of the loans. They immediately curtailed $60 million in short-term and commercial and inter-bank credits, and the advisory committee to the banks refused to endorse Brazil's request for a sixty day renewal of short-term commercial lines of credit, leaving the decision to individual banks.[92] The banks decided to renew Brazil's short-term credit lines that were due to expire on 31 March for only thirty days. Then, on 1 April, U.S. banks put Brazilian loans on a non-accrual status,[93] which led to the downgrading of some of the banks' own debt and a fall in their share prices. In a parallel move, the U.S. Inter-agency Country Exposure Risk Committee (ICERC) classified Brazilian loans as substandard.[94]

Second, the banks moved to preempt a spread of the moratorium by completing pending negotiations with other debtors, thus helping to isolate Brazil. Within days after the moratorium was declared, commercial banks allowed Chile to 'retime' its interest payments and granted Venezuela a reduction on its spread over LIBOR interest rates (after having ignored

Venezuela's demands for ten months), while creditor governments cooperated in securing a bridging loan for Argentina.[95]

Third, individual banks began to exercise their relative power to defend their assets and their remaining foreign loans. The primary policy move for many large banks was the provisioning of capital in order to reduce their exposure in relation to their total assets. On 19 May 1987, Citicorp was the first major bank to allocate a substantial provision against possible losses on its outstanding loans. By setting aside $5 billion (a 150 percent increase in its loan-loss reserves), Citicorp sought to protect itself directly against the possibility of borrowers' defaults. By the end of 1987, U.S. banks had added $19 billion to their loan-loss reserves.[96]

As Brazil's confrontational stance continued through 1987, international banks solidified their position against the government by drawing on their relative strength. They imposed severe cuts in trade lines to Brazil, which worsened the country's balance-of-payments position, since it had to draw funds from its foreign reserves to cover the trade credit gap. The banks also doubled the spreads on trade finance loans as a response to their perception of a greater sovereign lending risk. Recognition surfaced in the private sector that Brazil was denying itself necessary access to external sources of capital. With both a constriction and increased costs of obtaining trade credit, Brazilian private firms did not have sufficient funds to finance capital goods imports. Thus, the international commercial banks took the hard-line tactical position of squeezing Brazil's traders and government in order to force a resumption of interest payments.[97]

However, by fall 1987, there were indications that both sides had shifted in their *tactical responses* to each other's position and were willing to make some concessions. Given the international banks' short-term priority of resuming interest payments, the lead banks began to soften their hard-line stance. The moratorium was costing the creditors around $500 million a month, which by September 1987 amounted to a total of $3.5 billion in interest arrears.[98] The rupture in interest payments brought down the price of bank shares, and the continual erosion through discounting of the value of loans resulted in a critical review of bank portfolios by U.S. bank regulators.[99]

The costs to Brazil were also high. According to a U.S. bank's internal memo, both the World Bank and various export credit agencies had cut disbursements to Brazil leading to a shortage in trade credit.[100] William Rhodes of Citibank calculated that the interest payment moratorium cost Brazil some $1.5 billion in lost interest rate reductions from delayed restructuring, cancellation or higher costs of trade lines, loss of new funds from multilateral agencies, and capital outflows.[101] According to a U.S. Treasury official involved in these negotiations, Brazil's short-term financial status in November was vulnerable to bank leverage. During the October stock market crash, banks withdrew money from Brazil to obtain cash for their shareholders. Moreover, the cutting of trade lines resulted in a drop of trade loan maturity to only fifteen days, which constrained Brazilian traders. Without sufficient short-term loans, Brazilian inter-bank funds were drying up, affecting their capacity to finance Brazilian projects.[102]

By the time of the ICERC meeting in fall 1987, the injection of regulatory agencies examining the classification of loans and the threat of their being reclassified as 'value-impaired' forced Brazil and the banks to the negotiating table by winter.[103] In the face of these pressures, both sides sought to find common interests to ratify an agreement.

Finance minister Luis Carlos Bresser Pereira maintains that by August he had realized that the conventional approach of interest financing with adjustment had failed, and that a new approach, based on some type of debt relief, would be required. Increasing loan-loss reserves is quite a different tactic from actually writing down the debt. Although Bresser Pereira became aware of various solutions involving conversion of the debt to discounted bonds guaranteed by the creditor countries through the IMF and World Bank, and in fact proposed the creation of a debt authority in September 1987, he also knew he could not wait for global consensus on a new approach. He therefore presented a proposal to the bank advisory committee for a 'partial and negotiated conversion of present debt into new bonds, either with the same face value but fixed rates of interest below market rates, or with a discounted value and interest at market rates.'[104]

From Bresser Pereira's perspective, the banks felt threatened and the U.S. government considered itself challenged by a debtor country taking a new initiative on the debt problem: namely, the need for a mandatory discount on the debt. But, the banks were not ready for such an innovation, and they rejected the proposal out of hand. By October, Bresser Pereira had another plan ready which called for new credits of $10.4 billion to finance the interest due with no spread over LIBOR and with voluntary rather than mandatory conversion. Although this plan was supported by both business and military leaders in Brazil, the banks' reaction still remained noticeably cool. Nevertheless, Bresser Pereira's rapid presentation of alternative plans indicated his desire to find an acceptable compromise.

It is interesting, at this point, to compare briefly the skills of the finance ministers in Brazil, Kenya, and Zimbabwe in designing and implementing debt management strategies. Both George Saitoti of Kenya and Bernard Chidzero of Zimbabwe long have been recognized as superb economic technocrats who work well and easily cooperate with officials from the

IFIs. Their common drawback is the political and financial constraints which impair the implementation of any bargaining strategy. As Paul Volcker, former chairman of the Federal Reserve Board recently said in comparing the Latin American and African economic crises, 'Africa is a different kind of situation. It never has had implications for the world financial system. It is not a financial crisis in the same sense (as in Latin America). It is a development crisis.'[105] Neither Saitoti nor Chidzero are in a strategically powerful bargaining position with international banks.

The banks held firm in their demand for a resumption of interest payments prior to any rescheduling agreement. They demanded, and received, a 'token' payment of $500 million by late October. This payment and a later one of $1 billion were held in escrow until agreement was reached on Brazil's debt and on lifting of the moratorium. The stalemate between the banks and Brazil finally ended in November 1987 with the signing of a short-term package serving as an interim debt agreement. Brazil obtained a short-term loan of $3 billion from the banks, carrying a 0.875 percent spread over LIBOR and payable by 30 June 1988, when the longer-term finance package would be in place. In exchange for the short-term loan, Brazil resumed interest payments, agreed to consult with the IMF, paid all interest in arrears, and provided a 0.25 percent fee, plus an additional 0.25 percent fee to banks for early participation.[106]

Bresser Pereira privately decided with Sarney that, if an agreement was not reached by 29 January 1988, Brazil would dismiss the advisory committee and negotiate the conversion approach with individual banks.[107] Bresser Pereira did not have a chance to complete these negotiations, however: domestic opposition to his policies grew, with political leaders calling the interim accord a capitulation to the banks, inflation continuing to resist efforts at control, and resentment intensifying toward his new wealth tax plan. On 20 December 1987, he resigned when he became convinced that, in his words, the government was not 'ready to seriously fight the public deficit by demanding effective sacrifices from workers and from business enterprises.'[108] From his perspective, Brazil needed, first, to adopt strong measures vis-à-vis creditors to reduce the external debt *and*, second, to pursue internal adjustment. This public statement was one of the first to recognize the crucial linkage between domestic economic adjustment and foreign debt management. Interestingly, his understanding reflects the basic argument made by this study.

Frustrated by the lack of progress on all sides, President Sarney apparently decided in favor of a more orthodox approach to Brazil's debt problems. He replaced Bresser Pereira with Mailson Ferrera da Nobrega who moved quickly: in February 1988, he reached a tentative agreement

The State and Debt Management Strategies 149

with the bank advisory committee by which the banks would provide $5.8 billion in new loans to refinance the past due interest, restore short-term credits, and reschedule $61 billion of Brazil's long- and medium-term debt. In return, Brazil brought its 1988 interest payments up to date and moved to make some domestic economic reforms. In a separate negotiating process, Japan reportedly was insisting on a prior accord with the IMF, commercial creditors, and the Paris Club before committing up to $4 billion in loans for investment projects.[109] Since, however, as one banker mentioned, '75 percent of the game of lending is interest repayment,' Brazil's acceptance of keeping interest payments current had lessened the urgency of an IMF plan.[110] During this preliminary discussion, Brazilian officials made it clear that the government would accept a rescheduling agreement only if it allowed Brazil to *consult* with the IMF on economic policy issues instead of imposing on it a strict commitment to a traditional IMF austerity program. The banks were willing to cast aside the traditional linkage of an IMF austerity package with a new money accord in order to be repaid, and Brazil agreed to begin talks with the IMF.

In this instance, the relative bargaining strength of Brazil clearly dwarfs that of the African cases. While Brazil could persuade international banks that a prior agreement with the IMF was not necessary, neither Kenya nor Zimbabwe have the power resources to successfully separate an IMF accord from any other creditor agreements. Although Kenya has been allowed some slippage in implementing adjustment, such slippage only has taken place within an IMF-approved program.

Brazil was seeking a general plan of adjustment without having to set specific economic targets for each component. Although they still needed some agreement with the IMF to help the negotiations with creditor banks, the Brazilian authorities understood that the possibility of the debt being declared 'value-impaired' posed in some ways a greater threat to the banks than to themselves.[111] Brazil was betting that if it undertook some economic reforms without any firm IMF agreement, the banks would finalize a major rescheduling and refinancing package. Nobrega therefore proposed to freeze public sector wages (including those of the armed forces) and to sell off public firms to reduce the large government budget deficit. His efforts were initially stymied, however, as Bresser Pereira's had been earlier. President Sarney, under heavy pressure from military ministers, state officials, the labor minister, the PMDB, and even producers who feared a fall in consumers' purchasing power, authorized wage increases over Nobrega's threat to resign.[112]

After an intense week of pork-barrel politics and executive distribution of 'favors,' accompanied by rumors of a military coup if a parliamentary system were adopted, the constituent assembly approved, with a surprisingly large majority, a five-year presidential system rather than a parliamentary system with a four-year presidential term. This personal victory gave Sarney some much-needed political room to maneuver and was a crucial condition in the movement toward a debt agreement because he no longer had to contend with the issue of the length of his term and could negotiate without fear of immediate electoral consequences. At this point, he did heed Nobrega's advice and announced a two-month freeze on public sector wages, hoping to spur the banks on to approve the debt accord. In May 1988, an IMF mission arrived in Brazil to work out the basis for a new IMF loan and to conclude an agreement with the commercial banks which were still demanding IMF approval before signing the debt accord. In early June, the IMF agreed to grant Brazil a stand-by loan of $1.5 billion, half of which was to be paid upon signature of the agreement in July or August.[113] Then, on 23 June, the bank advisory committee signed the debt accord, rescheduling $62 billion and providing $5.2 billion of new credits. In July, the IMF letter of intent was signed and, by September, a sufficient number of banks had agreed to the debt accord to ensure its approval. The first disbursement of $4 billion of new money was made in November 1988.[114]

Similar to Mexico's 1986 accord, this agreement placed emphasis on a multi-year rescheduling strategy in contrast to refinancing every one or two years. Thus, Brazil and the banks agreed to reschedule $62 billion, equivalent to 95 percent of the medium- and long-term debt owed to international banks, over twenty years, with an eight-year grace period, at an interest rate margin of 13/16 percentage points over LIBOR. This figure was significantly lower than the average Latin American margin of about 1.7 percentage points and Brazil's previous margin of 1.5 percent.[115] It represented a compromise between Bresser Pereira's proposal of no spread, and the previous spread of 1.5 percent, over LIBOR.

Under the accord, Brazil received $5.2 billion in new money to refinance interest due in 1987, 1988, and the first half of 1989 also at a 13/16 percent per year spread above LIBOR, to be repaid over twelve years with a five-year grace period. This package contained four different options to attract bank participation: a) $750 million in co-financing with the World Bank; b) $2.85 billion in parallel financing with the World Bank; c) a new $600 million medium-term credit line to finance exports and imports; and d) a subscription of $1 billion in new money bonds.[116] An expanded menu of options offered a greater range of choices for individual banks as they decided whether to provide new money or to exit from the agreement. These options included exit bonds, debt-equity conversions, and up-front commissions to banks that agreed to the accord quickly.[117] Although the banks had rejected Bresser Pereira's attempt at debt relief through a debt-bond conversion for half of Brazil's commercial debt, they responded positively to the much more limited relief implied in the exit bond deal. Finally, Brazil immediately resumed interest repayment by remitting $1.35 billion to cover interest accrued in the first part of 1988.

Nevertheless, implementation of the international accord proved difficult within Brazil as the government's ability to sustain its own austerity policies was challenged. The wage freeze implemented by Nobrega in April and May 1988 was ruled unconstitutional and was undermined when individual ministers granted unauthorized wage increases. Under the new constitution, Congress was granted the authority to approve cuts in federal government subsidies to states, which it was reluctant to do. A battle over congressional approval of a reduced budget loomed in October 1988, and negotiations of an anti-inflation social pact between unions and the private sector broke down in the same month. Brazil, at this time, was representative of what Stephan Haggard and Robert Kaufman refer to as an 'unconsolidated democracy' in which newly elected leaders face challenges in implementing economic adjustment programs.[118]

Indeed, in the year following the signing of the debt accord, actions on both sides of the negotiating table demonstrated the problems of continued support and implementation of the agreement. In early 1989, the World Bank refused to release a $600 million loan package for the refurbishment of the country's power system since Brazil was unwilling to guarantee that the funds would not be used to build a nuclear power plant. The failure to approve this sector loan put in jeopardy another $600 million commercial bank loan package and a $450 million co-financing loan agreement from the Japanese government, both of which were signed in September 1988.[119] The government used this rupture with the World Bank as a means to place pressure on its other creditors. It argued that without their funds, the government would lack the capacity to pay during the upcoming bunching of payments. The government forecast $11 billion in interest payments due between April and December 1989, yet, these payments would not reduce the total debt outstanding.[120] Brazil then used the refusal by the World Bank and its depleting foreign reserve level as justification for having to suspend debt interest payments. This so-called *white moratorium* linked payments of debt interest directly to Brazil's foreign reserves position. In July 1989, Brazil suspended a $812 million interest payment to its Paris Club creditors; another delay in paying $980 million followed in January 1990.[121]

Debt Management Strategies of the 1990s

Brazil's next bargaining move was the suggestion that it would resume interest payments when the IMF provided $600 million in emergency financing. The creditors were anticipating an IMF agreement since, with that package, Brazil would be provided the funds to clear its growing arrears with the external creditors. The IMF reentered, once again, the complex negotiations with the government and with commercial banks. The IMF's involvement also reflected the tensions among the several types of negotiators over their objectives in these negotiations: the IMF sought domestic economic adjustments; the banks pursued the elimination of arrears; and the government focused on external accounts and the impact of negotiations of any debt agreement on the upcoming presidential election. The IMF agreement – the cornerstone of a more comprehensive debt rescheduling package – was not to be achieved until fall 1990.

Following the election of Fernando Collor de Mello as president and his appointment of Zelia Cardoso de Mello as finance minister, Brazil's debt bargaining strategy recognized both the important role of the IMF and the fragile relations among the international creditors. Cardoso de Mello stated that no formal talks with either commercial banks or Paris Club creditors would be held until the signing of an IMF agreement.[122] In addition, Brazil would continue its suspension of interest payments to the banks while maintaining current its payments to the IMF. In separating the IMF from other international creditors and in penalizing commercial banks by withholding interest payments, Brazil sought to divide and weaken the creditor bargaining position.

Yet, the issue of accumulated arrears surfaced as an immediate problem for Brazil and as a specific bargaining chip used by international banks. In July 1990, ICERC (the U.S. banking regulatory agency) lowered the rating of Brazil's foreign debt to value-impaired and ordered U.S. banks to write-off 20 percent of their outstanding loans. The lending banks struck back at Brazil along several fronts. Representatives of the bank advisory committee issued statements condemning Brazil's policy toward interest payments. A Bank of Tokyo official said that 'Brazil can no longer mock the banks.' John Reed, chairman of Citicorp, pointedly remarked that Brazil had lost $3 billion of short-term commercial and inter-bank credit lines during the payment suspension and, moreover, the banks had shortened the periods of maturity and increased the cost in providing loans.[123] The banks also sought to intervene in the negotiations between the IMF and Brazil by raising the issue of arrears as an obstacle to an IMF agreement. This issue, along with disagreements over the target figures for inflation rate and the public sector deficit, forced the temporary suspension of the debt negotiations.

By September, both the IMF and Brazil had returned to the bargaining table on the basis of each offering substantial concessions. The latter met a $30 million interest payment on exit bonds which were part of the debt agreement of 1988. The government also announced its intention of clearing arrears with the Paris Club creditors. The former provided its own concession by agreeing with Brazil that the $2 billion standby loan should not be tied to the accumulated arrears problem with the commercial banks.[124] The letter of intent, which was signed in mid-September, included no promise to resume interest payments to the banks. Brazil agreed to the IMF program because, according to Cardoso de Mello, 'the most important thing about the IMF agreement is not the amount but that it paves the way for negotiations with the Paris Club and the private creditors.'[125]

The 1990 IMF agreement permitted Brazil and its creditors to shift the focus of negotiations to the settlement of Brazil's debt with its private creditors. The stage thus was set for another round of debt negotiations, but the government and the banks were seeking two different objectives. The former sought to link the clearing of accumulated arrears to a wider agreement on its foreign debt. It realized that the banks were clearly concerned about the accumulation of arrears. The government hoped that, with offers to pay only some of the total arrears, the banks would be willing to make compromises on the bulk of the debt. The latter pressed for an immediate arrears agreement which, they argued, must be set prior to any other debt agreement.

Brazil issued the first negotiating proposal in October 1990. The Collor government argued that its 'capacity to pay' stood at $18.2 billion and most of this would be distributed to cover Brazil's internal debt service ($9.2 billion) and to bolster the country's foreign reserves ($2.4 billion). Only $1.9 billion of the total amount would be paid to Brazil's international commercial creditors. Both the banks and the U. S. government sent signals that the absence of any concession regarding the accumulated interest arrears could delay the signature of the IMF agreement with Brazil.[126] The banks countered with a demand of an initial payment on interest of at least $2.5 billion with the remaining $5.5 billion of accumulated arrears to be repaid by five-year bonds. The commercial banks then turned to government creditors to place pressure on Brazil. According to the *Latin American Weekly Report*, 'at the request of the Japanese government, with clear backing from Washington, the World Bank put off consideration of a US$450 million loan package' for a couple of weeks.[127] Although this delay lasted only for a few weeks, pressure from the U.S. continued into

December as the Bush administration called for a delay in the approval of an earlier IMF standby program.

The gap between the negotiators narrowed in February 1991 when each felt external constraints. The first of these constraints came from the government of Brazil's announcement that the 1990 trade surplus ($11 billion) was 31.6 percent lower than that of 1989. This figure strengthened the government's 'capacity to pay' argument. The bargaining position of the banks similarly was affected by signals from the U.S. government concerning an upcoming ICERC meeting. A senior banker reportedly stated that 'the only way to avoid it [a regulator-mandated write-down] is a breakthrough on the arrearages.'[128] In January, both sides apparently reconsidered their immediate objectives and each made limited concessions. Brazil agreed to partially lift its 18-month moratorium on interest payments by raising its repayment offer to $1.5 billion. The banks were willing to accept this small amount provided the government separated this arrears agreement from a major restructuring program. This initial accord developed by April into a formal agreement on the arrears issue. The agreement stated that 25 percent ($2 billion) of the overdue interest would be paid in 1991 with an immediate instalment of $900 million as soon as the agreement was formally signed, and another $1.1 billion in monthly instalments between May and December of that year. The remaining $6 billion would be exchanged for bonds maturing in ten years.[129]

With the resolution of the accumulated arrears problem, the most recent concern for Brazil and its creditors has been the restructuring and refinancing of Brazil's outstanding foreign debt and another negotiating round with the IMF. Parallel discussions started once again in 1991 and continued into 1992 with international banks and the IMF. Although Brazil had signed a letter of agreement with the IMF in September 1990, it was not approved by the Fund's board. The issue for the latter was not the accumulated arrears, but it rather concerned Brazil's failure to meet agreed economic targets. Since the commercial creditors were unwilling to commit themselves to a major debt agreement prior to an approved IMF deal, the government worked hard to rewrite a new and more realistic letter of intent. The agreement with the IMF, reached in October 1991, emphasized a major reduction in the monthly inflation rate (from 16 percent at that time to 7 percent in 1992 and to 2 percent by mid-1993) and significant cuts in the budget deficit.[130]

Armed with this letter of intent, Brazil returned to the creditor banks with a wide-ranging debt proposal. Brazil was hopeful that, with a commitment to fiscal adjustment reforms, as stipulated by the IMF, the creditor banks and the U.S. government would agree to a debt agreement linked directly to the Brady Plan. The overall bargaining objective for Brazil focused on a significant reduction in interest payments over the course of a multi-year rescheduling agreement. In order for commercial creditors to accept this proposal, Brazil took a 'menu of options' approach by offering creditors several options. During the latter part of 1991, the negotiating positions taken by the two sides demonstrated their mutual support of the menu approach. The year ended with both actors transmitting counter-proposals incorporating relatively minor alterations to the menu agreement.[131]

At the beginning of 1992, Brazil's debt bargaining strategy has focused on the 'normalization' of relations with the IFIs by reaching agreements with the IMF, the Paris Club, and, finally, international banks.[132] In January 1992, Brazil signed a $2.1 billion IMF stand-by agreement which will be given to Brazil in seven parcels during the next 18 months. The agreement was meant to release another $7 billion worth of trade and investment credits that were being held by several financial institutions.[133] The IMF stipulated that the conditionalities were binding only through June 1992 after which Brazil's economic performance was open to review.[134]

Paris Club negotiations followed the agreement with the IMF. On 27 February 1992, Brazil reached an agreement under which the government will pay $4.1 billion in 1992 and 1993 with the remaining outstanding debt of $20 billion to be rescheduled over the next 14 years.[135]

The third phase of Brazil's current bargaining strategy was the completion of negotiations with international bank creditors. Brazil was seeking a comprehensive agreement that would 'address the external financing requirements in the program period, while satisfactorily contributing to a viable balance of payments position in the medium term.'[136] Creditor banks rejected this sweeping framework and, instead, focused more specifically on the amount of money to be deposited by Brazil to serve as a guarantee against any future default. Brazil proposed a reserve account equivalent of six months' interest, while the banks responded with a recommendation of 15 months' interest.[137] Finally, on 9 July 1992, Brazil and the bank advisory committee reached an agreement that will reschedule and reduce its $44 billion debt owed to international commercial banks. The negotiators agreed that the guarantee fund should have $3.2 billion, far below the proposal by the banks. The agreement is subject to approval by the Senate in Brazil and by the hundreds of Brazil's creditor banks. Each bank will choose among six options, including the reduction of the unpaid principal of existing loans by 35 percent, reduction of interest owed by a similar amount, and offering new loans.[138]

The bargaining strategies of both Brazil and international creditors became clear following the moratorium of 1987 and the debt agreement of 1988. In the years following these events, Brazil has emphasized the importance of its *external accounts*, while the creditors often have focused on the country's *internal accounts*. Specifically, the Brazilian negotiators have argued that their capacity to pay the interest to creditors is based on the size of the trade surplus and of the foreign reserve level. During years with a declining surplus and/or reserves, Brazil has argued that it prefers additional credit from creditors to drawing from its own resources. The creditors, however, have followed a bargaining strategy that relies more on the current state of the domestic economy and on the policy reforms called for by the IMF to resuscitate the economy. Creditors often point to specific economic targets such as the inflation rate or the budget deficit. While there may be some conflict between creditor institutions over priorities (international banks favor immediate payments to erase any accumulated arrears; the IMF seeks economic policy reforms), there is now a fundamental convergence of views over their bargaining tactics as witnessed by the 1992 debt agreements.

Brazil's bargaining tactics during the late-1980s and early 1990s are derived from two sources: the perception of economic strength in the external accounts and the perception of domestic political weakness. The government has used the threat of a moratorium during periods of accumulated trade surplus or foreign reserves. From this position of relative strength, the government sought to impose pressure on its creditors. Second, it also used the potential instability arising from the transition to civilian and democratic rule to its advantage. It has argued that at this time the government must respond to the economic demands of the population. While some members of government may agree with the long-term objectives and goals of the IMF (eg, sustainable economic growth), they also may express their concern over the short-term and adverse effects of IMF programs upon the domestic economy. Both the Sarney and Collor administrations have argued that, while hyperinflation and massive budget deficits clearly are destructive, the creditor proposals that would control those problems have not been sufficiently sensitive to the political costs arising from the resultant recession.

CONCLUSION

Indebted development is a condition that fosters *challenges and opportunities* for states pursuing adjustment and debt management strategies.

All of these states, no matter how powerful or weak, seek to take advantage of this condition. However, each state brings with it to the debt negotiating table differing power resources and bargaining skills in an effort to manipulate and, perhaps, regulate the adverse outcome of the negotiations. In comparing the three cases presented in this chapter, we must consider the range of their power capabilities. A state's ability to effectively use their power depends on the size of their overall debt, the viability of alternative sources of financing, their geostrategic relationship to powerful creditor governments, and their competence and experience in international debt negotiations.

Kenya has followed a generally consistent orthodox strategy toward international creditors. There has been a very strong congruence of interests shared by the state and by the IFIs. Both accept the financing role of foreign capital in the adjustment process and the maintenance of a creditworthy debt management strategy with external creditors. The state has cooperated with most creditors (and particularly the IMF) as a means to enhance its bargaining power from within an orthodox strategy. One might argue that cooperation for Kenya simply implies an inability to implement a strategy of 'defection.' Yet, until very recently, Kenya has had considerable success in obtaining foreign credits while ignoring specific components of conditionality.

In contrast to Kenya, *Zimbabwe* pointedly pursued a different bargaining strategy. For ideological and pragmatic reasons, the government sought to avoid heavy financial reliance on the IMF, while keeping out of debt arrears with international commercial banks. By doing so, the state was fairly successfully in attracting private credit without IMF conditionality. With varying degrees of success through the 1980s, Zimbabwe used this capital to finance its 'home-grown' version of economic adjustment and thus to remain relatively independent from external creditors. But with the high cost of private international capital, mounting international and national economic constraints, and the emphasis on economic liberalization pushed by creditor governments, Zimbabwe's options narrowed and, by 1991, began an its own neo-orthodox SAP.

As a country with a diversified economic base, expansive economic potential, and a massive foreign debt, *Brazil* is in a stronger position to maneuver and to bargain with external creditors than the African countries. Given its substantial need for net capital inflow, the state has contracted loans from a variety of sources. In part, this tactic has added to its bargaining strength since it can, simultaneously, make promises and threats to different creditors in an attempt to divide and weaken their bargaining position. Brazil's debt negotiations have been much more complex and, in relative terms, much more important to international creditors than those of nearly any other African country. Brazil's relationship with its creditors is a prime example of what Jonathan Aronson referred to as a 'mutual hostage' condition, in which both the state and the creditors oppose each other while also needing each other to complete an agreement.[139] Cross-conditionalities, imposed on debtors by the IFIs, are less consequential for Brazil than for the African cases. In recognizing this symbiotic relationship, Brazil is in a position to resist the creditors' efforts in forming an effective and cohesive creditor regime.

While Kenya, Zimbabwe, and Brazil differ in terms of their power capabilities, each also share some similarities. Although they differ in regards to the specific *content* of their strategies, all three states repeatedly have attempted to exert control over the *timing and direction* of their economic adjustment strategy. In recent years, the IFIs (especially the IMF) have allowed considerable slippage within approved adjustment programs as long as the governments appear to be making progress toward economic adjustment objectives. That is, the IFIs generally have permitted disagreements over the specific targets and priorities within programs if the states have accepted the principles (and language) of orthodox adjustment and debt management.

In all cases, the state, in contracting and bargaining with external creditors, must take into account the domestic political reaction of the agreements. Thus, this chapter and the previous one comprise two sides of the same coin; that of indebted development. The next chapter will analyze the distributive outcomes of this indebted development condition.

NOTES

1. Republic of Kenya, *Statistical Abstract* (Nairobi: Government Printer, 1984), p. 10.
2. Republic of Kenya, *Budget Rationalization Programme* (Nairobi: Government Printer, 1986), pp. 5-6.
3. Republic of Kenya, *National Development Plan, 1989-1993* (Nairobi: Government Printer, 1988), p. 71.
4. Economist Intelligence Unit, *Kenya: Country Report*. 3 (London, 1990), p. 10.
5. External debt data presented in the following paragraphs are from

studies by the Institute of International Finance, *Kenya: Country Report* (Washington, D.C.: IIF, 1991).
6. Clifford Clift, *Aid Coordination in Practice: Are There any Lessons to be Learnt from Kenya?* (London: Overseas Development Institute, 1987), pp. 9–10.
7. Economist Intelligence Unit, *Kenya: Country Profile, 1991–92* (London: EIU, 1991), p. 35.
8. Economist Intelligence Unit, *Kenya: Country Report*, 1990, p. 21.
9. Institute of International Finance, *Kenya*, 1991.
10. Economist Intelligence Unit, *Kenya: Country Report*, 1990, p. 12.
11. *Africa Research Bulletin*, 'Five Year Economic Reform Program,' 28 (February 16, 1991).
12. Clift, *Aid Coordination in Practice*, p. 8.
13. USAID, Commerce Department, and Congressional officials, June 1988, November 1987.
14. Commerce Department official, November, 1987.
15. Jennifer A. Widner, 'Kenya's Slow Progress Toward Multiparty Politics,' *Current History* 91, 565 (May 1992), p. 217.
16. Tony Hawkins, 'Donors Face up to the Realities,' *Financial Times* (8 January 1992), p. III.
17. For an assessment of the role of the IMF in Kenya during the late 1970s, see Tony Killick, 'Kenya, 1975–81,' in Tony Killick, ed., *The International Monetary Fund and Stabilization: Developing Country Experiences* (New York: St. Martin's Press, 1984) and, for the early 1980s, see Martin Godfrey, 'Stabilization and Structural Adjustment of the Kenyan Economy, 1975–85: An Assessment of Performance,' *Development and Change* 18, 4 (1987).
18. US Treasury official, June 1988.
19. Economist Intelligence Unit, *Kenya: Country Report*, 1990, p. 11; *Africa Research Bulletin*, 'Five-Year Economic Reform Program.'
20. *Africa Research Bulletin*, 'Kenya: Funding Breakthrough,' April 30, 1989, p. 9499.
21. *African Business*, 'Kenyan Economy Faces Further Problems,' 162 (February 1992), p. 7.
22. *Africa Research Bulletin*, 'Kenya: Funding Breakthrough.'
23. IMF economist, June 1988.
24. Kenyan embassy officials, June 1988.
25. British economist and former advisor to Kenya, July 1988.
26. During the mid-1980s, an IMF consultant monitored Kenya's financial policies from within the Central Bank.
27. IMF economists, November 1987; June 1988.
28. Lloyds Bank economist, 1984.
29. Recent government documents include Republic of Kenya, *Development Plan, 1984–1988* (Nairobi: Government Printer, 1983); *Budget Rationalization Program*, 1986; *Economic Management for Renewed Growth* (Nairobi: Government Printer, 1986); *Development Plan,*

1989–1993 (Nairobi: Government Printer, 1988).
30. Paul Mosley, 'The Politics of Economic Liberalization: USAID and the World Bank in Kenya, 1980–1984,' *African Affairs* 85, 1, (1986), p. 112.
31. World Bank economist, June 1988. See also the World Bank's report on this program in World Bank, *Kenya: Second Structural Adjustment Loan and Credit: Program Performance Audit Report* (Washington, D.C.: World Bank, 1985), p. 10.
32. Kenya's level of indebtedness to multilateral organizations (including the World Bank) made a two and one-half fold jump between 1981 and 1988, up to $2.2 billion.
33. Paul Mosley, 'Kenya,' in Paul Mosley, Jane Harrigan, and John Toye, *Aid and Power: The World Bank and Policy-Based Lending*, Vol. 2 (London: Routlege, 1991), p. 291.
34. *New York Times*, 'Citing Corruption by Kenya Officials, Western Nations are Canceling Aid,' October 21, 1991, p. A9.
35. Geoffrey King, 'World Bank Backs Kenya, but Paris Donors' Meeting Chooses to Wait and See for Six-month Period,' *African Business* 161 (January 1992), p. 19.
36. In 1984, Kenya negotiated a £60 million loan guaranteed by the state to purchase patrol boats. The Kenya Coffee Board received a $36 million one year trade finance loan in 1985. Also, banks provided a large loan to Kenya Airways to purchase two new aircraft from Airbus.
37. Barclays Bank director, July 1988.
38. A Lloyds banker even commented in July 1988 that he would not be surprised if a coup took place the day after the interview.
39. Midland Bank manager, July 1988; British financial journalist, July 1988.
40. Managing Director of a Kenyan commercial bank, February 1985.
41. See Martin Meredith, *The Past is Another Country: Rhodesia, 1890–1979* (London: A. Deutsch, 1979).
42. For several recent analyses, see I. Mandaza, ed., *The Political Economy of Transition, 1980–86* (Dakar: CODESRIA, 1986); World Bank, *Zimbabwe: A Strategy for Sustained Growth* (Washington, D.C.: World Bank, 1987); O. I. Nyawata, 'Macroeconomic Management, Adjustment, and Stabilization,' in Colin Stoneman, ed., *Zimbabwe's Prospects* (London: Macmillan, 1988); Roger C. Riddell, 'Zimbabwe,' in Roger C. Riddell, ed., *Manufacturing Africa: Performance and Prospects of Seven Countries in Sub-Saharan Africa* (London: James Currey, 1990); Colin Stoneman, 'The Impending Failure of Structural Adjustment: Lessons from Zimbabwe,' paper presented at the Canadian Association of African Studies (May 1990); Stoneman, 'Zimbabwe Opens Up to the Market,' *Africa Recovery* 4 (October–December, 1990); Christine Sylvester, *Zimbabwe: The Terrain of Contradictory Development* (Boulder: Westview Press, 1991).

The State and Debt Management Strategies 161

43. In the 1978/79 fiscal year, the government obtained a $290 million foreign loan designed to bolster its balance of payments position. See Whitsun Foundation, *Money and Finance in Zimbabwe* (Harare: Whitsun Foundation, 1983), p. 119. Drawings of $195 million were arranged, but the changed political conditions after 1980 prevented the use of the balance.
44. World Bank, *World Debt Tables* (Washington, D.C.: World Bank, 1987).
45. Institute of International Finance, *Zimbabwe Country Report* (Washington, D.C.: IIF, 1991).
46. World Bank, *World Debt Tables, 1991–92* (Washington, D.C.: World Bank, 1991).
47. Institute of International Finance, *Zimbabwe: Country Report* (Washington, D.C.: IIF, 1990).
48. Tony Hawkins, 'On Course for More Growth,' *Financial Times* (August 30, 1991), p. 24.
49. *African Economic Digest*, 'Zimbabwe: On Course for More Growth,' 13, 4 (February 24, 1992), p. 5.
50. ZIMCORD, *Let's Build Zimbabwe Together* (Harare: ZIMCORD, 1981).
51. Senior official in the Ministry of Finance, April 1985.
52. Ibid.
53. International Monetary Fund, *Direction of Trade* (Washington, D.C.: IMF, 1988).
54. *African Economic Digest*, 'Zimbabwe: On Course for More Growth,' p. 5; Economist Intelligence Unit, *Zimbabwe: Country Report* #2 (London: EIU, 1992), pp. 12–13.
55. *African Economic Digest*, 'Zimbabwe: On Course for More Growth,' p. 5.
56. International Monetary Fund, *Zimbabwe: Staff Report for the 1982 Article IV Consultation.* SM/82/187 (IMF: Washington, D.C., 1982), p. 16.
57. April 1985.
58. April 1985.
59. Colin Stoneman, 'The World Bank and the IMF in Zimbabwe,' in Bonnie K. Campbell and John Loxley, eds., *Structural Adjustment in Africa* (New York: St. Martin's Press, 1989), p. 44.
60. Institute of International Finance, *Zimbabwe Country Report*, 1991, p. 5.
61. Stoneman and Cliffe offer a critical analysis of the indirect effects of 'IMF-induced' conditions upon Zimbabwe's economy and the general welfare of the population. See Colin Stoneman and Lionel Cliffe, *Zimbabwe: Politics, Economics, and Society* (London: Pinter, 1989), pp. 41–44.
62. *Africa Research Bulletin*, February 16, 1991, 28, 2, p. 10295.
63. *Africa Research Bulletin*, May 31, 1989, 26, p. 9538.

64. World Bank economists, November 1987, June 1988.
65. Republic of Zimbabwe, *Economic Policy Statement: Macro-Economic Adjustment and Trade Liberalisation* (Harare: Government Printer, 1990).
66. Economist Intelligence Unit, *Zimbabwe: Country Report* #2 (London: EIU, 1992), p. 12.
67. As a total of its total external debt owed to private creditors, Zimbabwe owed 85 percent in 1981 and 73 percent in 1982. This figure has been dropping steadily to a projected 23 percent in 1992. See Institute of International Finance, *Zimbabwe Country Report*, 1991.
68. Zimbabwe's total external debt had jumped in just three years (1981–84) by almost 60 percent, while official reserves fell by about 75 percent. The country's debt service as a percentage of exports also increased quickly from 14.5 percent to 30.5 percent in the same period. See Institute of International Finance, *Zimbabwe* (Washington, D.C: IIF, 1988).
69. Institute of International Finance, *Zimbabwe*, 1990.
70. Bankers Trust official in London, July 1988. As of 1986, the public sector in Zimbabwe owed 96 percent of the total external debt (Institute of International Finance, *Zimbabwe*, 1988).
71. *African Economic Digest*, 'Special Report: Zimbabwe,' 1987 (April), p. 1.
72. Institute of International Finance, *Zimbabwe Country Report*, 1991.
73. The government has enacted several measures regulating the loan agreements with international banks: 1) according to a Reserve Bank economist in 1985, the government requires Reserve Bank approval for any foreign loan over Z $2.5 million, whether the loan was projected for use by the private or public sector; 2) the government only accepts standby loans providing they bridge the balance of payments gap or generate exports and foreign exchange; 3) after projecting the debt burden, the government further decided to accept non-standby loans only with a maturity of more than five years; and 4) the government maintained the right to turn down loans with unacceptable terms. A former senior official in the Ministry of Finance recalled in an interview that between 1983 and 1984, the government turned down Z $100 million in foreign bank loans since they would have jeopardized Zimbabwe's repayment capacity (April 1985).
74. *Africa Research Bulletin*, 28, 6 (June 16, 1991), p. 10442.
75. See Jeffry A. Frieden, 'The Brazilian Borrowing Experience: From Miracle to Debacle and Back,' *Latin American Research Review*, 22:1 (1987), pp. 95–131.
76. Debt data are from World Bank, *World Debt Tables* (Washington, D.C.: World Bank, 1990) and from the Institute of International Finance, *Brazil: Country Report* (Washington, D.C.: IIF, 1991).
77. James Dinsmoor, *Brazil: Responses to the Debt Crisis* (Washington, D.C.: Inter-American Development Bank, 1990), p. 31.

The State and Debt Management Strategies 163

78. *Macroeconomic Control Plan* (Brasilia: Ministry of Finance, July 1987), p. 14.
79. World Bank, *World Debt Tables* (Washington, D.C.: World Bank, 1985), p. 173.
80. Institute of International Finance, *Brazil*, 1991.
81. Ramesh S. Garg, 'Brazilian External Debt: A Study in Capital Flows and Transfer of Resources,' *Journal of Inter-American Studies and World Affairs* 20, 3 (August 1978), p. 342.
82. *World Financial Markets*, 'Stabilization Policies in Brazil,' Morgan Guaranty Trust, (July 1984), p. 3.
83. These figures as well as those in the next paragraph are from the Institute of International Finance, *Brazil*, 1991.
84. Dinsmoor, *Brazil*, p. 35.
85. Eliana A. Cardoso and Albert Fishlow, 'The Macroeconomics of the Brazilian External Debt,' in Jeffrey D. Sachs, ed., *Developing Country Debt and Economic Performance*, Vol. 2 (Chicago: University of Chicago Press, 1990), p. 298.
86. Data for much of this paragraph is from the Institute of International Finance, *Brazil*, 1991.
87. Cardoso and Fishlow, 'The Macroeconomics of the Brazilian External Debt,' p. 352.
88. Alan Riding, 'Brazil, Fearing Reprisal, Seeking Debt Accords,' *New York Times*, February 23, 1987, p. 23.
89. *Atlanta Journal and Constitution*, February 2, 1987.
90. Eul-Soo Pang, 'Debt, Adjustment, and Democratic Cacophony in Brazil,' in Barbara Stallings and Robert Kaufman, eds., *Debt and Democracy in Latin America* (Boulder: Westview Press, 1989), p. 136; *Latin American Times*, 7, 10 (March 30, 1987), p. 10.
91. Guillermo O'Donnell has argued that the rational interest of creditors is not so much to 'maximize what they can collect from debtors, but to prolong the imbalance of forces entailed by the fact that, while debtors are locked in a 'prisoner's dilemma' [perpetuated by their inability to act collectively], the creditors themselves are cartelized' in 'Brazil's Failure: What Future for Debtors' Cartels?' *Third World Quarterly* 9 (October 1987), p. 1159.
92. Ibid., p. 1160.
93. Interest income recorded only when actually received.
94. *Latin American Weekly Report*, April 16, 1987, p. 7. The classification 'substandard' is a step before the more serious 'value-impaired' classification. The substandard category applies when a) a country is not complying with its external service obligations, as evidenced by arrearages, forced restructuring, or rollovers; b) the country is not in the process of adopting an IMF or other suitable economic adjustment program, or is not adequately adhering to such a program; or c) the counry and its bank creditors have not negotiated a viable rescheduling program and are unlikely to do so in the near future. See

Inter-agency Country Exposure Risk Committee, 'Inter-agency Statement on Examination Treatment of International Loans,' (Washington, D.C., December 15, 1983).
95. *Latin American Weekly Report*, March 12, 1987, pp. 6–7.
96. Seamus O'Cleireacain, *Third World Debt and International Public Policy* (New York: Praeger, 1990), p. 189. It is important to note the distinction between writing down a loan and establishing a provision for a loan. The former refers to a reduction in the book value of the asset in the creditor's balance sheet to a level that reflects the asset's real net present value. Creditors make 'provision against loans by putting aside reserves in low-earning but risk-free assets in order to cover the possibility that repayments of principal or payments of interest might not be made.' See Graham Bird, *Commercial Bank Lending and Third World Debt* (New York: St. Martin's Press, 1989), p. 51. If a default occurs, the bad debt is charged against the previously established reserves rather than against the banks' income or capital base. So long as the banks estimate these losses adequately through the reserve account, current earnings are unaffected. However, banks incur indirect costs in forgone additional loans and potential income. Indirect costs may mount because, according to most national bank regulations, provisions must be maintained for at least five years after the most recent rescheduling agreement or episode of payment arrears.
97. Paul Luke, *The Latin American Debt Problem: An Evaluation* (London: Libra Bank, 1988), p. 31.
98. *Latin American Markets*, 'Debt Crisis,' September 21, 1987, p. 2.
99. U.S. Treasury, 'Proposal with Respect to Certain Brazilian External Debt Held by Commercial Banks,' September 25, 1987, p. 2.
100. Internal memo, July 21, 1987.
101. William R. Rhodes, 'An Insider's Reflection on the Brazilian Debt Package,' *Wall Street Journal*, October 14, 1988, p. 13.
102. Author's interview, November 1987.
103. Author's interview with a senior vice president of a U.S. bank, June 1988.
104. This citation and the ones in the following paragraph are from Luis Carlos Bresser Pereira, 'A Brazilian Approach to External Debt Negotiation,' *LASA Forum* 19 (Winter 1989), p. 7.
105. Jonathan Fuerbringer, 'Brazil and Banks Reach Agreement on Reducing Debt,' *New York Times*, July 10, 1992, pp. A1, C2.
106. Katherine Sieh, 'New Debt Agreement Reached,' *Infobrazil*, November 1987; *Latin American Regional Reports: Brazil*, 'Deal with Banks Ends Moratorium,' November 26, 1987, p. 6.
107. Bresser Pereira, 'A Brazilian Approach to External Debt Negotiation,' p. 7.
108. Ibid., 7.
109. *Latin American Regional Reports: Brazil*, July 7, 1988, p. 5.
110. Author's interview with a British bank economist, June 1988.

111. Bresser Pereira was aware of the impact of this regulatory classification when he remarked in October 1987 that 'I am interested in getting out of the moratorium, but the banks are even more interested than I am.' See *Latin American Regional Reports: Brazil*, 'New Plan Suggests Thorny Debt Talks,' October 22, 1987, p. 6.
112. *Latin American Weekly Report*, March 17, 1988, p. 9.
113. *Latin American Weekly Report*, April 21, 1988, pp. 10–11; *Latin American Weekly Report*, June 16, 1988, p. 7.
114. Ruben Lamdany, 'The Market-Based Menu Approach in Action: The 1988 Brazil Financing Package,' *Discussion Papers* 52 (Washington, D.C.: World Bank, 1989), p. 4.
115. Stephen Fidler, 'Banks Agree 'Innovative' Approach,' *Financial Times*, June 23, 1988, p. 3. Some economists argued that the reduction in interest rates spreads achieved after a year of negotiations had in September 1988 already been wiped out by the rise in the LIBOR. See *Latin American Regional Reports: Brazil*, October 20, 1988, p. 2.
116. *Gazeta Mercantil*, 'Debt Rescheduling Accord Ready,' June 27, 1988, p. 3.
117. First, Brazil issued $5 billion in exit bonds carrying a six percent interest rate over twenty-five years. Banks can exchange a loan for bonds issued by Brazil, but at a lower interest rate. Banks can then reduce their loan exposure and Brazil can reduce its indebtedness. Over one hundred banks have subscribed to the exit bonds, as compared with only two banks under the 1987 Argentine accord. For a complete discussion of exit bonds, see Lamdany, 'The Market-Based Menu Approach in Action,' p. 6. The second option is the debt-equity conversion, in which a bank may exchange a loan at market (discounted) rates for local currency that it can use to invest in the debtor nation. A 1988 report by the advisory committee comprising the leading commercial banks with exposure in Brazil urged the government to expand its debt-equity program. See Peter Truell, 'Brazil Could Cut Foreign Bank Debt by $19 Billion by 1994, Study Says,' *Wall Street Journal*, August 23, 1988, p. 6. Finally, as an incentive to obtain the required 90 percent of Brazil's seven hundred creditor banks, the Brazilian government agreed to pay 3/8 percent and 1/8 percent commissions, respectively, to banks that adhered by August 5 and September 2, 1988.
118. Stephan Haggard and Robert Kaufman, 'The Politics of Stabilization and Structural Adjustment,' in Jeffry D. Sachs, ed., *Developing Country Debt and Economic Performance* (Chicago: University of Chicago Press, 1989), p. 243.
119. *Latin American Weekly Report*, March 9, 1989, p. 4; *Latin American Regional Reports: Brazil*, February 9, 1989, pp. 2–3.
120. *Latin American Weekly Report*, May 4, 1989, p. 8.
121. *Latin American Regional Reports: Brazil*, August 10, 1989, p. 5; October 19, 1989, p. 6; February 15, 1990, p. 5.

122. *Latin American Regional Reports: Brazil*, June 7, 1990, p. 5.
123. *Latin American Regional Reports: Brazil*, August 16, 1990, pp. 5, 7.
124. *Latin American Weekly Report*, October 11, 1990, p. 7.
125. *Latin American Regional Reports: Brazil*, October 25, 1990, p. 5.
126. *Latin American Weekly Report*, November 8, 1990, p. 7.
127. *Latin American Weekly Report*, November 29, 1990, p. 7.
128. *Latin American Regional Reports: Brazil*, March 21, 1991, p. 5.
129. *Latin American Regional Reports: Brazil*, May 2, 1991, p. 1.
130. *Latin American Regional Reports: Brazil*, October 24, 1991, p. 5.
131. Brazil's initial bargaining position provided four options: 1) the conversion of debt at par into 30-year bonds with a reduced annual coupon of 5 percent; 2) the exchange of existing debt at a discount of 37.5 percent on face value for 30-year bonds paying interest of 3/16 of a point above LIBOR; 3) fresh lending equivalent to 33 percent of existing exposure; and 4) the exchange of debt for temporary interest reduction bonds for 25 years. See *Latin American Regional Reports: Brazil*, September 19, 1991, p. 5. The banks countered with their own menu of options. They proposed: 1) instead of 30-year bonds with a discount of 37.5 percent on face value, they want 25-year bonds with a discount of 32.5 percent; 2) on the interest-reduction option, the banks want to set the reduced rate at 6.2 percent instead of 4.8 percent; 3) the banks have suggested the addition of a new option that would reduce interest rates for six years followed by a return to market rates; and 4) the banks have asked Brazil to set up a fund to guarantee interest payments. See *Latin American Regional Reports: Brazil*, October 24, 1991, p. 5.
132. 'Letter of Intent from Brazil to the IMF,' December 2, 1991; published as part of *Brazil: Economic Program*, Vol. 31, December (Brasilia: Central Bank of Brazil, 1991), pp. 24–5.
133. $3 billion from the World Bank; $1.5 billion from the Inter-American Development Bank; $1.5 billion from the Japanese Export-Import Bank; and $1 billion from the U.S. Export-Import Bank. James Bruce, 'IMF Approval of Reforms Aids Brazil's Trade Plans,' *Journal of Commerce*, February 3, 1992, p. 5A.
134. Economist Intelligence Unit, *Brazil: Country Report* #1 (London: EIU, 1992), p. 4.
135. Danielle Robinson, 'Brazil's Day of Redemption,' *Euromoney* (March 1992), p. 64.
136. 'Letter of Intent', 1991, p. 25.
137. Economist Intelligence Unit, *Brazil: Country Report*, 1992, p. 14.
138. Jonathan Fuerbringer, 'Brazil and Banks Reach Agreement on Reducing Debt,' p. C2.
139. Jonathan David Aronson, 'The Politics of Private Bank Lending and Debt Renegotiations,' in Jonathon David Aronson, ed., *Debt and the Less Developing Countries* (Boulder: Westview Press, 1979).

5 The State's Distributive Policies Under Indebted Development

The previous two chapters set the stage for the current discussion of the distribution of resources among domestic interests in Kenya, Zimbabwe, and Brazil. Chapters Three and Four specified the two aspects of indebted development within which the state operates. In considering the selection and implementation of adjustment strategies in the Third World, it is critical to analyze the role of the state as the main intermediary between societal interests and external creditors. The state is at the locus of interaction with the *former* in assessing and distributing the costs of adjustment and with the *latter* in identifying a debt management strategy as a means to protect state interests. With this place and role of the state in mind, an adjustment strategy becomes a series of policies and choices made by the state as it responds to the cross-cutting pressures and demands from both levels. The adjustment process is a political process in that the state simultaneously pursues policies that will benefit some groups and hurt others. Both domestic and external groups use their relative power capabilities to incorporate their interests into the adjustment strategy and to affect the implementation of relevant portions of the strategy. Ultimately, economic adjustment implies the allocation of scarce resources to certain beneficiaries and of distributing the economic costs of adjustment to other actors.

For Kenya, Zimbabwe, and Brazil, the distribution of scarce resources within society is of paramount importance. While all three cases have *outlined* their adjustment objectives in numerous public documents, the *actual distribution* of resources better reflects the impact of indebted development on domestic interests. Given pressure from international and national interests, the allocation of state funds committed to public investment, parastatals, and budget expenditures indicate the adjustment selection by these indebted states. This chapter will consider and evaluate the *role of the state in the allocation of resources*. Since the state remains the fundamental actor in the adjustment process, analysis will focus on the tension between public sector and private sector investment, the state's relationship to parastatals, and its policy toward its budget deficit.

DISTRIBUTIVE POLICIES OF KENYA'S ADJUSTMENT STRATEGY

My argument, then, is that the state, acting as an intermediary actor, is buffeted by the demands and constraints of international creditors and domestic economic interests. The state is under direct pressure from those groups as they press it to make concessions favorable to their own position. For example, Kenya's response to these pressures in the form of an adjustment strategy primarily has been, on the one hand, to *reward* international creditors with interest payments, agricultural exporters with incentives and capital, and specific parastatals with increased subsidies and, on the other hand, to *penalize* the lower classes and importers of capital inputs.

Kenya's adjustment strategy contains a long-term objective of establishing a base for liberal economic development. The most recent national development plan reaffirms this strategy in which the state is expected to shift investment resources from the public sector to the private sector and, in particular, the export-oriented agricultural sector of the economy. Government development statements stress the importance of the private sector and the need to eliminate state firms.[1] Yet, as Kenya continues to grapple with insufficient resources, political instability, and lingering budget deficits, the government remains an active agent in redirecting scarce resources to public sector firms, especially those in agriculture that promote export-oriented growth. The 1986 government document on which the current IMF program is based – *Economic Management for Renewed Growth* – was solely concerned with constructing the foundation for IMF-sponsored growth.[2]

In order to analyze and understand the distributive policies of Kenya's adjustment strategy, we first need to review the financial performance of the central government. The main characteristic of this performance is the tendency towards increased budget imbalances. Under pressure from the IMF, the government repeatedly has targeted budget deficit reduction as a major priority. However, the government has had limited success in bringing the deficit down. Indeed, between 1989 and 1990, the deficit actually increased by over 12 percent. Yet, as the economic growth rate hovered around five percent during the late-1980s, the deficit as a percentage of GDP slightly dropped, but it is expected to rise again to 5.3 percent in the 1991/92 fiscal year.[3] Government policy toward the budget deficit during the 1980s and early 1990s has been to promote the agricultural export sector and to make significant cuts in social welfare expenditures, while avoiding interest arrears. Central Bank and Ministry of Finance officials, agricultural exporters, and international bankers publicly have favored a redirection in government subsidies toward foreign exchange-generating parastatals, and away from basic goods state enterprises. Yet, as IMF and World Bank officials have observed, Kenya has failed to restructure parastatals that directly benefit agricultural exporters.[4]

Parastatal Policy

A major government response to mounting budget deficits has been a series of evaluations of its role with parastatal firms. A critical component of both the state's orthodox adjustment strategy and the IMF's programmatic guidelines is the curtailing of government involvement in the economy. During the 1970s, the government made an effort in the redirection, but not the elimination, of public investments to parastatals. Yet, the state continues to intervene in favor of parastatals that are considered integral to national 'security' (airlines, railroad), infrastructural development (steel, construction), and exports (marketing boards). Furthermore, the government has centralized the decision-making process of guaranteeing foreign loans made to these parastatal firms. The government's strong financial and political support for parastatals has brought adverse reaction by official creditors and weakens the government's claim that it is pursuing a strategy of liberalization.

Moreover, the government has failed to monitor properly its investments of parastatals and to supervise the repayment of loans and dividends to the Treasury.[5] The absence of reports and adequate accounts of financial transactions prompted the central government in the early 1980s, strongly supported by the Central Bank and the IMF, to set a new strategy towards parastatals. The Ndegwa Report, published in 1982, laid out new regulatory guidelines to streamline parastatals and to make them more efficient and profitable. Although the report called for placing some agencies on the open market, the government did not identify those 'marketable' firms. The study reported that 'some parastatals have exceeded their original mandates and have made investments in commercial and industrial activities that should be left entirely to the private sector.'[6] The report argued that state firms had become inefficient largely because of the intrusion of domestic political interests in the commercial decision-making process. These vested interests are generally of two kinds: domestic economic groups in the manufacturing sector and Africans benefiting from the anti-Asian stance of the government. Several commercial bankers and IMF officials agreed in interviews that one of the most serious problems is the friction between manufacturers close to the government and international institutions pressing for economic liberalization.[7] The selling of key parastatals would undermine the short-term benefits of local industrialists and local politicians, many of whom are close to the administration.

The second important domestic constraint has been the antagonistic relationship between Africans and Asians. The extension and protection of state firms initially employed many workers, but these firms also represented local African control of key financial and industrial resources. A liberalization of the local market would increase Asian opportunities to advance their economic interests. According to several respondents, the Asian community still maintains controls over commercial and industrial sectors, especially in vital export-oriented firms.[8]

Another government report issued in 1986 made specific recommendations toward the restructuring of state-owned enterprises. As a major component of the budget rationalization program, parastatals were recognized to cause considerable strain on scarce resources. The statement issued a number of objectives that, in theory, would eliminate parastatals which were inefficient and whose projects equally could be achieved by private sector interests. The remaining state firms would be required to improve their productivity and become self-financing in the activities which can be operated on a commercial basis. The government also established administrative control over the firms' budgets in order to have them stay within their budget and, in particular, to stabilize parastatal borrowing of foreign capital.[9] Yet, rather than dissolve or sell parastatals to private interests, the government sought only to reform the existing state controls over parastatal behavior. In the late-1980s, the government restructured the National Cereals and Produce Board and the Kenya Meat Commission. Additionally, in 1989 it even expanded the public sector by creating new parastatals, including the Nyayo Tea Zone and Nyayo Bus company.

The most recent attempt by the government to restructure and reform state enterprises occurred in July 1991 when President Moi appointed a *parastatal reform committee*. The committee's primary objective is to supervise and coordinate the implementation of parastatal reform and, specifically, to determine the terms and conditions of sale of each specified state enterprise.[10] The reform program was written in collaboration with the United Nations Development Program and the World Bank as part of Kenya's commitments made to its international donors. More specifically, the long-term schedule of the reform process is to make the distinction between strategic enterprises ('vital to national security or contingency and those providing essential goods and services') and non-strategic enterprises. The firms that fit into the first category (such as Kenya Railways and the Ports Authority) will undergo internal restructuring aimed at improvements in their efficiency. Those firms that fall into the second category either will be liquidated or sold to the private sector.[11] So far, the results have been minimal. The committee has formulated a timetable for reform implementation and has drawn up a list of 139 state firms identified as potentially 'divestible.' The government recently reported that 32 investments have been divested or are in the process of being sold, while 14 have been liquidated. The government also has contracted with several foreign consulting groups with expertise in corporate restructuring and privatization to conduct independent valuations of several other state firms.[12] The government also has informed its international creditors that Kenya Airways will be privatized by the end of 1993.[13]

Significant evidence is mounting that clearly supports a major privatization effort. During the 1990/91 fiscal year, Kenya spent Ksh 1.1 billion (about US $38 million) merely for servicing the debts of parastatals. In this same fiscal year, the unpaid or late taxes of these state firms amounted to more than Ksh 500 million.[14] According to another source, parastatal losses account for about 20 percent of the budget deficit, while their borrowings make up 17 percent of Kenya's foreign debt.[15] Given the lengthy history of the government's efforts to reform the public sector even with the financial support and economic advice of international financial institutions, the prognosis is far from clear. Recent evidence suggests that Kenya's privileged status with donors and the IFIs is in jeopardy and its ability to make promises without actual reform implementation is threatened.

Parastatal Borrowing Controls

By far, the most critical controls affecting state firms have sought to regulate their borrowing from foreign creditors. Several respondents would agree with a remark made by a Kenyan vice president of Citibank in Nairobi that 'the government is the first and last guarantor of bank loans made to state-owned enterprises.' The state currently controls parastatal borrowing through a set of criteria reviewed by the Treasury. Through state guarantees, the government seeks to redirect scarce foreign resources to state agricultural export firms, national security parastatals, and national development agencies. This process demonstrates the state's capacity to protect what it considers to be important domestic interests through a form of government subsidy. By controlling borrowing practices of state firms, the central government can obtain foreign currency directly from parastatals and, through currency conversion, it can transfer the loans to Treasury in exchange for domestic currency. Parastatals receive Kenyan shillings while the Treasury obtains foreign currency which it passes on for debt repayment or investment in the export sector.

Although state borrowing controls over parastatals are meant to regulate indebtedness, in practice their own ministries and the Ministry of Finance have allowed widespread borrowing. The Central Bank criticized the development of parastatals as argued in the *Working Paper* document which recommended sweeping divestments of the government's equity investments in commercial and industrial enterprises.[16] While private sector and IFIs objected to the inefficient and costly management of state firms, the central government continues to support public sector indebtedness.

The state also has assumed increased control and responsibility over foreign loans undertaken by agricultural interests. In this way, bank risk is transferred to the state by guaranteeing the production of the good that is to earn foreign exchange. One example of this arrangement was a large loan transaction made between the Coffee Board and a British bank syndication in 1985. The $40 million loan fixed at about $1\frac{1}{2}$ percent over LIBOR matured in one year. The state-guaranteed loan financed the 1986 coffee production by paying farmers for that year's harvest. In effect, according to the executive director of a British bank involved in the transaction, the government assumed responsibility for the following year's coffee production. Other Kenyan bankers, however, claimed the arrangement was a 'bloody scandal.' Two reasons were given. The amount of the loan could have been raised internally from domestic banks at a lower rate. More importantly, reliance on foreign sources of capital increases the foreign exchange risk. The foreign loan was converted into the local currency to pay the farmers, but the foreign currency became part of Kenya's foreign reserves. 'Kenya is now,' a Kenyan banker said in an interview, 'quite vulnerable to currency fluctuations affecting exchange payments.'

The government also has assumed central borrowing control for such important national firms as Kenya Airways, the national railway system, the Post and Telecommunications agency, and major electrification projects. The majority of these loan transactions is grouped into a category of long-term, limited foreign exchange-earning commitments. State guarantees permit it not only to oversee parastatal borrowing procedures, but they are also meant to facilitate its control over parastatal economic performance. Kenya Airways has been involved in several off-shore loans all of which have been guaranteed by the state. Banks do not fear the risk of default since the burden falls on the shoulders of the state. A Kenyan banker mentioned that the government can always raise the price of the product, say the price of stamps, to avoid a threat of default. State guarantees, on the one hand, permit a broader agreement with international banks to involve state agencies and projects that would not otherwise be funded. On the other hand, by accepting the maturity and interest conditions, the central government assumes the responsibility and the risk of foreign loans.

The state additionally regulates the finances and activities of industrial and manufacturing parastatals. As a means to consolidate state authority, the government has established and centralized agencies that coordinate infrastructural development of the country. The evolution of state development agencies has been shaped by the differing development priorities emphasized since independence. In Kenya's case, development corporations were established in industrial and manufacturing sectors to coordinate the international financing of development projects.

Two main parastatal financial agencies serve the industrial and manufacturing sectors. The state regulates their finances and activities through the Ministry of Commerce and Industry and through state guarantees of foreign bank loans administered by the Ministry of Finance. One main financial institution is the Industrial and Commercial Development Corporation (ICDC). The ICDC is a major vehicle for government participation in industry. It coordinates for the government the purchase of equity shares of firms. As a senior official of the ICDC remarked in an interview, 'all loans must have state guarantees' in order for the agency to accept them. The ICDC actively seeks foreign involvement especially in the more profitable endeavors financed by the corporation.

A second important development agency is the Development Finance Company of Kenya (DFCK). It is an investment company owned by its international shareholders (70 percent) and the state (30 percent). Much of its money comes from international development banks in Germany and Britain. For many years, the DFCK refused to accept the unsuitable terms of foreign bank loans. Yet, since 1982, the agency took on the burden of foreign commercial loans indirectly as its foreign shareholders borrowed off-shore and then lent that capital to the DFCK at high rates. Foreign loans contracted with the DFCK must be repaid in foreign currency, but with fluctuating exchange rates and a high exchange risk, repayment becomes expensive. The burden of repayment, according to the general manager of the Development Finance Company of Kenya, is shared by the DFCK and the Ministry of Finance. As the financing has shifted toward the external market, so has the investment priorities of the DFCK. While a more complete discussion of Kenya's economic adjustment strategy is found in Chapter Three, it should be pointed out that recent DFCK policy is to encourage export-sector growth. According to the general manager of the DFCK, through its central control over this agency, the state has channeled funds to the agricultural, mining, industrial, and tourism sectors. The financial base of the investment company will continue to rely on state-guaranteed loans.

Sectoral Allocation

Another indicator of the economic priorities set by Kenya during periods of economic adjustment is the sectoral allocation of state-guaranteed loans.[17] First, during the mid- to late-1970s, the state and external financial institutions agreed to disburse capital primarily to the infrastructural sector. The infrastructural sector covers a wide range of major areas utilizing large-scale projects, such as transportation, communication, and energy. Between 1976 and 1979, around 60 percent of all foreign loans were allocated to infrastructural projects. These projects included massive modernization alterations in the development of the railway and port systems and the construction of an oil pipeline. State-owned enterprises were the primary beneficiaries and coordinators of these large capital outlays. Second, the state has used its power to issue loan guarantees to generate foreign exchange from an expanded export-oriented economy. The development strategy pursued by the state called for a substantial reorientation of the economy towards the international market. Government leaders sought means to direct the flow of exportable goods along refurbished transportation routes to the seaports. More specifically, the politically powerful agricultural sector benefited from the distribution of foreign capital. The most significant investments were disbursed for the revitalization of the sugar industry, a major export crop. Nearly two-thirds of the loans supplied to the agricultural sector during the late-1970s were used by the state-subsidized sugar factories.

The industrial sector received much less attention from the state during this period. The only recipient agency in the industrial sector was the Industrial Development Bank, a state corporation established to facilitate small indigenous projects. Discussions with Kenyan policy-makers support the contention made by the development plans of this time that Kenya lacked the technological expertise and capital resources to produce competitive industrial products for regional and international markets.

An examination of the distribution of loans during the 1980s suggests continuation for the most part of the allocation priorities within each sector. Railway and harbor expenditures maintained their dominant position within the infrastructural sector, followed by communication investments in

The State's Distributive Policies 175

Table 5.1 *Sectoral Distribution of External Loans Guaranteed by Kenya, 1977–1983 (Ksh million and in percent)*

	1977	1978	1979	1980	1981	1982	1983
Infrastructural	55.2	82.1	121.9	112.7	77.3	92.1	204.4
(% of external loans)	52	66	67	61	47	49	50
Agricultural	40.8	27.9	40.8	46.3	56.3	68.0	69.8
(% of external loans)	39	22	23	25	34	36	17
Industrial	4.9	6.1	9.4	12.6	15.6	18.3	107.4
(% of external loans)	5	5	5	7	10	10	26
Other	5	8.7	8.5	13.1	14.3	20.4	26.2
(% of external loans)	5	7	5	7	9	11	6
Total External Loans	105.9	124.8	180.6	184.8	163.5	188.8	407.8

Source Republic of Kenya, *The Appropriation Accounts for the Controller and Auditor-General* (Nairobi: Government Printer, various years).

Note Total percentages may not equal 100 percent due to rounding.

Kenya's Post and Telecommunications agency. Much of the difference was picked up by increases to the agricultural sector and less to the industrial sector. A significant boost in the agricultural allocation further supported both the tea and sugar industries. The Kenya Tea Authority, which had languished for several years, took off in the early 1980s. The Tea Authority consumed one-quarter of the agricultural sector's loans and, by 1983, its allocation had increased to 33 percent. The Industrial Development Bank's use of external loans continued to grow at a steady though marginal rate. The government had sought external financing for factory construction and development corporations. The former's allotted portion amounted to over Ksh 61 million, equivalent to 58 percent of the industrial sector's foreign financing. The state also had committed its guarantees to cover investments in the development of the industrial, tourism, and commercial sectors. While the relative proportion of infrastructural investments remained at about 50 percent, its rate of growth doubled. The foreign element of the financing of the railway and port systems stood at Ksh 140 million, or 34 percent of the total external loans guaranteed by the state. The Post and Telecommunications' position also grew as its foreign loan portion nearly doubled.

The government's protection of influential supporters in the 1980s has not changed much since the 1970s. A 1985 example was a large loan transaction made between the Kenya Coffee Board and a British bank syndication. Another was a similar $40 million state-guaranteed loan mentioned above that financed the 1986 coffee production by paying farmers for that year's harvest. By the late-1980s, capital disbursements continued to support the foreign exchange-generating export sectors. Railway and harbor expenditures maintained a dominant position within the infrastructural sector followed by a significant boost in the agricultural allocation for tea and sugar industries.[18] The government also has covered foreign credit for such firms as Kenya Airways and electrification projects. During the current adjustment period, the government seeks to restrain state enterprises producing basic goods that are both inefficient and are unable to earn foreign currency, while protecting state export firms that may be inefficient but are important generators of foreign exchange.

Budget Allocation

We are now ready to turn to an examination of the government's budget allocation. An examination of the functional distribution of the central government expenditure reveals that, from the 1970s until the present, education, defense, and interest payments have made up the largest components of total expenditure. Overall, current expenditure increased at a yearly rate of 20 percent, and only two sectors recorded an above average growth rate: defense and interest payments. Defense spending increased dramatically during the latter half of the 1970s, but it reached a plateau during the early 1980s. The rapid expansion of external indebtedness prompted an escalation in annual growth rates for interest payments beginning in 1981. The average yearly rate between 1980 and 1984 was 36.5 percent and forty percent between 1985 and 1989.

Three relevant implications can be drawn from this data. First, *interest payments* provided the most significant growth change during this period. As Kenya embarked on periodic credit expansion, various debt indicators revealed a deteriorating situation. An increasingly large portion of total expenditure was allocated to interest payments. As a percent of total expenditures, interest payments increased from seven percent to over 18 percent between 1980 and 1986. More recently, the growth of interest payments in terms of total expenditures has slowed down. However, the 1992 forecasted portion of expenditures committed to interest payments is nearly fifteen percent.[19]

Second, while agricultural subsidies, interest payments, and defense benefited from Kenya's strategy, the costs of austerity were imposed on domestic social welfare sectors. Between 1980 and 1985, *basic needs expenditure* (education, health, housing, and social welfare) increased by only fourteen percent, a significant reduction over the twenty-two percent annual growth rate from 1964 to 1974. When the inflation rate of thirteen percent per year between 1974 and 1984 is considered along with the population growth rate of four percent, real basic needs services per capita in 1985 had fallen by more than twenty-five percent below their 1974 level.[20] During the latter part of the 1980s (1985/86 to 1990/91), the basic goods sector expenditure only was raised by about 14 percent per year. Moreover, the percentage of total expenditures allocated to basic goods has fallen from 31 percent in 1985/86 to 26 percent in 1990/91.[21] As the poor rely more heavily on basic needs services, this expenditure drop tends to place a significant share of the adjustment burden on the poor. Alleviation of those cutbacks have been considered inappropriate until growth and debt repayment goals are met. In the 1991 Budget Speech, there is no mention of the distributive consequences of adjustment. Yet, explicit recommendations recently have been made by the agreement between the IMF and the government concerning the reduction of the budget deficit. The government intends to curb wage increases among public sector employees, reduce the number of lower level public employees, and limit the growth in the number of teachers.[22]

Third, during the late-1970s, the government pumped nearly 60 percent of all development expenditure into agricultural, energy, roads, and communication sectors.[23] Expenditure patterns in these areas represent the government's adjustment to pressures of indebtedness. Projects in these sectors were intended to generate large amounts of foreign exchange in order to maintain Kenya's credit standing.

Kenyan authorities generally recognize these pressures inflicted on the state by the competing interests of domestic and foreign groups. The growing budget deficits, the costs of indebtedness, and the increasing budget allocation to non-productive sectors (such as defense and interest payments) have not gone unnoticed by state officials. They have called for a period of development retrenchment that is expected to continue into the 1990s. Themes of the most recent budget statement include the rationalization of the tax structure and stricter control of government expenditure.[24] At a more general level, the 1991 Budget Speech encouraged a development strategy centered on the private agricultural sector, the containment of public sector expenditure levels, and the maintenance of a favorable relationship with international commercial banks and the international financial system; that is, an export-oriented development strategy in alignment with policies of economic orthodoxy promulgated by IFIs.

Table 5.2 Expenditure by Function of Kenya's Central Government, 1970–1989
(as percent of total expenditures)

Year	Public Administration	Defense	Interest Payments	Education	Economic Service	Agriculture
1970	16.4	4.4	5.1	18.9	38.1	
1971	17.8	5.4	5.1	19.6	36.1	
1972	15.8	6.1	5.5	20.8	36.9	
1973	15.2	6.4	5.4	20.6	36.8	
1974	15.0	6.3	4.8	21.2	34.7	
1975	19.5	5.5	5.2	19.4	33.3	
1976	15.3	10.5	5.8	19.7	31.6	
1977	15.6	13.5	5.6	16.0	32.3	
1978	13.9	14.4	5.7	15.2	35.5	
1979	14.1	11.0	6.5	18.0	33.4	
1980	16.9	9.2	7.0	18.1	30.4	
1981	14.2	11.4	10.6	17.6	27.7	
1982	11.7	11.6	12.3	17.3	22.9	
1983	9.4	13.8	14.6	20.6	22.0	10.1
1984	8.5	12.7	15.8	19.6	22.0	7.5
1985	10.7	8.6	15.1	19.6	26.1	10.3
1986	8.6	8.9	18.6	22.6	21.8	9.7
1987	12.1	9.1	16.4	21.2	20.1	11.4
1988	9.3	12.2	18.5	22.1	17.9	7.1
1989	9.4	7.8	17.9	19.8	26.6	14.6

Source International Monetary Fund, *Government Finance Statistics Yearbook, 1991* (Washington, D.C.: IMF, 1991).

DISTRIBUTIVE POLICIES OF ZIMBABWE'S ADJUSTMENT STRATEGY

In the case of Zimbabwe, distributive issues have been stressed repeatedly in several government documents beginning with the 1981 *Growth with Equity* statement, the 1982 *Transitional Development Plan*, the 1986 *Five-Year National Development Plan*, and through to the 1990 *Economic Policy Statement*. Historically, these documents seek to justify the government's decision to relax the strict focus on economic growth as practiced by Kenya on the grounds that equitable distribution will lay the foundation for sustained growth. But, the most recent budget speech (1991/92) makes a partial break from the previous documents. In conjunction with the new five-year Structural Adjustment Program (SAP), the government is seeking a mixture of tough restraints on public spending with tax breaks for taxpayers at the lower end of the scale. Actual distributive policies reveal that Zimbabwe has attempted to follow a two-pronged strategy. On the one hand, until the end of the 1980s, the government determined that the relative benefits from international borrowing were greater than either implementing serious incentives for multinational corporations or subscribing to IMF-sanctioned adjustment programs. Since Zimbabwe must remain creditworthy to obtain additional loans (when necessary), the government has implemented prompt repayment schedules to international creditors. On the other hand, Zimbabwe is under no delusion that the country should not make profound adjustments. The government, however, has sought to pursue self-imposed adjustment according to the distributive objectives determined by itself. According to government documents, the so-called 'home-grown' adjustment strategy should remain sensitive to domestic social welfare demands and expectations from the public even to the extent of rising budget deficits.

One critical factor in the rapid rise of the budget deficit has been the extensive participation of the state in the economic arena. The government has allowed the expansion of the budget deficit to remain at or above ten percent of GDP since the mid-1980s despite being attacked by the IMF and the World Bank for undertaking irresponsible fiscal actions. However, under the current SAP as expressed in the 1991/1992 budget, the government intends to stabilize the economy in part by reducing the budget deficit from 10.5 percent of GDP to 7.5 percent by the the end of 1993. A primary policy to accomplish this is the cutting of subsidies to parastatal firms and a freeze on government employment.

A government with self-proclaimed socialist intentions that inherits an economy with capitalist features undoubtedly faces a significant dilemma concerning its role in the mounting budget deficit and its participation in the economy. Radicals in government (many of whom fought during the civil war) pushed for sweeping nationalization of the financial, mining, and manufacturing sectors. To do so, according to the pragmatic faction, would have had several adverse implications. First, nationalization (without compensation) would have broken the Lancaster House Constitution which led to Zimbabwe's independence and, if compensated, the action would have cost the government around $2.5 billion.[25] Second, leaders of the pragmatic group (such as Finance Minister Chidzero) realized that nationalization would have incurred the anger and likely punishment of the West. Any move toward taking over the private sector during the early years would have jeopardized the Zimcord aid negotiations. Moreover, since the majority of foreign firms operating in Zimbabwe at the time of independence were South African, many government leaders feared economic reprisal and attempts to destabilize the new regime.

Despite what might be called these structural constraints against government policies, the new government embarked upon both an indirect and direct approach toward regulating private (mainly white) capital interests. In particular, the government has used the financial sector as a channel for its monetary policy. The state's main agent is the Reserve Bank working in close partnership with the Ministry of Finance. The Reserve Bank administers a complex network of exchange control regulations and governs the allocation of foreign exchange to the private sector. According to an early study, the private sector received a thirty-six percent increase in foreign exchange allocations in 1979 over the previous year, which jumped by another forty-seven percent in 1980, but followed by only a twenty percent rise in the following year.[26] The restrictive policy toward the private sector continued, since between 1982 and 1985, that sector's foreign exchange allocation dropped by 30 percent. Given the government's official ideological predisposition toward the peasant class and the export strength of white commercial farmers, foreign exchange allocations have benefited the agricultural sector to the detriment of industrial and manufacturing interests. Foreign exchange allocation was slashed during the first six months of 1987 to industrial and commercial sectors by forty percent and fifty-five percent, respectively.[27]

Parastatal Policy

Implicit in the government's controls of private sector investment is a government effort to regulate foreign (mainly South African) firms embedded in the private sector. The government has established a number of parastatals in an attempt to assert control over key economic sectors partially influenced by South African companies. Among the most important state firms are the Industrial Development Corporation, the Zimbabwe Development Bank, the Minerals Marketing Corporation, and the most recent state firm, the Indigenous Business Development Centre. Each one seeks to develop specific economic sectors, but also to control the productive forces through the purchase of equity in foreign and private companies. Most of these parastatals have greater access to foreign currency than many private firms. According to a managing director of a British bank in Zimbabwe in 1985, the government pressured his bank to lend to industrial and agricultural parastatals. Pro-private sector economists from the Confederation of Zimbabwe Industries (CZI) and the World Bank were both critical of this policy. Each argued that as the government clamps down on foreign currency allocation and redirects it to the public sector, the consequences will be two-fold: the private sector's share of foreign currency will be squeezed and foreign investment will decrease.

The government also heavily uses its power to extend *subsidies to parastatals* as a direct tool of influence. Between 1981 and 1985, public subsidies amounted to an average forty-two percent of the budget deficit.[28] By 1987, that figure had jumped to sixty percent.[29] The policy reforms since 1988 have helped to lower the percentage to around 40 percent of the 1991/92 budget deficit.[30] The absolute total of subsidies have risen steadily since the beginning of independence. By 1984, government subsidies to parastatals had tripled. The next six years experienced another jump which more than doubled state subsidies. With the advent of the SAP, the government intends to reduce its subsidy support by about ten percent during the 1991/92 fiscal year. Moreover, one of the financial targets determined by the SAP focuses on the reduction of subsidies to a maximum of Z$40 million by 1994/95.[31] In order to achieve this objective, the government will raise prices of goods produced by parastatals, privatize some state firms, and reduce the public sector work force. Still, the bulk of these subsidies are allocated to inefficient parastatals which have consistently lost money. Since independence, each of the nine major parastatal firms has run an accumulated overall deficit of around Z$100 million. According to Riddell, their operating annual deficits rose from just under five percent of GDP in 1980 to nearly seven percent in 1986/7.[32] The largest requirement for subsidies by a single parastatal is from the National Railways of Zimbabwe which amounts to more than 40 percent of total subsidies. Agricultural marketing boards consume another 30 percent followed by ZISCO (the state-owned steel company) with 15 percent of total subsidies.[33] Unlike Kenya's and Brazil's rapid pace towards privatization, Zimbabwe is taking

Table 5.3 Subsidies in the Zimbabwe Economy, 1980/81–1984/85, 1989/90–1991/92
(Z$ million)

	1980/81	1981/82	1982/83	1983/84	1984/85	1989/90	1990/91	1991/92
Total	106.1	138.1	156.1	269.5	312.6	450.0	654.0	598.0
Food Subsidies	73.5	100.5	125.6	150.5	149.7	–	–	–
National Railways	36.0	37.6	28.0	24.0	31.3	–	281	–
ZISCO Steel	–	–	–	52.0	76.0	–	100	–
Air Zimbabwe	–	–	–	–	18.0	–	13	–
Exporters	5.6	–	2.5	10.0	15.0	–	–	–
Assistance to Industry	–	–	–	20.0	5.3	–	–	–
Reserve Bank of Zimbabwe	–	–	–	10.0	13.6	–	–	–
Zimbabwe Broadcasting	–	–	–	3.0	3.7	–	–	–
Agricultural Marketing Boards	–	–	–	–	–	–	220	–
Agricultural Finance Corp.	–	–	–	–	–	–	40	–
Ratio of Total Budget (%)	8.3	8.2	6.9	10.3	11.1	–	10.0	–
Ratio of Budget Deficit (%)	–	44	33	43	48	–	58	40
Ratio of GDP (%)	2.9	3.3	3.3	5.2	5.2	–	5.4	–

Source 1980/81–1984/85: Anthony Hawkins, *Public Policy and the Zimbabwe Economy* (Harare: USAID, 1985); 1990/91: Republic of Zimbabwe, *1990 Budget Statement*, (Harare: Government Printer, 1990); 1991/92: *African Business*, 'Purge of Parastatals Seeks to Reduce Public Losses,' 158 (October 1991), p. 19.

Table 5.4 *Public Sector Investment Program Expenditures, 1980–84, 1990*
(in Z$ million)

Sector	1980	1981	1982	1983	1984	1990
Infrastructural	207	331	217	250	262	1159
Agricultural & Rural Development	52	97	132	180	171	345
Social Services	108	163	–	125	260	93
Administrative Services	–	90	–	47	–	–
TOTAL	367	681	349	602	693	1597

Source   Ministry of Finance, *Budget Statements* (Harare: Government Printer, various years).

a more cautious approach. Although the government has created a special committee to determine which state firm should be privatized, a more likely scenario is broadening the range of options to include joint-ventures and leasing to the private sector.[34]

Another area of government economic involvement is the *Public Sector Investment Program* (PSIP). The PSIP allows the state to play an especially significant role in the development of the country as it finances major development projects in the infrastructural, agricultural, and social services sectors. The PSIP, in the words of the Minister of Finance in 1981, is 'the Government's principal tool for restructuring the economy, correcting, influencing development and possible distortions in production as well as achieving an equitable balance within and among sectors of the economy.'[35] The initial priority of the early PSIP was the rehabilitation of the warring groups and the reconstruction of the country following many years of civil war. Within one year, priorities shifted as a response to the public's demands for increased social services and land distribution, and for infrastructural development of the transportation, communication, and energy sectors. The first PSIP budget in 1980 directed 55 percent to infrastructural projects, including railway electrification and the construction of the Wankie Thermal Power Station. But, by 1984, that proportion of the PSIP budget had fallen to 34 percent. The slack was taken up by projects in the agricultural and rural development sector (25 percent of total) and the social services sector (38 percent).

Data from the 1990/91 PSIP budget reveal another shift that returns the budgetary emphasis back to infrastructural development. As recurrent expenditures and the budget deficit rose during the late-1980s, the government altered its PSIP allocation to benefit the infrastructural sector (72 percent of total) while diminishing the social services sector (6 percent).

These changes in distributive priorities reflect two objectives: the government's attempt to reduce the overall budget deficit by restraining expenditures and its renewed concern over structural constraints affecting economic growth.[36] The PSIP priority shift was an outcome of intra-government debates concerning the relative value of investments in productive or consumption sectors of the economy. Economists urged a growth pattern based on productive development led by the state but in conjunction with the private sector. A senior official in the Zimbabwe Banking Corporation commented in an interview that 'the growth impetus should shift from education and public services to basic rural development.' In his presentation of the 1983 Finance Bill and again in the 1990 Budget Statement, the Minister of Finance found the 'asymmetry between the rapid expansion of the non-material sectors, notably education, health, and public administration, and the sharp declines in the material sectors' to be an 'extremely disconcerting feature of the growth pattern.'[37]

Parastatal Borrowing Policy

Zimbabwe also has used its authority to guarantee the loans of the public sector and parastatal firms as a means to obtain private and official credit. The government long has relied on state-guaranteed loans to finance and manage the expansion of parastatal operations. The government's total long-term loans to parastatals in 1991 amount to more than Z$1.5 billion.[38] This policy proceeded with the full backing of both international private creditors and members within the government. From the perspective of private creditors, state guarantees were crucial in extending credit to the state. One British banker even suggested in an interview that 'the key to lending was the general guarantee by the state.' A state-guaranteed loan can either be sustained by the project's capacity to earn foreign exchange or by the borrowing of additional capital. Bankers generally have expressed a preference for the former, but since a large number of loans have been invested in non-productive sectors or for balance of payments financing, private banks, in practice, rarely have been affected by the actual disbursement of their capital.

A closer examination of private bankers' attitudes toward state-owned enterprise borrowing is insightful. The pervasive notion, among bankers, that state firms are poorly managed and inefficient firms headed by corrupt officials chosen because of political patronage rather than business aptitude, has not seriously affected bank-state firm relations. Private bankers repeatedly expressed their interest in maintaining business ties with these firms while acknowledging their generally unprofitable performance. A statement made by a Barclays banker is indicative of most bankers' attitude toward parastatals: 'given state guarantees, banks are quite willing to do business with state-owned enterprises.' A Standard and Chartered banker mentioned that 'what is not that important is the massive state subsidies of state-owned enterprises or their actual balance sheet performance . . . All loans have to be state-guaranteed. These loans can only be commercial (ie, profitable for the lending bank) if state-guaranteed.' The use of state guarantees releases the banks from sharing the risk of their investments with indebted states. The primary risk of non-repayment due to project failure or increasing state deficits has been assumed by the government's acceptance of bank risk. 'State-owned enterprises, like the state,' claimed one British banker, 'could never go bankrupt and thus agencies could not be placed in liquidation.' The ideological disposition of Zimbabwe failed to persuade at least one major international bank's to weaken its relationship with the government. A bank official with Barclays said that 'no matter the rhetoric, if their loans are guaranteed by the state, the bank will continue to be well served.'

Sectoral Allocation

A primary issue for the state is the means by which foreign loans can be channeled to state firms according to its own distributive priorities. Zimbabwe's adjustment strategy has sought to incorporate state guarantees as a means of controlling parastatal indebtedness and their vulnerability to international economic conditions. A senior economist in the RAL Merchant Bank in Zimbabwe pointed out in an interview that the government considers the state guarantee mechanism as a potential control over state firms in particular sectors. The government has overseen and guaranteed the capital investments in a number of sectors managed, in part, by the state. The central government has created new and expanded old parastatals, such as the Electricity Supply Commission, the National Railways, the National Pipeline, Air Zimbabwe, ZISCO Steel, and other major infrastructural firms. Private creditors have expressed much interest in extending credit to infrastructural projects so long as they can be guaranteed repayment and the development efforts strengthen foreign exchange earning capabilities.[39]

During the period of the Unilateral Declaration of Independence, the settler state carried a small burden of state-guaranteed debt. The external loans were contracted before the installment of the Smith regime. The ratio of state-guaranteed external loans arranged for the public sector to the total public sector debt did not vary much between 1973 and 1980, averaging 48 percent.[40] The Central African Power Corporation was the main beneficiary of state-guaranteed loans. Its portion of these loans from

1973 to 1980 amounted to 92 percent, or to over Z $150 million. By the late-1970s, the government began to inject large sums of capital in support of the war effort as well as to establish a more efficient industrial base.

Since independence, the state began to guarantee loans to an expanding number of state-owned enterprises. The Central African Power and the railways had their support continued, but other agencies in energy, transportation, and agricultural sectors received large external loans backed by the state. Energy and transportation agencies received 86 percent of all state-guaranteed external loans between 1981 and 1983. Agricultural loans also received state-guarantees since, in the long run, the projects could become self-sufficient and could lead to foreign exchange earnings. The state, playing a dominant role in agricultural development, exercised control, in 1982, over 60 percent of the commercial farming sectors via its marketing agencies.[41] Much of the financial control stems from the state's role in guaranteeing about 60 percent of the Agricultural Marketing Authority's (AMA) borrowings.[42] The burden of the risk attached to indebtedness based on vacillating price structures and export volumes was not a major concern for a senior AMA official. 'The question of risk does not affect the AMA, as long as the government fulfills its obligation.' International creditors were only too pleased by the upsurge in state-guaranteed loans and the repayment responsibility shifted to the central government.

A similar position was held by a senior director of the Mineral Development Corporation, a parastatal organized as a primary investment instrument of the state. He recognized the inherent risks in lending foreign capital to the mining sector. The short-term maturity structure of the loans do not usually reflect the length of the projects. Short-term loans also have high premiums which the corporation will pay through state guarantees and subsidies. 'The financial risks derived from borrowing,' according to this official, 'rest with the government.' The alternative borrowing route is to guarantee foreign exchange earnings generated by long-term mineral contracts. Given the deteriorated economic status of the mineral industry, any financial support in the intermediate future will continue to come from the central government.

Budget Allocation

Up until the late-1980s, the government unequivocally attempted to meet the public expectations that arose from independence by a considerable expansion in the budget allotment for basic needs. In the 1980/81 budget, education, as a proportion of recurrent expenditure, received 15 percent. However, *interests payments* and *defense* expenditures also combined for another large component of the government budget; throughout the 1980s, they accounted for over one-third of it. Annual interest payments on the foreign debt amounted to nearly seven percent of the total government expenditure in the fiscal year 1988/89. By the 1991/92 fiscal year, this figure is expected to rise to almost 13 percent.[43] The persistent security problem along the border with Mozambique has meant also that defense expenditures continue to be a major drain on the budget. The defense component of the current budget is about thirteen percent.

Emphasis on the *basic needs sector* continued in the late-1980s. In the fiscal year 1987/8, education consumed about seventeen percent of the budget while health accounted for nearly six percent.[44] The 1989/90 budget called for an increase in education spending to 19 percent of the budget. In response to inflationary tendencies in the economy, the government froze both wages and prices in May 1987 only again to raise wages by fifteen percent in March 1988 while only permitting a five percent rise in prices. As a further support for workers, the government is enforcing labor regulation that restricts the laying off and firing of workers. These distributive policies continued in the face of strong objections by the World Bank and international private banks.[45] Since the government embarked on an adjustment strategy in the early 1980s that could be considered heterodox, the budget's allotment to the social services is not surprising. Neither is the significant portion of the budget allocated for interest payments because of the government's objective of maintaining strong credit relations with international creditors.

The Zimbabwe government further has relied on state subsidies to acquire small and medium-sized manufacturing businesses and to establish numerous state-owned enterprises. Subsidies help to keep low sales prices to consumers (mainly for wheat and milk products), permit more rapid increases paid to producers relative to international levels, and to secure employment. Subsidies also have supported nonagricultural parastatals that suffer from losses, operating inefficiency, and inadequate pricing structures.

Additionally, though the government has not conducted a policy of sweeping nationalization, it has intervened consistently in the economy in its pursuit of the 'Zimbabweanization' of the productive capital stock. Through direct investment, sometimes on a joint-venture basis, or through indirect investment, using the state-owned Industrial Development Corporation, the government has used its authority in an attempt to shape the economic structure. The government followed such a policy despite the reliance on foreign loans to finance this move. Of the total foreign loan obligations in mid-1987, 28 percent were liabilities of state-owned companies.[46] In 1983, the government acquired a forty percent equity

Table 5.5 *Expenditure by Function of Zimbabwe's Central Government, 1982–1989 (as percent of total expenditures)*

Year	Public Service	Defense	Interest Payments	Education	Economic Affairs	Agriculture	Health
1982	11.8	17.3	9.1	21.9	24.2	10.4	6.4
1983	11.7	18.3	10.7	21.5	20.8	6.1	6.2
1984	11.5	16.2	11.3	20.4	26.0	10.9	6.2
1985	11.2	15.6	13.0	21.0	25.9	10.9	6.5
1986	10.3	16.5	13.3	22.2	25.5	11.7	6.7
1987	12.5	17.1	13.3	21.0	24.0	9.9	6.8
1988	11.1	16.3	14.1	22.0	23.1	11.0	7.6
1989	11.2	16.5	15.5	23.4	22.4	11.1	7.6

Source International Monetary Fund, *Government Finance Statistics Yearbook, 1991* (Washington, D.C.: IMF, 1991).

interest in the Hwange Colliery. In 1984, it purchased all shares of Lancashire Steel. A 1985 study found that the government's investment in the private sector covered a wide spectrum, including holdings in newspapers, banks, and manufacturing industries.[47] More recently, government purchases of shares in foreign companies that wanted to disinvest in 1987 and 1988 have contributed to the $54 million in net foreign disinvestment outflows in those years.[48] A senior economist in RAL Merchant Bank suggested in an interview that 'through these bureaucratic regulations, the government has all of the power with nationalization, but none of the initial costs of responsibility.' A 1989 confidential U.S. bank study noted that 'paradoxically, the government is encouraging new foreign investment while at times expanding its control over the private sector which it considers to be dominated by foreign ownership.'

What is of particular interest is the shift in the distribution of expenditures as the government began an ambitious neo-orthodox strategy of economic adjustment in the late-1980s that has accelerated into the 1990s. A primary target under the SAP is a major reduction of the budget deficit. A result of the government's early 'home-grown' adjustment strategy has been budget deficits running near 10 percent of GDP. As we have seen in Chapter Four, the central concern among the more orthodox groups (including international donors, private creditors, foreign investors, and the domestic private sector) is the adverse impact of the deficit on the availability of capital for 'productive' investments made by the private sector. While budget statements historically have called for fiscal restraint, policy measures only recently have been taken to reduce the budget deficit. The government's aim is to reduce the deficit by two percent of GDP per year until it reaches five percent by 1994/95.[49]

The government intends to reverse its decade-old strategy by eliminating significant portions of the government bureaucracy and by reducing subsidies to parastatals. The government reported that 41 percent of recurrent expenditures in 1989/90 were committed as salaries for civil servants.[50] The objective in the current budget is to make a 25 percent cut in civil service staff levels in all divisions, with the exception of education.[51] That is, adjustment under the SAP is expected to increase unemployment by 25,000 civil servants, 20,000 from the private sector, and a minimum of 2000 parastatal employees although President Mugabe recently said that rather than retrenching these civil servants, they will be 'redeployed.'[52] State support for parastatals also will be affected under the current adjustment strategy. One policy is to clear parastatals' losses by the end of 1994/95, 'except only in exceptional cases, where subsidies will be directed towards target groups.' A second policy is to progressively lower the ceiling limit of government subsidies to parastatals so that by the end of 1994/95, parastatals will be operating without direct government support.[53]

Social services, the heart of Zimbabwe's 'home-grown' adjustment program, will not escape the scrutiny coming from fiscal pressures. Although education in the 1991/92 budget is allotted 32 percent of the total (a ten percent increase over the previous year), user fees in both education and health will reduce those who are eligible.[54] In broad terms, the government recognizes some of the social costs of its economic adjustment strategy: more unemployed, higher prices, and more people in need of basic services. As an attempt to protect at least the fired civil servants, the government, in conjunction with the African Development Bank, is establishing a *Social Development Fund*. The government is supplying $44 million of the $80 million needed to cover the first two years of the SAP.[55]

Even with a Social Development fund to cushion the results of Zimbabwe's adjustment program, the long-standing distributive priorities will be threatened. As one observer writes, 'compensation for less than 4 percent of the formal sector work force pales into insignificance when set against unemployment growth of at least 200,000 a year over the next five years.'[56] One study noted that the government will require a substantial inflow of capital to generate new jobs. The study reported that between 1989 and 1991, $750 million managed to create only 40,000 jobs. Creating formal sector employment for 200,000 new job-seekers each year implies an investment of $3.75 billion annually – 75 percent of Zimbabwe's GDP.[57]

Domestic opposition to Zimbabwe's economic adjustment program also is mounting. With a projected inflation rate of 30 percent in 1992 cutting into incomes, salaried workers and civil servants and their trade unions are voicing their dismay. The secretary general of the Zimbabwe Congress of Trade Unions commented that 'trade unions should not be expected to abide by wage restraint policies that they had not been party to.'[58] Members of the business community also have expressed their concerns about the effects of the SAP. Standard Chartered Bank warned in February 1992 of the 'possibility of widespread bankruptcies and a general deterioration of the business climate because of high interest rates as the government implemented a tighter monetary policy.'[59]

One of the most important distributive policies of Zimbabwe's early development plan concerns land reform. The current drought, which some claim to be the worse in 30 years, has made the issue of land redistribution more urgent and controversial. The Land Acquisition Bill is designed to enable the government to acquire land owned mainly by white farmers, through compulsory purchase with a controversial compensation scheme. Although white commercial farmers account for 40 percent of exports, the law would redistribute one-half of their land to small black farmers.[60] Although this bill has incurred the wrath of the Commercial Farmers' Union, the government, according to one report, has tried to soften the radicalism by claiming the bill would not affect any other assets in the economy.[61]

Zimbabwe's response to the distributive consequences of economic adjustment illustrates several important differences from Kenya's strategy. For most of the 1980s, public sector development projects in Zimbabwe were extended into areas of the society left untouched by the Smith regime under UDI. Government policy allocated capital for national development and basic goods objectives, while it allowed central government deficits to climb. The government was willing to risk the costs of deficit financing and the deterioration of its international credit standing in order to advance a transformation of the society. However, after several recent and consecutive years of drought and a foreign exchange drain for the purchase of food imports, the socialist and nationalist development plan of the early 1980s has been scaled down. Zimbabwe presents a clear case in which *economic growth* objectives rest in a precarious balance with *social distributive* objectives. In 1992, Zimbabwe's economic adjustment strategy now must respond to increasing internal demands from domestic exporting interests and international credit interests who are calling for a more liberal economic and political policy.

DISTRIBUTIVE POLICIES OF BRAZIL'S ADJUSTMENT STRATEGY

In order to understand the Brazilian state's role in allocating resources we first need to examine the relationship between the private and public sectors. The distributive impact from Brazil's twin strategies of economic adjustment and debt management differs in some respect from that of Kenya and Zimbabwe. Overall, Brazil has been more successful than Kenya in turning indebtedness into an advantage for the state and the public sector. Another important factor that distinguishes Brazil from the African cases is the traditional role of the strong state dating back to its colonial period and, more currently, to the 1930s and the formation of the Estado Novo under Vargas.[62] Vargas' administrations were responsible for, and succeeding regimes refined, the creation of an enormous social welfare system backed by a rapid growth of government agencies and state firms. Yet, even with this foundation for centralized state control, many important state-owned enterprises developed their own political and economic power base often working for their own representatives rather than for the central government. An independent course of action was taken, in particular, by the energy sector, led by Petrobras. Its fiscal and borrowing policies have been regulated weakly by state authorities. The Brazilian public sector is not only very large, but extremely complex. It consists of the general government and a number of state-owned enterprises. The general government itself is comprised of the federal government, the state governments, and the municipal governments. The federal government accounts for about 70 percent of revenues and 65 percent of expenditures of the consolidated government. It alone encompasses approximately 600 decentralized agencies and partially controls some 400 firms. The public sector in Kenya or Zimbabwe has neither the historical experience nor the absolute size of that in Brazil.

Allocation between Public and Private Sectors

In addition to a massive public sector, the Brazilian state also has supported an active private sector in the domestic capital market. A distinct division of labor emerged by which the state allowed the private sector to intercede in the low-risk and short-term areas of consumer credit and to channel government and foreign loans to private borrowers. The public sector's capital investment initiative followed high-risk and long-term credit markets in the agricultural, housing, and industrial sectors.[63] Investment through the private sector soon came to represent the production of capital goods and their distribution as export items to international markets, whereas public sector investment focused on national development projects and the domestic market.

During the so-called 'miracle' period of the late-1960s and early 1970s, the two sectors worked in conjunction in an environment of increasing consumption and growing indebtedness as foreign loans were used to finance deficits in the trade account. The areas of government responsibility overlapped into the ministries overseeing internal development and external accounts. The Ministry of Planning and the Central Bank positioned themselves to use international credit for across-the-board investment objectives without regard to their political and economic consequences. This represented, on the one hand, the ability of Brazil's strategy to attract foreign bank capital, and yet, this apparent success in influencing international creditors in the 1970s was tempered by the debt management problems of the 1980s and continuing into the 1990s. As the flow of foreign credit diminished and as combined interest payments and trade deficits grew, the investment decision-making process became more conflictual for both the public and private sector.

The major impetus behind public sector growth was a massive investment plan for the capital goods sector during the 1970s. The intended consequences of the plan, however, fell to the wayside as a deeper transformation occurred. 'What began as an institutional reform,' wrote two scholars, 'to promote the low cost capitalization of private sector growth has in effect become a vehicle for public financing policies.'[64] The plan forecast a $43 billion investment program for the capital goods sector. The estimate was based entirely on state enterprises, including those firms producing exportable goods in electricity, steel, and petrochemical industries, and on their ability to seek financing from domestic capital markets and to earn foreign exchange through the sale of their products. In contrast to the 1950s when the public sector's share of gross fixed capital investment stood at 25 percent, by 1960 it had expanded to 48 percent and, by 1980, it had risen to 60 percent.[65] The capital goods sector benefited most from Brazil's economic adjustment strategy. Unlike the decline in the state's participation experienced by the consumer goods sectors, public assistance given to the capital goods sector rose from five percent of the total investment in 1973 to 18 percent in 1977.[66] Resolution 9 submitted by the state's Economic Development Council in 1977 reaffirmed the measures for the support of capital goods production. The state intended to promote participation by the domestic private sector in these production projects. Yet, the bulk of financing remained in the public sector's budget and various investment projects. Given the deterioration of the world economy, the decline in the latter part of the 1970s in domestic demand and production, and the level of unused industrial capacity, both the revenues and self-financing ability of the public sector were reduced.

The financial position of the public sector also was affected heavily by the second oil price hike and the deep international recession of the early 1980s. The government in 1979 sought immediate relief through the establishment of a state agency given power to monitor the approval and implementation of state enterprise budgets (Secretariat for the Control of State Enterprises, SEST). In comparison to Kenya and Zimbabwe, Brazil moved faster and more formally in regulating parastatal financial activities. Nevertheless, by the early 1980s, all three governments had created institutional authorities to oversee parastatal operations. The effects of this state policy was felt almost immediately. The public sector deficit, which had stood at 9 percent of GDP in 1980, fell to 7.1 percent in 1981 and to 6.2 percent in 1982.[67] Yet, by the early 1990s, failure to rationalize parastatal financial activities and to control parastatal borrowing led to a widening of the public sector budget deficit. Due to higher interest rates on the internal debt, the deficit is expected to grow to 36 percent of GDP in 1991.[68]

Brazil's policy toward the public sector and its budget deficits has been influenced by two significant groups. On the one hand, an outward-looking set of interests made up, in part, by Central Bank officials and international creditors, seek the elimination of the *trade deficit*, while Ministry of Planning officials often place more emphasis on the elimination of the *public sector budget deficit*. The former looks to the international export sector with trade finance loans and short-term roll-overs as means to establish creditworthiness. International bankers in interviews gave the impression that the effect of budget deficits on their credit determination is minimal and they would rather see greater public and private sector commitment toward Brazil's export capacity. Their management policy, as reflected by the position of the National Monetary Council (an agency under the control of the Ministry of Finance), encourages the private sector to seek foreign resources, promotes the intensive use of suppliers' credit to finance imports, and urges the constant search for new sources of capital.[69]

The Ministry of Planning, on the other hand, presents other measures to control the foreign public debt. They include the cutting of parastatal expenditures, the reduction of their credit subsidies, and the maintenance of strict control on the amount of credit available to parastatal firms. Public sector finances have come under the direct control of the Ministry of Planning, from regulating staff levels to the external debt of state firms. Since, at the beginning of the debt crisis, state enterprises accounted for 70 percent of public sector expenditures and over 70 percent of the foreign debt, the management of credit allocation became an important objective of the Ministry of Planning.[70] A primary goal of the 1981 SEST budget then was 'to make the expenditure programs of the state enterprises compatible with the real availability of financial resources' and, at the same time, to minimize their dependence on foreign sources of credit.[71]

These two groups and their economic policies represented for one observer the 'ongoing contradiction in the bosom of the government itself, which supported a developmentalist, interventionary policy, on the one hand, and a conservative monetarist policy, on the other.'[72] By the 1980s, the 'contradiction' was at least temporarily resolved when the state, in seeking to boost trade surpluses, intervened directly in the external sector by supporting an outward-looking trade strategy. The government established sets of policies in an attempt to limit the deteriorating economy and to strengthen the state's control over its international credit rating.

In seeking to manage a growing debt burden, the exchange rate has been one of the state's main instrument for promoting exports and discouraging imports. The 30 percent devaluation in 1979 and again in 1983 raised the cost of the dollar in cruzeiro terms; the latter devaluation increased by 289 percent in the twelve months prior to 1983, compared with a rate of inflation of 211 percent for the same period.[73] The government continued its aggressive devaluation policy into the 1990s. The cruzeiro fell by fifteen percent on September 15, 1991 followed by an additional decline of 12.5 percent by the end of the year.[74] While these large devaluations improved the value of Brazilian exports, there also was the danger of increasing the country's debt-servicing burden and the large proportion of internal government debt which is pegged to the dollar. The double-edged sword of devaluation hampered any overall improvement in the balance of payments.

The government also has relied heavily on export and import policies as means of improving the country's cash-flow position. As stated by the National Monetary Council, the country's export credit policy in the 1980s was based on the financial assistance given by international creditors. A close collaboration between foreign creditors and the state in facilitating international trade supported, according to the government in the early 1980s, the 'continued diversification of products and markets, in such a way as to ensure export growth.'[75] By the 1990s, the strategy has shifted towards a liberalization of import controls. The Brazilian government committed itself in the 1991 Letter of Intent to the IMF that the maximum tariff is to be reduced from 105 percent in 1990 to 85 percent in 1991 and to 40 percent by January 1994.[76] Yet, as in both the Kenya and Zimbabwe cases, the government in Brazil recognized early the necessity in encouraging strong export performance. As one study noted, 'manufactured export growth is also important to alleviate the adverse effect on employment of the current contractionary demand management, which may be made worse by the increase in import penetration.'[77]

One of the most prominent formal attempts encouraging the growth of exports was the Befiex program. Since its inception in 1972, this program had a significant influence in the expansion of manufacturing exports. In its first six years, those exports grew to over $1 billion.[78] In exchange for signing long-term export commitment contracts with the government, firms were exempted from the payment of import taxes on raw materials and capital goods incorporated in the exported products. After approval of the project by the Ministry of Industry and Commerce, firms would then earn import tax reductions of 70 to 90 percent. Most Befiex projects benefited the automotive industry and foreign firms because of the government's central role in increasing the level of foreign capital investment. The current implementation of the Befiex program continues to be successful. In 1991, about 70 percent of Brazilian manufactured exports were made under Befiex contracts.[79] The level of state participation in the subsidies of export firms also has acted as an incentive for increased foreign bank lending. A U.S. banker, who has worked in Brazil, said in an interview that banks lend, for example, to the steel sector under the condition that the state finances the exports and subsidizes the firm in addition to the interest paid to the banks.

The government sought to allay the fears of exporters in other sectors by administering credit incentives for only exports. One type of incentive provides credit for export sales by lending money at interest rates below the international rate. CACEX (the Foreign Trade Department of the Central Bank) subsidizes the gap between commercial and official rates of interest for export firms. Another incentive plan encourages export production. The government contributes 15 percent of a firm's export value to the firm when export earnings are converted into the local currency. Thus, the government acquires foreign exchange and the export sector obtains Brazilian currency.

State-Guaranteed Loans

Another factor that reflects Brazil's distributive orientation is its policy toward the sectoral allocation of state-guaranteed loans. The role of state guarantees, as in the cases of Kenya and Zimbabwe, has evolved into a major force in the centralization of control for the Brazilian state. First, during the early 1980s, all foreign loans had to be submitted 'to the demands of the administration of external debt and to the priorities of economic policy.' The government then exerted 'rigid control' over the credit operations of parastatal firms.[80] The government also consolidated the budgets of these public sector firms under the aegis of the Ministry of Planning. The Planning Secretariat controlled the budgets of all ministries and regulated the ceiling of indebtedness for state firms. Currently, the Secretariat for the Control of State Enterprises directs the borrowing requirements of state firms.

Second, all public sector loans and, in particular, loans to state firms, must have guarantees that are also backed by international reserves. The state, in the late-1970s, sought to maintain at least one dollar of reserves for every five dollars of foreign debt.[81] As the applicability of this goal became less feasible, international creditors demanded guarantees at a greater cost to the state. Brazil, then, was placed in a position where it had to not just improve the country's general economic condition, but it had to take on, as a sovereign entity, the risk of public sector loans. An 'on-line' official for Bankers Trust in Brazil said that banks prefer lending to state firms because 'sovereign risk improves as the country risk weakens.' As long as the state and, in particular, the Central Bank as administrator, guarantees foreign loans, 'state-owned enterprises,' according to several American and British bankers, 'are a very secure destination of bank loans.'

Apart from the IMF and many industrialized states, the Brazilian government and international banks believed that linking external loans to state-guarantees was an appropriate policy. The state centralization of public financing facilitated a substantial inflow of foreign resources into the state treasury and the means to sustain ambitious capital formation programmes. Yet, at the same time, the state-guaranteed debt aggravated the pattern of dependence on foreign sources of capital and the need to service that debt. In 1981, the debt load of over 500 parastatals accounted for $29.3 billion, that is over two-thirds of the public sector foreign debt. Not surprisingly, the greatest growth in state-guaranteed debt by these firms occurred in foreign exchange-generating sectors such as in the electric energy, steel, oil, mining, and transportation sectors. It is not coincidental that all but one of these debtor firms (steel) placed among the ten largest state enterprises in the 1970s.[82] Not only have international banks stipulated lending to state-guaranteed firms, but Brazil showed its willingness to risk its subsidization of the export sector by promoting state guarantees.

Public Sector Reforms

As discussed in Chapter Four, in its debt negotiations with the IMF, the government of Brazil is expected to undertake fiscal adjustment reforms that would include a new emphasis on reforming and restructuring state-owned enterprises. Calls for privatization, especially from the international financial community, resonated throughout the 1980s and have not let up in the 1990s. As the number of public sector firms quickly grew (150 new firms were added in the 1960s and another 215 in the 1970s), concern was expressed about their relative profitability.[83] One study noted that the profits of public enterprises were only about half of those of multinational firms operating in Brazil in 1978.[84] In 1981, the government issued two decrees that established restrictions on the creation of state firms and further established guidelines on the transfer of those firms to the private sector. In light of the decline of the GDP by 11 percent from 1981 to 1983 and in the face of a politically charged environment against the possible expansion of foreign firms in the economy, this early attempt at privatization failed.

A second attempt in the mid-1980s also sought to create a list of firms for privatization and procedures for their sale. By 1987, the Privatization Council had constructed a list of 179 firms for sale that either were not considered strategic or did not provide essential services.[85] Despite the rhetoric of privatization, between 1981 and 1987 the government only sold 35 small firms.[86] Indeed, from 1980 to 1989, the accumulated sales from privatization amounted to just $800 million.[87]

During the fall of 1988, the Sarney administration created a new *Federal Council on Privatization* that was charged with objectives similar to those of its predecessor. The newly revised list included 100 firms though many of them had appeared on earlier lists. The first wave of sales would be from the manufacturing sector, followed by the privatization of the ports systems.[88] The new guidelines issued in August 1990 allowed foreign investors to be able to buy up to 40 percent of the voting capital of the privatized companies and up to 49 percent of privatized forms on a resale.[89] Yet, there was still a wide gap between the *expected financial pay-off* from the privatization process and the *actual payments*. According to the Council director in 1989, he anticipated that privatization for that year would generate $3 billion from the sale of state firms.[90] In 1990, the government originally sought to raise at least $7 billion from sales through its privatization program. However, a number of delays during the year interrupted it. The government initially intended to sell eleven firms in 1990, but subsequently that number was reduced to eight.[91] According to another statement offered by the head of the privatization program, the government is hoping to raise $17 billion between 1990 and 1992 from the privatization of 40 state firms. Most of these estimates have proven inaccurate. The first wave under the privatization program again was postponed until October 1991 when the major steel firm (Usiminas) was sold to a consortium of private firms for $1.1 billion. Earlier in the year, the government expected the sale of Usiminas to yield $3 billion.[92] By the end of 1991, three other companies were sold, with total proceeds exceeding $1.2 billion. This year-end total sales figure and the estimated figure for 1992 of between $2 and $3 billion are both well under the earlier projections.[93] A 1988 study on the privatization program in Brazil correctly anticipated its minimal impact. The author wrote that 'given that relatively few public sector companies are attractive to the private sector, and that substantial political hostility remains toward the privatization process, it is unlikely that Brazil's privatization policy will be more than a footnote to the country's economy in the foreseeable future.'[94]

Budget Allocation

A brief review of the expenditure patterns of Brazil's central government reveals an interesting trend. During the 1980s, as the government agreed to and implemented a series of economic adjustment programs with its foreign creditors, social welfare and infrastructural sectors received a declining portion of the total expenditure. The percentage provided to the education and health sectors declined during the mid-1980s, but both have shown slight improvement in recent years.

Brazil's distributive policies share with those of Kenya and Zimbabwe the need to respond to domestic economic and political groups affected by economic adjustment strategies. A two-level analysis of the interaction between the state and domestic groups also is broadly applicable to Brazil as well as to the African cases. However, analysis of more specific distributive policies in Brazil illustrates some differences. The state has used its considerable financial resources and economic potential to its own advantage by creating and sustaining a massive public sector based on numerous state-owned firms. The Brazilian state considers its economic diversity to be a powerful factor against the restrictive conditions imposed on it by international creditors. Its adherence to this bargaining tactic has allowed the state to diversify the economy, expand the export sector, and control the borrowing process of state firms. It has controlled parastatal borrowing in order to transfer funds to the treasury of the central government. Although it attempts to manipulate international creditors, it nevertheless works within the rules set by the IFIs, and it seeks to strengthen its collaboration with those organizations. As the state has become faced with mounting budget deficits, it has had to make some adjustments in its support of privatizing public sector firms. However, it has done so not with the intention of dismantling the public sector through privatization. Rather, the intent is to manage the domestic conflict between the outward-oriented interests who are concerned with the trade deficit and other groups who have emphasized the control of the budget deficit.

CONCLUSION

Discussion on the distributive policies of economic adjustment strategies indicates that all three states are struggling in the grips of indebted development. The policies of these economic adjustment strategies can be understood by analyzing the capabilities of the state to allocate scarce resources to groups within society. The state is crucial in allocating resources, determining the balance between private and public sectors, and influencing the extent of public sector reforms. A two-level analysis as used in this book is helpful in understanding and explaining these policies that arise from strategic bargaining between the state and its domestic constituency. While this method of analysis may be considered too complex in relation to the unitary actor model, it does present a more complete and accurate account of the consequences of economic adjustment.

Given the need for some degree of economic adjustment, the primary issue for these indebted states concerns their ability to influence and manipulate the distributive effects of adjustment. A common thread that links these three countries then is their similar overall reaction to the orthodox and liberalization pressures imposed on them from international and national groups. Each state has sought to centralize its power in order to channel scarce resources to economic sectors and political groups which fit into the adjustment priorities determined by the state. Indeed, adjustment reforms often have been used by state authorities as a cover to direct and allocate funds to groups that support its development objectives. Slippage has become a common practice for all three states as they claim to carry out fiscal, monetary, and parastatal reforms. Yet, now that all three states have IMF funding programmes, the question is how much longer the IMF and other IFIs will continue to support these regimes.

In a way, all three states are walking a tightrope between various groups and interests and yet they have reacted differently to specific constituent demands. *Kenya* has responded to its budget deficits by attempting

Table 5.6 Expenditure by Function of Brazil's Central Government, 1975–1989 (as percent of total expenditures)

Year	Social Security/Welfare	Defense	Education	Health	Transportation/ Agriculture	Communication
1975	38.5	6.1	6.8	6.5	7.5	14.6
1976	36.4	6.5	5.8	7.5	5.5	11.4
1977	35.4	5.0	5.0	6.9	3.0	6.3
1978	35.6	4.3	3.5	7.3	5.3	5.8
1979	37.8	4.1	5.4	7.4	5.0	5.5
1980	33.0	3.5	3.4	6.5	6.6	3.9
1981	34.6	3.4	3.8	7.4	7.2	4.6
1982	35.3	4.3	4.6	7.8	6.3	3.2
1983	34.9	4.1	3.7	7.3	7.7	3.7
1984	31.2	3.9	3.1	7.4	4.5	3.4
1985	23.4	3.0	3.0	6.4	4.2	3.6
1986	22.7	3.2	3.3	6.1	6.3	2.3
1987	23.7	4.0	4.8	9.5	3.8	3.7
1988	20.3	4.4	4.1	6.3	1.8	2.2
1989	19.9	4.2	5.3	7.2	1.7	2.0

Source International Monetary Fund, *Government Finance Statistics Yearbook, 1991* (Washington, D.C.: IMF, 1991).

to balance the financing of export-oriented, agricultural interests while depriving large segments of the population of basic goods. *Zimbabwe* represents a contrasting distributive strategy by its continued emphasis on basic goods allocation. Yet, it too is caught on a tightrope between the pragmatists who push for economic growth and the radicals who focus on social welfare distribution. The regime's commitment to the ideals (public sector employment, basic goods, and land reform) promulgated during the civil war of the 1970s is in doubt. *Brazil*, too, is walking a tightrope, but one held by groups favouring a reduction in the trade deficit and by others committed to a reduction in the budget deficit. However, neither of these states has articulated or implemented clear and consistent guidelines to assist in distributing resources. Each has made policy decisions based on the specific context of the state-domestic interests relationship and, in particular, the relationship between the public and private sectors.

NOTES

1. Republic of Kenya, *Development Plan, 1989–1993* (Nairobi: Government Printer, 1988).
2. Republic of Kenya, *Economic Management for Renewed Growth* (Nairobi: Government Printer, 1986).
3. Economist Intelligence Unit, *Kenya: Country Profile, 1991–92* (London: EIU, 1991), p. 28; *African Economic Digest*, 'Saitoti Tinkers but Privatization Looms,' 12:21, 1 July 1991, p. 7.
4. IMF and World Bank economists, June 1988.
5. Interviews with several Kenyan bank and government officials.
6. Philip Ndegwa, *Report and Recommendations of the Working Party* (Nairobi: Government Printer, 1982), p. 40.
7. IMF economist; Standard Chartered economist; Bankers Trust banker; Barclays Bank economist, 1988.
8. Kenya Association of Manufacturers official and senior officer of Barclays Bank in Kenya, 1985.
9. Republic of Kenya, *Economic Management for Renewed Growth*, p. 41.
10. *Africa Research Bulletin*, July 16–Aug. 15, 1991, p. 10475.
11. *Africa Research Bulletin*, April 16–May 15, 1991, pp. 10369–70.
12. Tony Hawkins, 'Donors Face up to the Realities,' *Financial Times* 8 January 1992, p. III.
13. Institute of International Finance, *Kenya: Country Update*, (Washington, D.C.: IIF, 1991), p. 10.
14. *African Business*, 'Privatisation Opens Up Investment Opportunities,' 158, October 1991, p. 21.
15. Hawkins, 'Donors Face up to the Realities.'

16. Ndegwa, p. 19.
17. Data are from Republic of Kenya, *The Appropriation Accounts for the Controller and Auditor-General* (Nairobi: Government Printer, various years).
18. Ibid.
19. Institute of International Finance, *Kenya*, 1991.
20. R. Van der Hoeven and J. Vandemoortele, *Kenya: Stabilization and Adjustment Policies and Programmes* (Helsinki: World Institute for Development Economic Research, 1987), p. 7.
21. Economist Intelligence Unit, *Kenya: Country Profile, 1991–92*, p. 29.
22. Institute of International Finance, *Kenya*, 1991, p. 8.
23. Republic of Kenya, *Economic Survey* (Nairobi: Government Printer, 1984).
24. *Africa Research Bulletin*, July 16–Aug. 15, 1991, p. 10473.
25. Jeffrey Herbst, *State Politics in Zimbabwe* (Berkeley: University of California Press, 1990), p. 116.
26. Whitsun Foundation, *Money and Finance in Zimbabwe* (Harare: Whitsun Foundation, 1983), p. 120.
27. *African Economic Digest*, 'Special Report: Zimbabwe,' April 1987, p. 1.
28. Anthony Hawkins, *Public Policy and the Zimbabwe Economy* (Harare: USAID, 1985).
29. *African Economic Digest*, 'Special Report: Zimbabwe,' p. 2.
30. Institute of International Finance, *Zimbabwe Country Report* (Washington, D.C.: IIF, 1991), p. 6.
31. *African Business*, 'Purge of Parastatals Seeks to Reduce Public Losses,' 158, October 1991, p. 19.
32. Roger C. Riddell, 'Zimbabwe,' in Roger C. Riddell, ed., *Manufacturing Africa: Performance and Prospects of Seven Countries in Sub-Saharan Africa* (London: James Currey, 1990), p. 371.
33. Republic of Zimbabwe, *1990 Budget Statement* (Harare: Government Printer, 1990), p. 31.
34. *African Business*, 'Purge of Parastatals Seeks to Reduce Public Losses,' p. 19.
35. Republic of Zimbabwe, *Budget Statement* (Harare: Government Printer, 1981), p. 896.
36. Republic of Zimbabwe, *1990 Budget Statement*, p. 33.
37. The Minister noted that the rate of material growth was only one percent while the non-material rate grew 14 percent in Republic of Zimbabwe, *Finance Bill* (Harare: Government Printer, 1983), p. 913.
38. *Southern African Economist*, 'Close to the Bone,' 4:4, August–September 1991, p. 15.
39. External borrowings, particularly if guaranteed by the state, may be acceptable if proportional foreign exchange can be secured. Many capital investment programs cannot be expected to provide sufficient returns within the repayment period. The construction of infrastructural

projects require many years of committed expenditure prior to the realization of a return. The state guaranteeing of foreign bank credit became a powerful instrument in the hands of those foreign banks. The absence of a secure repayment package based on immediate returns, requires the collateral of the public sector in the form of state guarantees.

40. Data are from annual reports published by the Comptroller and Auditor-General (Harare).
41. USAID, *Country Development Strategy Statement* (Washington, D.C.: USAID, 1982), p. 10.
42. Interview with an administrator of the Agricultural Marketing Authority.
43. Institute of International Finance, *Zimbabwe*, 1991.
44. Economist Intelligence Unit, *Zimbabwe: Country Report*, #4 (London: EIU, 1987), p. 17.
45. World Bank, *Zimbabwe: A Strategy for Sustained Growth* (Washington, D.C.: World Bank, 1987), p. 54.
46. Riddell, 'Zimbabwe,' p. 371.
47. Hawkins, *Public Policy and the Zimbabwe Economy*, p. 27.
48. Institute of International Finance, *Zimbabwe* (Washington, D.C.: IIF, 1989), p. 13.
49. Republic of Zimbabwe, *1990 Budget Statement*, p. 6.
50. Ibid., p. 10.
51. *Africa Research Bulletin*, 'Five Year Economic Reform Programme,' February 16, 1991, p. 10295.
52. Tony Hawkins, 'On Course for More Growth,' *Financial Times*, 30 August 1991, p. 24.
53. Republic of Zimbabwe, *1990 Budget Statement*, p. 8.
54. *Africa Research Bulletin*, July 16, 1991, p. 10478.
55. Economist Intelligence Unit, *Zimbabwe: Country Report*, 2 (London: EIU, 1992), p. 13.
56. Hawkins, 'On Course for More Growth,' p. 24.
57. Brian Moyo, 'Coping with SAP,' *West Africa*, 3866, 14 October 1991, p. 1729.
58. Economist Intelligence Unit, *Zimbabwe: Country Report*, p. 14.
59. Ibid., p. 13.
60. *African Economic Digest*, 'Zimbabwe's Controversial Land Reform,' 13:5, 9 March 1992, p. 6.
61. *African Economic Digest*, 'Zimbabwe: On Course for More Growth,' 13:4, 24 February 1992, p. 5.
62. For an historical analysis of statism in Latin America, see Claudio Veliz, *The Centralist Tradition in Latin America* (Princeton: Princeton University Press, 1980) as well as the classic book on this period by Thomas Skidmore, *Politics in Brazil, 1930–1964: An Experiment in Democracy* (New York: Oxford University Press, 1967).
63. Sylvia Ann Hewlett, 'The State and Brazilian Economic Development:

The Contemporary Reality and Prospects for the Future,' in William Overhold, ed. *The Future of Brazil* (Boulder: Westview Press, 1978), p. 181.
64. Jose Roberto Mendonca de Barros and Douglas H. Graham, 'The Brazilian Economic Miracle Revisited: Private and Public Sector Initiative in a Market Economy,' *Latin American Research Review* 13:2 (1978), p. 10.
65. Jeffry A. Frieden, 'Third World Indebted Industrialization: International Finance and State Capitalism in Mexico, Brazil, Algeria, and South Korea,' *International Organization* 35:3 (1981), p. 418.
66. Philippe Faucher, 'The Paradise that Never Was: The Breakdown of the Brazilian Authoritarian Order,' in Thomas C. Bruneau and Philippe Faucher, eds. *Authoritarian Capitalism: Brazil's Contemporary Economic and Political Development* (Boulder: Westview Press, 1981), p. 21.
67. Inter-American Development Bank, *External Debt and Economic Development in Latin America* (Washington, D.C.: IADB, 1984), p. 164.
68. Institute of International Finance, *Brazil Country Report* (Washington, D.C.: IIF, 1991), p. 8.
69. National Monetary Council, *Foreign Sector Policy* (Brasilia, 1981), p. 3.
70. Eul-Soo Pang, 'Debt, Adjustment, and Democratic Cacophony in Brazil,' in Barbara Stallings and Robert Kaufman, eds., *Debt and Democracy in Latin America* (Boulder: Westview Press, 1989), p. 129.
71. Secretariat of Planning, *Fiscal Policy* (Brasilia, 1981), p. 5.
72. Luiz Bresser Pereira, *Development and Crisis in Brazil, 1930–1983* (Boulder: Westview Press, 1984), p. 177.
73. Lloyds Bank, *Brazil: Economic Report* (London: Lloyds Bank, 1984), p. 21.
74. Institute of International Finance, *Brazil*, 1991, p. 10.
75. National Monetary Council, *Foreign Sector Policy*, p. 2.
76. 'Letter of Intent from Brazil to the IMF,' (2 December 1991) published in *Brazil: Economic Program*, 31 (Brasilia: Central Bank of Brazil, 1991), p. 11.
77. Economist Intelligence Unit, *Brazil: Country Report*, 1 (London: EIU, 1992), p. 18.
78. William G. Tyler, *Advanced Developing Countries as Export Competitors in Third World Markets: The Brazilian Experience* (Washington, D.C.: CSIS, Georgetown University, 1980), p. 46.
79. Economist Intelligence Unit, *Brazil: Country Report*, p. 19.
80. Secretariat of Planning, *Third National Development Plan, 1980–1985* (Brasilia, 1979), pp. 36–7.
81. Sidney Dell and Roger Lawrence, *The Balance of Payments Adjustment Process in Developing Countries* (New York: Pergamon Press, 1980), p. 40.

82. Ricardo Luz da Costa Lobo, 'State and Accumulation in Contemporary Brazil, 1964–1978.' Unpublished Ph.D. dissertation. (New School for Social Research, 1982), p. 162.
83. Ethan B. Kapstein, 'Brazil: Continued State Dominance,' in Raymond Vernon, ed., *The Promise of Privatization* (New York: Council on Foreign Relations, 1988), p. 131.
84. Ibid., p. 132.
85. Ibid., pp. 135–136.
86. Ben Ross Schneider, 'Partly for Sale: Privatization and State Strength in Brazil and Mexico,' *Journal of Interamerican Studies and World Affairs* 30:4 (Winter 1988/89), p. 98.
87. Economist Intelligence Unit, *Brazil: Country Profile, 1991–92* (London: EIU, 1991), p. 14.
88. *Latin American Regional Reports: Brazil Report*, August 16, 1990, p. 7.
89. *Latin American Weekly Report*, September 6, 1990, p. 8.
90. Schneider, 'Partly for Sale: Privatization and State Strength in Brazil and Mexico,' p. 100.
91. Institute of International Finance, *Brazil: Special Report* (Washington, D.C.: IIF, 1990), p. 5.
92. *Latin American Regional Reports: Brazil Report*, February 14, 1991, p. 4.
93. Institute of International Finance, *Brazil*, 1991, pp. 6, 14.
94. Kapstein, 'Brazil: Continued State Dominance,' p. 145.

6 Conclusions: The Process of Indebted Development

This study has utilized an analytical framework which, by focusing on strategic interaction and bargaining, examines the two major economic crises facing Third World states in the 1980s and continuing into the 1990s: economic adjustment and debt management. In contrast to most other studies, this one considers these economic crises as two sides of the same coin; one that I have characterized as *indebted development.* Nearly all debtor regimes are faced with the near impossible task of accumulating scarce resources and of distributing funds in sufficient quantities in an attempt to satisfy domestic constituents (via economic adjustment strategies) and foreign financial interests (via debt management strategies). The state, considered from this two-sided perspective, stands at the center of a very difficult and controversial relationship with domestic and foreign groups.

My study can be considered as part of a third wave of studies that has occurred since the outbreak of the debt crisis in the early 1980s. The *first wave* was dominated by proponents of strict economic orthodoxy as a prescription for the ills of indebtedness. The problems of indebtedness at this time were associated with short-term solutions of liquidity. It was assumed that with a sufficient inflow of capital into these countries combined with 'getting the prices right,' the governments would sustain an environment favorable to foreign investment, fiscal responsibility, strengthened balance of trade, and manageable inflation rates. Through concerted lending the IMF attempted to increase the flow of international bank capital to help finance orthodox adjustment programs in the Third World. From looking at the economic adjustment crisis, the IMF and other supporters of economic orthodoxy similarly perceived the internal economic problems of borrowing countries to be short-term in duration and in solution.[1] As Chapter Two demonstrates, however, this short-term response to indebtedness by international creditors proved inadequate.

Studies in the *second wave* of literature generally focused on the failure of strict adherence to orthodoxy as applied to many indebted states. These studies often took two different approaches. On the one hand, some of them argued that failure to implement IMF adjustment programs implied a lack of political will. Research emphasized the inability of indebted states to implement orthodox economic programs due to specific domestic political variables, such as the relationship between political regime type and the implementation of IMF-supported programs.[2] On the other hand, some studies emphasized the relative power capabilities that external creditors maintained over debtor states. They argued that state capacity is severely constrained by the state's relationship with the IMF.[3] Other studies have documented the efforts (many of which have failed) by indebted states to shift the focus of indebted development away from economic orthodoxy to the social effects of adjustment programs.[4]

Most studies from this second wave viewed the effects of indebtedness and the policies implemented from the perspective of either debtors or creditors. The mid-1980s was a period of strong *debtor response* to the imposition of orthodoxy by the IMF. Debtors sought to use their indebtedness as a source of power against the international financial institutions.[5] Another set of studies from this time centered attention on the *creditors' response* to their exposed foreign loan position. Charles Lipson presented some of the first arguments concerning the policies of international creditors during this period.[6]

The *third wave* of studies beginning in the late-1980s abandoned this 'either/or' approach by imposing more of a comprehensive framework upon the action and reaction of debtors and creditors alike. Because of the length of the debt crisis, some observers have used variations of learning theory in analyzing the shifting policies of these actors.[7] Some have utilized this framework to examine the strategic interaction of debtors, while others have centered their research on the policies of creditors.[8] Another increasingly popular and useful tact has been applying negotiating theory to debt rescheduling. While negotiating implies the relationship between at least two actors, many studies often simplify their research by focusing on the bargaining stance of one of the actors.[9]

Combining these approaches into a *unified perspective* was one of the primary objectives of this study. Following some of the suggestions offered by Callaghy, Griffith-Jones, Haggard and Kaufman, and Mosley, et al, I have examined both economic adjustment and debt management strategies that define the debtor states' relationship to their creditors and to their domestic constituents.[10] I argue in this book that economic adjustment and debt management are closely intertwined. Indeed, by examining their specific ties as detailed in the three cases, I assert that they are strategically and integrally linked. All three debtor states have pursued complementary strategies: their economic adjustment strategies are directed to their domestic constituency, while debt management strategies are oriented to the demands and expectations of their international creditors. In today's economic and political reality, these debtor states have found that attempts to reduce their foreign debt are directly and explicitly related to efforts toward reforming the economy. In 'real' terms, economic reforms, more often than not, imply imposition of austerity measures in society which necessitates an examination of who is to be harmed.

I incorporated a methodological framework that best reflects the strategic interaction of groups at different 'levels.' This study moreover parts from many other studies by drawing on the literature concerning two-way strategic bargaining between these two levels of interests. In large measure, my approach has adapted and modified the two-level bargaining game as discussed by Robert Putnam.[11] My book considered strategic bargaining as a process involving negotiators bargaining with their opposites (negotiator as bargainer) and bargaining with their constituents (negotiator as representative).[12]

The *two-level game* provides a more complete (though necessarily more complex) analysis of strategic bargaining of creditors, debtors, and their constituents than does a *state-centric unitary model* of negotiations. First, strategic moves during the negotiation phase between the state and creditors (Level I in Putnam's terms) are influenced by the game between the domestic constituents and the state (Level II) because of the need for domestic constituents to ratify the final agreement at Level I. At the center of these interactions is political struggle and conflict. The two-level model offers an analytical framework for understanding policy outcome as a product of numerous political struggles among competing national and international interests.

In contrast to the two-level work, a unitary model assumes policy congruence which manifests itself as a coherent, distinct bargaining strategy. The state identifies a single national policy and strategy which can be explained by its interests and its relative sources of leverage (economic performance, size of foreign debt, strategic power) in the international system. However, an aggregate construction of the state inappropriately dismisses the importance of complex social and political realities within debtor countries. Level I analysis is necessary, but not sufficient in understanding and explaining the different policy outcomes over time. Another advantage in using the two-level model is the incorporation and analysis of the efforts by Level I negotiators to influence the Level II game of the other negotiator. By targeting their initiatives to the domestic political environment, Level I negotiators seek to increase the likelihood of a ratifiable agreement by influencing the preferences of constituents of the other negotiator.

Conclusions: The Process of Indebted Development

The two-level game thus provides a framework to allow the state to be considered as an actor with its own interests, objectives, and political capabilities. The state, though not simply an autonomous actor, is an entity with formal institutional capacities that either defend or promote its interests during the period of indebted development. Callaghy earlier noted this tension when he wrote that 'the success or failure of adjustment efforts to a large degree depends on a government's ability to insulate itself from – and buffer against and adjust to – threatening political, societal, and international pressures that might prevent the inherent economic logic of the adjustment process from coming into play to the extent necessary.'[13] Paradoxically, the indebted state has emerged from the debt crisis as a viable player in the adjustment process, using its leverage against its domestic constituents and international creditors. Both Callaghy and Biersteker have noted that a result of attempted economic reforms has not been a diminishment of state capabilities, but rather the state has become an integral actor in these reforms.[14]

The apparent *paradox of state power* in indebted states can be clarified by analysis of their adjustment and debt management strategies. These strategies clearly have unleased varied responses from domestic and foreign interests, some of whom seek to weaken the state while others attempt to align themselves with it. Through a mixture of economic orthodoxy and heterodoxy that most appropriately matches the dominant ideology in society, the state uses its power in an attempt to shape the adjustment process. The state utilizes its technocratic-administrative apparatus to design and implement development plans that reflect those governing societal interests. An important implication from this book is that the particular combination of economic adjustment strategies suggests that most economically precarious states attempt to implement policy reforms whether or not an IMF program is in place. The state uses its range of power capabilities in penetrating, extracting, or allocating scarce resources with the IMF or without the IMF. One finding from this study is that a concentration of state power is necessary for states (such as Zimbabwe) which make economic adjustments in spite of external pressures exerted by the IMF or other financial institutions. Another finding from Kenya's experience is its ability to use 'slippage' as a deliberate bargaining tactic in its relationship with the IMF and World Bank. A third finding from all three cases is the state's ability and willingness to manipulate the timing, scope, and content of the adjustment programs. Given the need for some degree of economic adjustment, the primary issue for these states concerns their ability to influence and manipulate the effects of adjustment.

All three states are making economic decisions that are constrained by a similar *dilemma*: to what extent should they enact policies that either respond to the demands of domestic constituents or to international creditors? None of these cases has illustrated the ease in finding a balance between these two economic forces. Indeed, all, with varying degrees of success, have attempted to define an uneasy and unstable balance whose success depends on the regime's willingness to implement conditionalities, the availability of alternative sources of capital, and the regime's own power resources.

Kenya's response to indebted development has been to aggressively attract all forms of foreign capital, publicly accept most terms imposed on loans, and speak the language of economic orthodox adjustment. Yet, a closer examination of Kenya's bargaining strategy suggests that the regime has succeeded in neglecting implementation of many conditions. Kenya is widely known for its policy slippage which is not surprising considering the regime's historic geostrategic and economic relationship with the IFIs and several donor governments. This state, widely identified as a conservative regime, often has used its power to manipulate international creditors and to award narrowly defined domestic interests. In what may be called a neo-orthodox approach, the state actively uses its regulatory power and legal controls to promote a growth-oriented economy based on the agricultural export sector. It further relies on its powers to only slowly make reforms in the parastatal sector since those state firms form the basis of a powerful patronage system controlled by the governing elites and that any dramatic change in the control of these state firms would seriously threaten the status quo. Yet, Kenya's debt management strategy favors most international creditors with its emphasis on punctual repayment, avoidance of arrears accumulation, and a willingness to borrow. Clearly, examination of its distributive decisions further indicates the state's broad agreement with its creditors. In order to meet certain IMF terms (ie, debt reduction), the costs of adjustment have been imposed on the basic goods sector and on parastatals that do not generate foreign exchange.

However, as Kenya's economic imbalance became more acute by the late-1980s, the state has followed a more cautious liberalization program. It has consolidated old controls and established new ones. However, foreign investment, borrowing, and public sector investment controls are not considered as long-term instruments of monetary and fiscal policy, but as temporary controls that are a 'necessary evil.' Instead of using negative controls as weapons against foreign investors, the state regards them as institutional incentives that should promote investments. Rather than using controls as means to block repatriated profits (as in Zimbabwe), the state seeks to manage indebtedness in order to attract additional foreign capital.

Conclusions: The Process of Indebted Development 211

The state is using its enhanced power to broaden its ties to foreign and domestic export-oriented, agricultural, and foreign exchange-generating firms. Yet, contrary to its stated orthodox objectives, the Kenya state still seeks to protect the domestic market, especially import-substituting industries and, rather than dismantle parastatals, the state only promises to restructure them. The future success of Kenya's bargaining strategies depends on two variables: a) the perception held by its international creditors is changing as Kenya refuses to implement genuine reforms. The policy of slippage, permitted for decades by donors and IFIs, is coming under vigorous attack and b) the government not only is being pressed by external creditors to liberalize the economy, but it is under rising pressure from domestic constituents calling for real political liberalization.

Zimbabwe also is currently burdened by this indebted development dilemma. Overall, the state has been seeking a balanced strategy between economic growth and equitable distribution. However, for much of the 1980s, the regime successfully avoided the harsh implications of indebted development by selectively drawing on international commercial banks for its financing requirements in an attempt to obtain foreign capital that offered the least resistance to its distributive objectives. In comparison to Kenya's distributive policies, Zimbabwe's policies contain a much stronger dosage of heterodox principles mixed with orthodoxy. The state's active intervention in the economy with foreign exchange, import, and price controls, and its support of parastatal subsidies and wage increases illustrates Zimbabwe's emphasis on a distributive model of adjustment rather than a pure growth model. Until the late-1980s, the government relied more on its authoritative powers of allocating foreign exchange and restricting outflow of capital than on a market system of allocation. The objective was to obtain foreign funds that did not impinge on either state behavior or the state investment of those funds. Unlike Kenya, it purposively (until 1992) avoided much financial reliance on the IMF, while studiously keeping out of debt arrears with international financial creditors.

Yet, my study confirms the incongruity in Zimbabwe's policies and bargaining strategies. While seeking to avoid the internal political ramifications of accepting IMF conditions, the government failed to attract sufficient foreign capital to serve the interests of the crucial private sector and, by depleting foreign reserves to finance a growing government budget deficit, the government is faced with serious economic dilemmas. Recently, the government has backed away from a clear anti-foreign capital stance as it realigns its strategy to fit the reality of insufficient amounts of foreign investment. Under the current SAP, the government is intending to liberalize international trade, deregulate prices and wages, and reform the public sector.[15] Given the government's historic inability to effectively reduce the budget deficit, international creditors and the indigenous business community have only given lukewarm support to the current programme. Moreover, the threat to government employees and to the increasingly large number of unemployed workers creates a problematic future for Zimbabwe's adjustment strategy. In addition to doubts about the government's adherence to economic liberalization, domestic and foreign groups have been critical of the internal political direction of the government. Caught in the cross-cutting pressures by seeking financial assistance from IFIs and by seeking political support from the marginalized groups in society, Zimbabwe's adjustment strategy remains at risk.

As with Kenya and Zimbabwe, *Brazil* also is grappling with indebted development. It too has sought to balance the dilemma between answering the demands of domestic constituents and those of its international creditors. In Brazil's case, the specific dilemma focuses on those groups favoring strengthened external accounts (namely, trade surpluses), while others emphasize control of internal accounts (namely, budget deficit reduction). Over the years, the government has sided with the former by attempting to take advantage of the perception of economic strength as indicated by large trade surpluses. By accumulating substantial surpluses, the government borrowed significant sums from international banks while keeping arrears to relatively small amounts.

Yet, it too needed to go to the IMF for standby arrangements which imposed conventional adjustment conditionalities. As with Kenya, Brazil was able to avoid significant components of policy implementation. Brazil's power capabilities are far more extensive and, in some ways, more permanent than those of the African cases. Brazil's negotiating experience, competent technocrats, economic diversity, alternative financing sources, size of its foreign debt, and its transition back to political democracy are components that have empowered the regime's bargaining strategy. The 1992 debt agreements with the IMF, the Paris Club, and international banks reflect Brazil's bargaining expertise and negotiating strength.

However, Brazil's relative success in its debt management strategy comes at a great expense to its economic adjustment strategy. Since 1985, Brazil's governments have imposed some half a dozen heterodox economic plans, none of which has resulted in long-term benefits. Brazil now is faced with rising inflation, budget deficits, weakening trade balance, and current account deficits. It has taken action, in part, by reducing government support of the basic goods sector. One of the strengths of Brazilian society, the corporatist relationship with the state, is in jeopardy as domestic opposition to government economic policy is rising. Indeed,

Conclusions: The Process of Indebted Development

this 'social pact' may come unglued, leading to political instability and, in the worse scenario, a return of the military to political rule.

While Kenya and Zimbabwe can be considered as representatives of middle-income countries in the developing world, Brazil is more representative of upper-income Third World countries. The state for these countries is not withering away as a result of economic and political instability. Although foreign indebtedness and economic deterioration have placed difficult constraints on state economic capacity to perform efficiently and equitably, state political and institutional powers, in some instances, have become strengthened and centralized under government authorities.

However, the analysis presented in this book should not imply that the 'hardening' of the state is the long-term trend. Indeed, in light of worsening economic conditions placed in the context of economic instability, ideological conflicts, and regressive patron-client relations, the state in the Third World remains in a precarious position. In Kenya's case, state intervention in foreign and domestic investment may be a last gasp effort by a desperate government to forestall collapse. It is not clear at this point if Zimbabwe's move toward economic liberalization portends a general transition to more integrated and liberal economic relations with the international economy and, if so, whether it will be successful. Brazil's fate is tied less to debt management, but more directly to its ability to manage domestic economic crises. The Third World state may be expanding its powers in seeking to respond to indebted development, but it has declining influence over such structural constraints as falling terms of trade, growing international protectionism, and rising potential for international recession.

This study has sought to examine issues of economic adjustment and debt management by focusing on the interactive and strategic relationship among the primary actors. While it is hoped that this framework may contribute to a better understanding of the three cases, more research along these lines should be encouraged in several areas. First, selection of three contrasting case studies was meant to highlight the broad *application of strategic bargaining to the problems of indebted development*. Certainly, Kenya, Zimbabwe, and Brazil fulfilled this objective with their vast differences in levels of absolute foreign debt, access to alternate sources of funds, reliance on official and private creditors, geostrategic importance, and bargaining strategies toward constituents and creditors. Yet, despite these differences, the condition of indebted development is prevalent in all three countries. Still, additional research is necessary that extends the framework of strategic bargaining to other categories of debtor states, especially the category of low-income countries who suffer (in proportional terms) more from indebted development than other countries.

Second, successful application of strategic bargaining would benefit from not only an *extension* to other countries, but from a more *intensive* analysis of state-society-creditor relations. Clearly, adjustments have been made by actors at different levels of analysis. A more complete understanding of the action-reaction process that cuts across linkages between levels is dependent on following the specific moves and counter-moves of the actors. States have undertaken a number of different policy moves that seek to influence the outcome of negotiations. Creditors also have made adjustments to strengthen their bargaining position. Moreover, the bargaining stance of important domestic groups, such as labor and business, must be clarified.

Third, economic adjustment and debt management strategies should not be relegated simply to the state, international creditors, and a few powerful domestic groups. Since the majority of the people in these debtor countries are *marginal to state-creditor negotiations*, these less powerful domestic groups often are overlooked. While this study has focused on adjustment and debt management as a product of negotiations, their impact reverberates throughout society and is widely felt by the more marginalized, less formal associations in the country. Future studies incorporating strategic bargaining would benefit from a more intensive examination of these groups.

Fourth, another research interest that derives from my argument is the prospect of and conditions for *social learning* among the negotiators. In many studies, the bargaining strategies, tactics, and objectives of the negotiators were seen as relatively static. Multilateral organizations wanted to see their programs implemented; creditor governments and commercial creditors wanted to be repaid as quickly as possible; and debtor governments wanted to balance repayment with economic growth and political stability.[16] Yet, as this study has shown, states and institutions have become much more willing and, in some cases, more able to shift their preferences and tactics in order to produce an acceptable and 'ratifiable' adjustment program. While at times tension and even conflict exists between and within the two levels of negotiations, one can also point to convergence of interests brought about by dialogue, commitment to joint problem-solving, and mutual adjustment.[17]

NOTES

1.   J. B. Zulu and S. M. Nsolui, 'Adjustment Programs in Africa. *Occasional Paper* 34 (Washington, D.C.: International Monetary Fund,

1985); Miles Kahler, 'Orthodoxy and Its Alternatives: Explaining Approaches to Stabilization and Adjustment,' in Joan M. Nelson, ed., *Economic Crisis and Policy Choice: The Politics of Adjustment in the Third World* (Princeton: Princeton University Press, 1990).

2. Stephan Haggard, 'The Politics of Adjustment: Lessons from the IMF's Extended Fund Facility,' in Miles Kahler, ed., *Politics of International Debt* (Ithaca, N.Y.: Cornell University Press, 1986); Joan Nelson, 'The Political Economy of Stabilization: Commitment, Capacity, and Public Response,' *World Development* 12:10 (October 1984); Karen Remmer, 'The Politics of Economic Stabilization: IMF Standby Programs in Latin America, 1954-1984,' *Comparative Politics* 19:1 (October 1986).

3. See the chapters in Bonnie K. Campbell , ed., *Political Dimensions of the International Debt Crisis* (New York: St. Martin's Press, 1989) and Bonnie K. Campbell and John Loxley, eds., *Structural Adjustment in Africa* (New York: St. Martin's Press, 1989).

4. Ishrat Husain and Ishac Diwan, eds., *Dealing with the Debt Crisis* (Washington, D.C.: World Bank, 1989).

5. The Cartegena Conferences, followed by initiatives by Nigeria, Peru, and Brazil, often constituted the focus of this research.

6. Charles Lipson, 'Bankers' Dilemmas: Private Cooperation in Rescheduling Sovereign Debts,' *World Politics* 38:1 (October 1985).

7. Miles Kahler, 'External Influence, Conditionality, and the Politics of Adjustment,' unpublished paper, 1990.

8. For debtors, see Stephan Haggard and Robert Kaufman, 'The Politics of Stabilization and Structural Adjustment,' in Jeffrey Sachs, ed., *Developing Country Debt and the World Economy* (Chicago: University of Chicago Press, 1989); Thomas Callaghy, 'Toward State Capability and Embedded Liberalism in the Third World: Lessons for Adjustment,' in Joan M. Nelson, ed., *Fragile Coalitions: The Politics of Economic Adjustment* (New Brunswick: Transaction Books, 1989). For creditors, see Graham Bird, *Commercial Bank Lending and Third World Debt* (New York: St. Martin's Press, 1989); Paul Mosley, *Conditionality as Bargaining Process: Structural Adjustment Lending, 1980-86*. Essays in International Finance 168 (Princeton University, 1987); Robert Devlin, *Debt and Crisis in Latin America: The Supply Side of the Story* (Princeton: Princeton University Press, 1989); Benjamin J. Cohen, *Developing-Country Debt: A Middle Way*. Essays in International Finance 173 (Princeton University, 1989).

9. On the IMF bargaining position, see Kendall W. Stiles, *Negotiating Debt: The IMF Lending Process* (Boulder: Westview Press, 1991); on the commercial banks position, see Bird, *Commercial Bank Lending and Third World Debt*; on the debtors' bargaining stance, see Haggard and Kaufman, 'The Politics of Stabilization and Structural Adjustment;' and on the various bargaining positions of commercial banks and creditor governments, see Matthew Martin, *The Crumbling*

Facade of African Debt Negotiations (London: Macmillan, 1991).
10. Callaghy, 'Toward State Capability and Embedded Liberalism in the Third World: Lessons for Adjustment;'; Stephany Griffith-Jones, 'Debt Crisis Management: An Analytical Framework,' in Stephany Griffith-Jones, ed. *Managing World Debt* (New York: St. Martin's Press, 1988); Paul Mosely, Jane Harrigan, and John Toye, *Aid and Power: The World Bank and Policy-based Lending*, Vol. 1 (London: Routledge, 1991); Haggard and Kaufman, 'The Politics of Stabilization and Structural Adjustment.'
11. Robert Putnam, 'Diplomacy and Domestic Politics: The Logic of Two-Level Games,' *International Organization* 42 (Summer 1988).
12. Daniel Druckman, 'Boundary Role Conflict: Negotiation as Dual Responsiveness,' in I. William Zartman, ed., *The Negotiation Process: Theories and Applications* (Beverly Hills: Sage Publications, 1977), p. 88.
13. Callaghy, 'Toward State Capability and Embedded Liberalism in the Third World: Lessons for Adjustment,' p. 120.
14. Callaghy, ibid., p. 116; Thomas J. Biersteker, 'Reducing the Role of the State in the Economy: A Conceptual Exploration of IMF and World Bank Prescriptions,' *International Studies Quarterly* 34:4 (December 1990), p. 477.
15. Several observers are critical of Zimbabwe's shift toward economic liberalization. Colin Stoneman, in particular, argues that, given Zimbabwe's economic success, there was no need to change strategy. He asserts that 'it may thus be one of history's ironies that the African country which best showed the vialbe alternative to World Bank structural adjustment policies, itself embraced them just before they became widely discredited.' See Stoneman, 'The Impending Failure of Structural Adjustment: Lessons from Zimbabwe,' paper presented at the Canadian Association of African Studies (May 1990), p. 6. Since my interpretation of Zimbabwe's adjustment strategy is found in Chapter Three, I shall only argue that the country's economic condition was far more serious than Stoneman's analysis. Despite the widely known negative consequences of economic adjustment programmes, Zimbabwe's Five-Year Economic Reform Programme incorporates many components of the state's earlier 'home-grown' liberalization strategy. For arguments similar to Stoneman's, see his 'Zimbabwe Opens Up to the Market,' *Africa Recovery* 4 (October-December, 1990 and Roger C. Riddell, 'Zimbabwe,' in Roger C. Riddell, ed., *Manufacturing Africa: Performance and Prospects of Seven Countries in Sub-Saharan Africa* (London: James Currey, 1990).
16. Martin, *The Crumbling Facade of African Debt Negotiations*, p. 320.
17. Kahler, 'External Influence, Conditionality, and the Politics of Adjustment;' and Mosley, Harrigan, and Toye, *Aid and Power: The World Bank and Policy-based Lending*, Vol. 1.

Index

adjustment process, 2, 4, 10, 13, 69, 82, 109
adjustment with debt reduction strategy, 31, 47
    criticisms of debt reduction, 37–9, 47
    support of debt reduction, 51, 52
adjustment with growth strategy, 31, 36, 46, 47, 55
Almond, Gabriel, 5
arrears, 41, 46

Baer, Werner, 99
Baker Plan, 37–9, 43, 47, 50, 52, 53, 56
bank regulatory authorities, 32, 40
basic needs sector,
    Kenya, 176, 177
    Zimbabwe, 186, 187
Basle Agreement, 40, 42
Beckerman, Paul, 99
Bennett, Douglas, 66
Biersteker, Thomas, 7, 209
Brady Plan, 30, 50, 52–6, 155
    menu of options, 31, 50, 56
Brazil
    arrears, 140, 141, 146, 148, 152–4, 156
    Bresser Plan, 103
    budget allocation, 199
    budget deficit, 193, 200, 201
    Collor Plan, 106–7
    Cruzado II Plan, 100–2
    Cruzado Plan, 99, 101, 102, 105
    debt burden, 141–2
    debt management strategies, 119, 120, 129, 138, 142–56
    debt moratorium of 1987, 144
    direct foreign investment, 93
    economic growth and structure of debt, 139–42
    investment program, 192
    national development plans, 93–6

Paris Club, 143, 149, 151–3, 155
    menu of options, 155
    privatization, 198–200
    public sector, 191–3, 195, 197–201
    relationship with the IMF, 93, 98, 99, 101–5, 108, 109, 128, 143, 145, 147–50, 152–6, 195–8
    relationship with private creditors, 139, 153
    relationship with the World Bank, 108, 145–7, 150–3
    repayment dilemma, 140, 141, 144, 149, 151, 154
    sectoral allocation, 196
    sources of foreign borrowing, 139
    state-guaranteed loans, 196
    Summer Plan, 104, 105
    trade policy, 193, 195, 200, 201
    White Moratorium, 151
Brazilian Democratic Movement Party (PMDB), 97, 98, 100–4
Bresser Pereira, Luis Carlos, 103, 147–51

Callaghy, Thomas, 3, 7, 12, 207, 209
capital provisions, 32, 34, 35, 37, 39, 40–6, 49, 52–54, 56
Cardoso, Eliana, 94
Cardoso de Mello, Zelia, 152, 153
Chidzero, Bernard, 138, 147, 148, 181
Cline, William, 37
Collor de Mello, Fernando, 106, 152
comparative analysis, 93, 102, 108, 147, 191
    case studies, 16–22, 109–10, 131, 157–8, 200–1, 210–14
    debt burden, 11, 16, 36, 45, 47–9, 52, 53, 56
    economic indicators, 15
Confederation of Zimbabwe Industries (CZI), 85, 88, 182
Corden, Max, 51, 53
cross-conditionality, 37, 38, 48, 126

217

CZI, see Confederation of Zimbabwe Industries

David, Wilfred, 67
debt data, 15–17, 122, 123, 131–2, 140, 142, 168, 175, 188, 189
debt management negotiations 1, 14
debt management strategies, 120, 129, 138,
dilemma, 141
Dell, Sidney, 94
devaluation policies, 73, 74, 90, 91, 93, 96
Brazil, 195
see Kenya: export incentives; trade liberalization
Development Finance Company of Kenya (DFCK), 173
Devlin, Robert, 34
DFCK, see Development Finance Company of Kenya
Dinsmoor, James, 139

economic adjustment strategies 2, 10, 13, 16, 64, 65, 68, 206, 207, 209
Brazil, 94, 97, 102
coalitions, 65, 66
definition, 3–4, 14
dilemma, 1, 2, 7, 10, 11, 210–12
Kenya, 69
negotiations, 1
Zimbabwe, 78
Enhanced Structural Adjustment Facility (ESAF), 45–6
Kenya, 125–6
Zimbabwe, 134–8
ESAF, see also Enhanced Structural Adjustment Facility

financing and adjustment, 31, 34, 35
innovations, 35, 36
Fishlow, Albert, 94
foreign exchange allocation, 72, 80, 83, 89, 90
see Kenya: foreign capital investment
FORD, see Forum for the Restoration of Democracy

Forum for the Restoration of Democracy (FORD), 78
Frieden, Jeffry, 94
Funaro, Dilson, 99, 101–3, 145

game theory, 13, 14
Gourevitch, Peter, 66
Green, Reginald, 33, 86
Griffith-Jones, Stephany, 207

Haggard, Stephan, 10, 151, 207
Hanlon, Joseph, 86
heterodox economic adjustment
Brazil, 22, 97, 99, 212
defined, 4, 67–8
strategy of, 64, 65, 109, 119, 209
Zimbabwe, 22, 79, 80, 187, 211

ICDC, see Industrial and Commercial Development Corporation
ICERC, see Inter-agency Country Exposure Risk Committee
ICO, see International Coffee Organization
IMF, see International Monetary Fund
indebted development, 2, 17, 109–10, 119, 158, 167, 200, 206–14
Brazil, 92, 138, 156
Industrial and Commercial Development Corporation (ICDC), 173
Inter-agency Country Exposure Risk Committee (ICERC), 39, 145, 147, 152, 154
International Coffee Organization (ICO), 76
international creditor regime, 30–4, 36, 40–9, 53, 55–6
definition, 32, 50
International Monetary Fund (IMF), 6, 7, 12, 22, 31, 32, 35, 37, 41–6, 50–4, 200
political role, 6, 44, 45
response to Brady Plan, 53–4
Investment Promotion Center (IPC), 74, 75
IPC, see Investment Promotion Center

Jessop, Bob, 9

Index

KANU, *see* Kenya African National Union
Kahler, Miles, 67
Kaufman, Robert, 151, 207
Kenya
  arrears, 120
  budget allocation, 176, 177
  budget deficit, 168, 169, 171, 177
  debt burden, 120
  direct foreign investment, 68, 69, 78
  drought conditions, 68, 76
  economic adjustment objectives, 69
  ethnic tensions, 70, 72, 169, 170
  export incentives, 72–5, 78
  foreign capital investment, 72
  national development plans, 69, 74, 168–76
  parastatal borrowing controls, 171
  parastatal policy, 169
  private sector investment, 69
  privatization, 171
  relationship with donor countries, 123–4, 125
  relationship with the IMF, 68–70, 73, 75, 77, 78, 121, 123, 125–7, 157, 168, 169, 177
  relationship with private creditors, 121, 123, 128
  relationship with the World Bank, 68, 69, 72, 121, 123, 125–7, 169, 170
  sectoral allocation, 174
  sources of foreign borrowing, 121
  state-guaranteed loans, 174
  trade liberalization, 77
Kenya African National Union (KANU), 78
Krasner, Stephen, 7

Latin American debt meetings,
  Acapulco, 48
  Cartagena Conference, 36, 48
  Declaration of Uruguay, 50
Lawrence, Roger, 94
loan-loss reserves, 39, 41, 42, 44, 51, 54
Loxley, John, 67

Marenin, Otwin, 65

Migdal, Joel, 6
Moi, Daniel Arap, 70, 78, 102, 106, 170
Mosley, Paul, 4, 207
Mugabe, Robert, 82, 84, 102, 189

Ndegwa, Philip, 70
Nelson, Joan, 4
Nobrega, Mailson Ferrera da, 104, 148–51
Nordlinger, Eric, 7, 8

OAU, *see* Organization of African Unity
OGIL, *see* Open General Import Licensing
Olson, Mancur, 66
Open General Import Licensing (OGIL), 91, 134
Organization of African Unity (OAU), 49
orthodox economic adjustment
  Brazil, 22, 98, 104, 109, 148
  defined, 2–3, 66–7
  Kenya, 17, 68, 69, 123, 157, 169, 177, 210, 211
  strategy of, 1, 4, 12, 17, 37, 50, 64–8, 72, 78, 119, 158, 200, 206–7, 209
  Zimbabwe, 22, 79, 80, 82, 89, 92, 157, 188, 211
Overseas Private Investment Corporation, 85

PMDB, *see* Brazilian Democratic Movement Party
paradox of state power, 1, 2, 4, 6, 208–10
Paris Club, 32, 53, 54, 56
  response to Brady Plan, 53–4
Putnam, Robert, 10, 208

Reed, John, 152
reserves, *see* capital provisions
Riddell, Roger, 85, 182
Rothchild, Donald, 5, 9

Sachs, Jeffrey, 52

Index

SAF, *see* Structural Adjustment Facility
Saitoti, George, 147, 148
SAL, *see* Structural Adjustment Loan
SAP, *see* Structural Adjustment Program
Sarney, Jose, 97–107, 145, 148–50, 156
secondary debt market, 41, 42, 53
Sharpe, Kenneth, 66
Singer, Paul, 100
slippage
 defined, 65
 Kenya, 31, 69, 78, 109, 119, 127, 209–11
 strategy of, 31, 65, 119, 149, 158, 200
Snider, Lewis, 9
state-owned enterprises, 67, 70, 96
 see Brazil: public sector
 see Kenya: parastatal policy
 see Zimbabwe: parastatal policy
state-society relations, 4, 7, 9, 209–13
Stoneman, Colin, 86, 135
strategic bargaining, 1, 12–14, 17, 23, 25, 64, 208, 213, 214
 components of, 6
 debtor governments 64
 model of, 13, 14
 utility of, 13, 14
Structural Adjustment Facility (SAF), 37, 45, 46
 Kenya, 125, 126
Structural Adjustment Loan (SAL), 127
Structural Adjustment Program (SAP), 91, 109
 Brazil, 93
 Kenya, 77, 78
 Zimbabwe, 91, 133–5, 138, 157, 180

Toronto Economic Declaration, 49
two-level bargaining game, 10, 208
 debtor governments, 3, 11, 12
 international creditors, 1–3, 10–13, 17, 22, 23, 25
 strategic dilemma, 10

Unilateral Declaration of Independence (UDI), 79, 80, 185, 190

Volcker, Paul, 148

World Bank, 4, 6, 7, 22, 32, 37, 43, 46, 50, 51, 53, 54, 182
 response to Brady Plan, 53–4

Zimbabwe
 arrears, 157
 blocked capital, 84
 budget allocation, 186
 budget deficit, 180–3, 188
 debt burden, 131
 debt management strategies, 129, 130–3
 direct foreign investment, 79, 83–5, 87–9
 drought conditions, 86
 economic adjustment objectives, 79
 foreign exchange allocation, 181
 foreign investment history, 136–8
 ethnic tensions, 86
 export incentives, 92
 national development plan, 80, 83
 privatization, 182
 Public Sector Investment Program (PSIP), 182–4
 'radical' vs 'pragmatic' factions, 180
 relationship with donor countries, 133, 134
 relationship with the IMF 79, 81, 83, 85, 89, 92, 131, 134–7, 157, 180
 relationship with private creditors, 131, 132, 136, 137, 138
 relationship with South Africa, 80, 81, 84, 86, 89, 90
 relationship with the World Bank 79, 81, 88–9, 92, 134–6, 180, 187
 sectoral allocation of loans, 185
 sources of foreign borrowing, 133–7
 trade liberalization, 90, 91
 state-guaranteed loans, 184–6
Zimbabwe Investment Centre, 87
Zimcord, 131, 133, 134, 137, 181